GCSE
Health & Social Care
for Edexcel

Mark Walsh

Published by
HarperCollins*Publishers* Limited
77–85 Fulham Palace Road
Hammersmith
London
W6 8JB

www.CollinsEducation.co.uk
Online support for schools and colleges

ISBN-13 978 0 00 731114 9

British Cataloguing in Publication Data
A cataloguing record for this publication is available from the
British Library

Cover design by Angela English
Book design and layout by Graham Brasnett
Cover picture by Getty Images
Picture research by Jill Thraves
Illustrations by Bethan Matthews
Index by Karen Seymour
Project managed by Emma Woolf
Production by Simon Moore
Printed and bound in China

www.fireandwater.co.uk
The book lover's website

CONTENTS

ACKNOWLEDGEMENTS

For Karen, Hannah and Barney

Thanks are due to everyone who has provided the help, support and hard work needed to get this book completed.

Mark Walsh

The publishers gratefully acknowledge the following for permission to reproduce photographs and other material. Every effort has been made to trace copyright holders, but if any material has been inadvertently overlooked, the publishers will be pleased to correct this at the earliest opportunity.

Alamy: Title page br, pp 9br, 42, 44c, 194c, 198b, 219,

Corbis: p 40

Getty Images: Title page tl, c, tr, pp 8tl, ct, cb, 9cr, 13b,17, 18, 21, 23b, 28b, 29c, 45b, 55b, 72, 74, 78, 79, 86, 88, 98, 99c, 101, 122, 126, 140cl, c, 155, 159, 184, 195t, br, 198t, 206, 210, 214, 221, 223, 228, 229, 233, 234, 246, 248, 251

iStockphoto: pp 8bl, 26, 28t, 32, 45b, 46, 49, 51, 55t, 58, 63, 69, 71, 75, 84, 93, 97, 99, 140bl, c, br, 143, 146, 156, 158, 167, 177, 180, 181, 194cl, b, 195cb, cr, 201, 203, 205, 208, 209, 240,

Rex Features: pp 230, 232, 249

Science Photo Library: pp 194t, 252

INTRODUCTION

Welcome to GCSE Health and Social Care for Edexcel!

The aim of this book is to help you to develop the knowledge and understanding that you will need to complete your GCSE Health and Social Care course. The book covers the following units:

- **Unit 1 – Understanding Personal Development and Relationships**
- **Unit 2 – Exploring Health, Social Care and Early Years Provision**
- **Unit 3 – Promoting Health and Wellbeing**
- **Unit 4 – Health, Social Care and Early Years in Practice**

You need to complete the first two units if you are taking the GCSE Single Award qualification. You need to complete all four units if you are taking the GCSE Double Award qualification. Each of the units in the book provides you with opportunities to develop the knowledge and understanding that will be needed to successfully complete the coursework assignments and external assessments that are part of your GCSE Health and Social Care award.

Features of the book

The book closely follows the specification (syllabus) of your GCSE Health and Social Care award. This means that all of the topics and issues referred to in the course specification are fully covered. You will find the following features in the book:

- **Topic Focus** – This is a short, introductory section at the start of each new topic that tells you what the topic or chapter you are about to study is going to focus on.

- **Over to you!** – These are activities that aim to get you thinking about an issue or topic. These short activities can usually be completed on the spot without doing any more research. You should try as many of them as you can as they are designed to boost your thinking and learning skills.

- **Investigate...** – These activities are designed to extend your knowledge and understanding by encouraging you to find out a bit more about a topic or issue that you have been learning about. Finding information in other books or on the Internet will help you to deepen and extend your knowledge and understanding of health and social care.

- **Knowledge Check** – This is a list of questions about the topic you have been studying. You should try to answer as many of these as you can to check your learning and understanding of the topics you have been studying. You might also want to try answering the Unit 1 and 4 questions again when you are revising for your externally assessed examinations.

- **Topic review** – You will find this feature at the end of each topic. It provides you with an opportunity to think about what you have been studying and to check that you have covered everything you need to. The topic review also provides you with brief information on how the topic you have been studying is assessed.

Assessment

The Edexcel GCSE Health and Social Care award is assessed through both coursework assignments and external tests.

- **Unit 1 Understanding Personal Development and Relationships** is externally assessed through a 1 hour and 15 minute written exam, with a total of 70 marks.

- **Unit 2 Exploring Health, Social Care and Early Years Provision** is assessed through an assignment set by Edexcel and marked by your tutor, with a total of 50 marks.

- **Unit 3 Promoting Health and Wellbeing** is assessed through an assignment set by Edexcel and marked by your tutor, with a total of 50 marks.

- **Unit 4 Health, Social Care and Early Years in Practice** is externally assessed through a 1 hour and 15 minute written exam, with a total of 70 marks.

I've tried to write a book that helps you to gain a good, clear understanding of a range of care topics and also to give you a taste of what to expect from a career in the health and social care sector. Taking a GCSE Health and Social Care course gives you an opportunity to decide whether this is an area of work that you are suitable for and interested in pursuing. Hopefully, you'll think about taking your interest in health and social care further when you've worked through the book and completed your GCSE. Good luck with your course!

Mark Walsh

Understanding Personal Development and Relationships

Introduction

This unit is about personal development and relationships across the lifespan. You will learn about:

- The way people grow and develop during each stage of life

- The factors that influence the way people grow and develop as they get older

- How people develop a self-concept and personal relationships throughout life

- The types of relationship that are important to personal development

- The life events and changes that can affect personal development during each stage of life

Health, social care and early years workers help people of all ages and backgrounds. Knowing about expected patterns of human growth and development can be important when people experience health problems or have care needs. Knowing what kinds of physical and language skills a two year old child normally has would help a children's nurse to assess a child in hospital or allow a playworker to plan suitable activities at a nursery, for example. This unit will give you a better understanding of human growth and development.

Topic 1.1

Human growth and development

Topic focus

How does a person grow and develop throughout the course of their life? People experience physical, intellectual, emotional and social development in each life stage. A **life stage** is a defined period of growth and development. This topic will focus on the patterns and processes of human growth and development that occur in the following six life stages:

- Infancy (0–2 years)
- Childhood (3–8 years)
- Adolescence (9–18 years)
- Early adulthood (19-45 years)
- Middle adulthood (46-65 years)
- Later adulthood (over 65 years).

Topic 1.1 will also focus on how the self-concept develops and changes across the life stages and the factors that affect this.

What are growth and development?

The term growth refers to an increase in size. Typically, a person will experience a gradual increase in their weight and height as they move from infancy through childhood and into adolescence and adulthood. Development is different to growth. **Development** happens when a person gains new skills, abilities and emotions. Typically, our skills, abilities and emotions become more sophisticated and complex as we progress from childhood through adolescence and into adulthood.

Developmental norms

Human growth and development tends to follow a pattern. Growth and **developmental norms**, sometimes also called 'milestones', refer to the points in a person's life where particular changes are expected to happen. For example, the point in infancy when you were first able to sit up unaided, when you took your first steps and when you said your first words will be relatively similar to the point at which other people of your age first did these

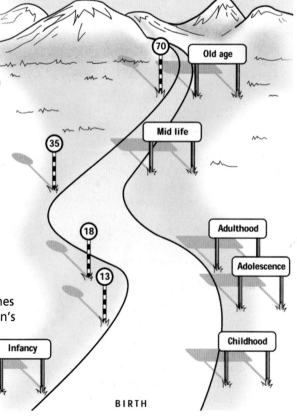

things too. Though human growth and development follows a relatively predictable pattern it is important not to think of this as an exact timetable that 'normal' people follow. An infant, child, teenager or adult is not abnormal if he or she reaches growth or developmental milestones at slightly different times to the expected pattern. A person's growth and development can be different to the 'norm' for a variety of reasons.

Figure 1.1 Examples of developmental norms.

Age	Developmental changes
3–4 months	Infants start on solid foods, develop better head control, can roll from side to side, reach for objects.
6–9 months	Teething begins, learns to sit unaided, lift their heads and look around, use thumb and index finger to grasp objects
9–12 months	Infants can crawl, chews food, use their hands to explore, can walk holding on to parent or furniture ('cruising'), may say a few words, know their name and start to understand their parents words
12–18 months	Toddlers learn to feed themselves, walk unaided, can understand simple requests – 'give it to me' – develops better memory and concentration
18–24 months	Toddlers can run, turn pages of a book, use simple sentences, have temper outbursts and know their own name
10 years (girls)	Puberty begins
12 years (boys)	
45–55 years	Menopause occurs

Investigate

Before you begin studying the five main life stages of human growth and development, go to **www.babycenter.com/pregnancy-fetal-development-index**. This website explains how development occurs in the womb during pregnancy. In small groups choose one trimester of pregnancy and investigate what is happening to both the mother and the baby. Summarise your findings in the form of a poster or leaflet.

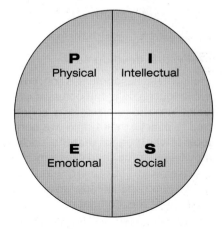

Using the PIES approach

Human growth and development has been studied in great detail by scientists and health and social care specialists for centuries. In the twenty first century we now have a detailed understanding of what happens to human beings in each life stage. One clear way of explaining the complex process of human growth and development is to identify four types of growth and development. This is known as the PIES approach. **PIES** stands for physical, intellectual, emotional and social development.

Physical growth and development

Physical growth and development refer to the way in which a person's body changes throughout their life. A person will experience most of their physical growth (in height and weight) during infancy, childhood and adolescence. Physical growth is a very rapid during infancy, slower but continuous during childhood and then very rapid again during adolescence when a final growth spurt occurs. A person generally reaches their

P Physical	**I** Intellectual
E Emotional	**S** Social

Figure 1.2 PIES.

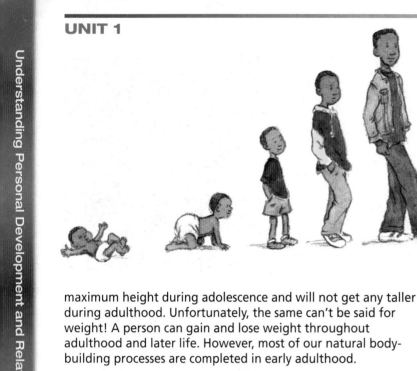

maximum height during adolescence and will not get any taller during adulthood. Unfortunately, the same can't be said for weight! A person can gain and lose weight throughout adulthood and later life. However, most of our natural body-building processes are completed in early adulthood.

Physical development, like growth, is a continuous process. Human beings begin developing physical skills from birth. We experience a peak in our physical abilities during adulthood. A slow and gradual decline in physical ability then occurs as we move into later adulthood.

The sequence of physical changes that happen in each life stage is known as **maturation**. This process is thought to be controlled by a biological 'programme' built into our genes. Though we all change physically as we grow older, the rate, or speed, at which people age varies. For example, some very old people remain physically active and mentally alert right up until the end of their lives. Other people lose their physical skills and mental abilities at a much earlier point in their life because they have aged more quickly. The rate at which a person ages is influenced by factors such as:

- whether the person inherits 'long life' genes from their parents
- the person's attitude to life
- the person's health and fitness routines
- the extent to which the person lives a stressful life.

Intellectual development

Intellectual development is concerned with thinking, memory and language skills and occurs in every life stage. This is sometimes also referred to as '**cognitive development**'. People used to believe that a child was born with a mind like an empty book. It was thought that the 'book' gradually filled up with knowledge as the child experienced the world around it. However, scientific research has shown that babies start learning in the womb and already have some basic abilities and lots of potential at the moment of their birth. Jean Piaget (1896 – 1980) a Swiss psychologist, first put forward the theory that we are born with basic intellectual abilities that improve as we experience different stages of intellectual development during infancy, childhood and adolescence.

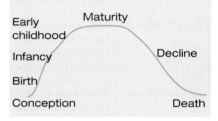

Figure 1.3 Development is a continuous process.

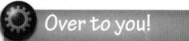

Over to you!

Have a look through your family photographs and identify the ways in which you and your family have changed as a result of 'maturation'.

Emotional development

Emotional development is concerned with a person's feelings. People experience emotional development in each life stage. We develop and express emotions, such as love, happiness, disappointment and anger, through the various relationships and social situations we experience. As we grow older we learn to recognise, understand and take into account other people's feelings too. The very early relationships we have with parents and close relatives, such as brothers, sisters and grandparents, play a vital role in our emotional development. Feeling loved, secure and cared for during infancy provides an important foundation for later emotional development. As we grow older the way that others treat us also has an effect on our emotional development. Emotional development involves:

- becoming aware of your '**self**'
- developing feelings about your 'self'
- working out your feelings towards other people
- developing a self-image and personal identity.

Social development

Social development is concerned with the relationships we create with others, the social skills we develop and learning the culture (or way of life) of society. Parents and teachers have a key role in our early social development. They teach us:

- the acceptable ways of behaving
- how to relate to others in everyday situations
- the importance of making and keeping good relationships with others.

This process of helping a person to develop socially is known as **socialisation**. Friends and work colleagues also become important sources of socialisation during adolescence and adulthood. Friends are particularly important during later adolescence when we are trying to create our own individual identity.

Knowledge Check

1 What does the term 'growth' refer to?

2 What is meant by development?

3 What are developmental norms?

4 Which four aspects of growth and development are referred to as PIES?

5 What does the term 'maturation' refer to?

6 What kinds of skills and abilities improve as a result of intellectual development?

7 What is emotional development?

8 What role do parents and other family members play during early socialisation?

Understanding Personal Development and Relationships

Infancy (0–2 years)

Infancy is the first human life stage that begins at birth and continues until about 2 years of age. A newborn baby will experience a huge amount of physical growth as well as physical, intellectual, emotional and social development during infancy.

Physical growth and development

Physical growth happens very quickly during infancy. A baby is born with a number of primitive reflexes but is largely helpless and dependent on others during the first year of life. **Reflexes** are automatic physical movements that a baby makes without intending to (see figure 1.4). As a result of rapid physical growth and development children quickly change from being small, very dependent babies into much larger, stronger and more capable 'toddlers' in the second year of their life.

Physical change in very young infants occurs from the head downwards and from the middle of the body outwards (see figure 1.5). As a result, a child is first able to hold their head up without help before they are able to use their body to sit up. Following this children are able to use their legs to crawl. A child's bones gradually grow and harden and their muscles get stronger in this same head-downwards, middle-outwards pattern during infancy. This allows the child to carry out new sorts of movement as their body undergoes physical development and change.

During their first 18 months infants gradually develop **gross motor skills**. These are whole body movements, such as sitting up, crawling and walking that depend on being able to control the large muscles in their arms and legs. By the end of infancy, most children also have some **fine motor skills**. These are manipulative movements that we make with our fingers which rely on control over smaller muscles and fine movement. The physical changes that infants experience transform their appearance as well as their movement abilities. They also provide the foundation for other forms of intellectual, social and emotional development to occur.

Moro (startle)

stimulus: insecure handling or sudden noise

response: the baby throws its head back, fingers fan out, arms return to embrace position and the baby cries

Grasping

stimulus: placing object in the baby's palm

response: fingers close tightly round the object

Placing

stimulus: brushing the top of foot against table top

response: the baby lifts its foot and places it on a hard surface

Walking

stimulus: held standing, feet touching a hard surface

response:the baby moves its legs forward alternately and walks

Sucking

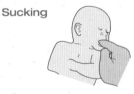

stimulus: placing nipple or teat into the mouth

response: the baby sucks

Rooting

stimulus: brushing the cheek with a finger or nipple

response: the baby turns to the side of stimulus

Figure 1.4 The reflexes of new babies.

Measuring physical change

A child's physical growth is usually measured by a health visitor during infancy. After weighing and measuring a child, the health visitor will record their details on a percentile chart (see figure 1.6). **Percentile charts** of weight and height have been compiled after studying and recording the growth patterns of thousands of children to work out average and expected patterns. There are different charts for girls and boys. When they are completed for a specific child, a percentile chart provides clear, visual information about their growth.

The bold line on the chart in figure 1.6 shows the average trend in weight gain expected in boys during the first 12 months of their life. This means that if a 4-month-old boy weighs 7 kg, on average 50 per cent of boys of the same age will weigh less than him and 50 per cent of boys of the same age will weigh more than him. If a boy weighs 13 kg at 11 months, then the graph says that 97 per cent of boys of the same age will weigh less than he does and 3 per cent will, on average, weigh more. Care practitioners, such as health visitors and GPs, use percentile charts to monitor progress and note whether a child's growth is following an expected pattern.

Intellectual development

Intellectual development refers to the development of thinking and understanding. It involves changes in a person's ability to make sense of situations, remember and recall things and use language. Intellectual development begins in the womb and never really ends until the person dies. A great deal of basic intellectual development happens during infancy.

The Swiss psychologist Jean Piaget identified a number of stages of intellectual development. He saw infancy as the period when children went through the **sensorimotor stage**. During this stage, infants learn about themselves and the world through their senses (touch, hearing, sight, smell, and taste – hence *sensori*) and through physical activity (also known as *motor* activity). As well as handling, listening to and looking at new things, infants often put objects into their mouths as a way of investigating and trying to understand them.

One very important lesson that children learn during this stage is that objects and people in the world continue to exist even when they can't be seen. This might seem obvious to you now, but it's not to a young baby. A child of 8 months or less won't usually search for an object that has been hidden or which they drop out of sight because, to the child, it no longer seems to exist. A child will search for 'hidden' objects in later infancy because they develop what is known as **object permanence**. This means that they learn that objects do still exist even though they can't see them.

Language development

Learning to speak is a key feature of intellectual development during infancy. People who are responsible for young children have an important role to play in helping them to communicate well and to

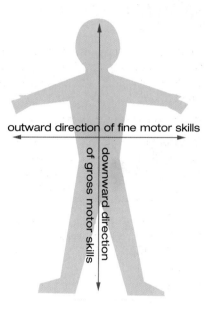

Figure 1.5 The direction of development.

Figure 1.6 A centile chart for a boy.

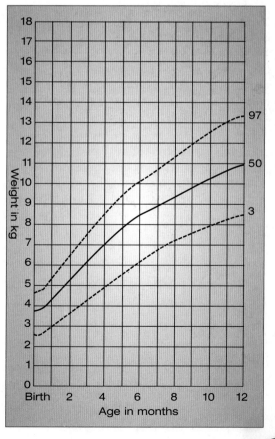

use language in a wide variety of ways. While children do not actually use their first proper words until they are about one year old, babies begin developing communication skills almost straight from birth.

A baby is, in fact, born with the ability to communicate in a range of ways, including through crying, babbling and using facial expressions. Infants acquire a better understanding of the world around them quite quickly as they begin to explore their surroundings and interact with their main carers. By the time they are 2 years old most children will point at and name familiar objects when they see them ('dog' or 'bus' for example) and be able to join a few simple words together ('go park' or 'shoes on', for example). However, whilst most children don't begin asking questions or using longer sentences until early childhood, the environment in which an infant lives can influence the speed and extent to which they develop intellectually. Stimulation, support and encouragement are all important features of this early learning.

Emotional and social development

Emotional and social development during infancy is extremely important. It is thought that a person's earliest relationships set the pattern for other relationships that they will go on to develop in each life stage. Ideally children should develop feelings of trust and security during infancy. This happens when a child establishes an **attachment relationship** with their parents or main caregivers in the first year of life. The parental response to this emotional linking is known as **bonding**. Attachment and bonding are needed for a first relationship to occur. The quality of the relationship between a baby and parent is influenced by:

- how sensitively the parent understands and responds to the baby's needs
- the personality of the parent or carer
- the consistency of the care that the baby receives
- the baby's own temperament.

We gradually expand our social circle during infancy by making relationships with brothers, sisters, other relatives and perhaps neighbours' children. These relationships are strongly influenced by the infant's emerging **communication skills**. A child is increasingly able to look at the world from the point of view of other people, becoming less **egocentric**, as they progress through infancy. This is demonstrated by the gradual changes that occur in the way in which children in this age group play.

Knowledge Check

1 What kinds of reflexes do newborn babies have?

2 What physical changes need to happen before a child can crawl?

3 Explain what gross motor skills are, giving examples.

4 Using examples, explain what fine motor skills are.

5 What is a percentile chart used for?

6 How do children learn during the sensorimotor stage of development?

7 What is an attachment relationship?

8 What factors help children to develop successful social relationships?

Investigate ...

Ask your parents about your own early growth and development. Try to find out whether you followed the expected pattern of development, when you reached different 'milestones' and what their memories are of you as a baby and infant.

0 – 1 year: solo play

Its difficult for me to think of people other than myself so I like to play on my own. I learn through exploring everything around me.

2 – 3 years: parallel play

I'm still mainly interested in myself and I can't see the sense of sharing yet. I am interested in other people so I like to be near them. I learn by imitating other people.

Figure 1.7 Early stages of play.

Case study

Luke is 18 months old. His mum, Cheryl, spends most time with Luke looking after him at home whilst his dad, Simon, is out at work. Cheryl has recently started taking Luke to a playgroup one day a week. Luke really enjoys this, running around, using the toys and playing alongside other children. Luke likes toys that he can pick up and hold, like teddies and small building blocks, as well as toys that he can push and move about, like toy cars and trains. Luke also likes dogs a lot. He will point and say 'dog' whenever he sees a dog on the television or whilst he is outside at the park or in his pram.

- Whom is Luke likely to have formed the strongest attachment relationship with?
- Give two examples of the gross motor skills Luke has developed.
- How does Luke use fine motor skills at the playgroup?
- What types of play does Luke take part in when he is at playgroup?
- Is Luke's language development appropriate for his age? Give reasons for your answer.

Early childhood (3–8 years)

Compared to infancy, childhood is quite a long life stage. Growth and development during childhood isn't as rapid as in infancy. However, a person will change a great deal in all of the PIES areas during their childhood.

Physical growth and development

If you go to a primary school you will see that learning activities in the reception and lower infant classes are often directed towards refining and expanding co-ordination and fine motor skills. Young children begin to gain greater control over their bodies and develop a range of complex physical skills during childhood. A child will improve their balance control and coordination early in childhood. This will allow them to develop more complex physical skills, such as skipping, catching a ball and riding a bicycle. A child's body changes noticeable in early childhood as they lose their baby shape and gradually develop the proportions of a small adult. Most children will experience a **growth spurt** in the middle part of childhood, though their rate of growth is slower in childhood than it was during infancy.

Intellectual development

According to Jean Piaget (see page 15), the second stage of intellectual development occurs in early childhood between the ages of 2 and 7 years. This is known as the **pre-operational stage**. In this stage children become less reliant on physical learning (seeing, touching and holding things) because they develop the ability to think about objects and **concepts** that are not actually there in front of them. Children need to understand concepts like numbers, letters of the alphabet and colours to be able to learn to read, write and tell the time. Intellectual development during childhood results in huge improvements in a child's thinking and language abilities and in their communication skills. In early childhood, children ask lots of questions in an attempt to understand more about their environment and the society in which they live. By the end of childhood a child will be able to use adult speech easily and will have vastly improved their knowledge and thinking skills.

Moral development

An important change occurs in a child's sense of values and in the way that they think about 'right' and 'wrong' and 'good' and 'bad' during early childhood. This is because a child's **conscience** is said to develop during this life stage.

During childhood children learn to base their judgements about right and wrong and good and bad on rules that they have been taught by people who have authority in their lives, such as parents and teachers. Children will generally obey rules if this means that they will avoid being punished or that they will receive rewards. The standards of morality that are taught or demonstrated by parents tend to have a big influence on young children who wish to be a 'good boy' or 'good girl'. This lasts until late childhood or early adolescence, when making a moral judgement becomes a more sophisticated process.

Emotional development

Children begin to learn to cope with their emotions and the feelings that others express towards them during early childhood. Controlling anger, jealousy and frustration and dealing with disapproval and criticism of their behaviour are part of emotional development during this life stage. A child's parents, siblings, teachers and friends all play a part in this process and also nurture a child's emotional development by offering love, acceptance and respect too. A child who feels encouraged and supported and who has good role models will develop self-confidence and a sense of independence more easily than a child who is criticized, discouraged and over-protected during early childhood.

Most children gradually increase their self-confidence, make friendships and become a little more independent at primary school. However, some children also find their first days at school are emotionally difficult and distressing. Children are able to cooperate, appreciate the viewpoints and feelings of others in ways that infants cannot. This enables children to play together and to join in groups and team games. Friendships become very important and can also be emotionally intense during childhood.

Social development

Children need to make relationships with people from outside of their own family during early childhood. They have to learn to co-operate, communicate and spend time with new people. Going to nursery and then primary school are two important ways in which children do this. Children's play changes from the **solo** and **parallel play** of infancy to **associative** and **cooperative play** during this life stage (see figure 1.8). Children are now able to choose their own friends and want their peers to like and approve of them. Successful social relationships among children are helped by:

- secure attachment in their early years
- mixing with other children, especially where this involves activities that require co-operation

Over to you!

What could a parent do to encourage a child to have a positive, happy attitude towards life?

Understanding Personal Development and Relationships

- the personality of the child: friendly, supportive and optimistic children make friends more easily than children who are negative and aggressive.

Most children develop a preference for same-sex friends and become very aware of and sensitive to differences between boys and girls.

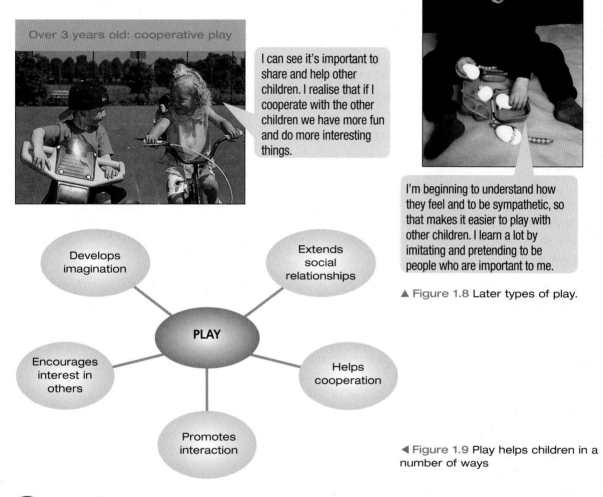

Over 3 years old: cooperative play

3 years old: associative play

I can see it's important to share and help other children. I realise that if I cooperate with the other children we have more fun and do more interesting things.

I'm beginning to understand how they feel and to be sympathetic, so that makes it easier to play with other children. I learn a lot by imitating and pretending to be people who are important to me.

▲ Figure 1.8 Later types of play.

PLAY

- Develops imagination
- Extends social relationships
- Encourages interest in others
- Helps cooperation
- Promotes interaction

◀ Figure 1.9 Play helps children in a number of ways

Case study

Hanif, aged 5, has recently started primary school. He was anxious at first but now he loves to go. He likes playing with other children, painting and listening to the stories that his teacher reads to the class. Hanif's teacher encourages him to take part in a range of practical activities and always praises him for doing his best and working with other children. Hanif is learning to name colours, write his name and count to ten. Hanif's teacher has noticed that he has made two friends in the class whom he likes to sit by and play with. Hanif and his two friends often chase each other around the playground and play imaginary games together.

- Which stage of intellectual development is Hanif in?
- What kinds of concepts will Hanif need to understand to be able to write a story and do basic arithmetic?
- How will the development of Hanif's conscience affect his behaviour during this life stage?
- What evidence is there that Hanif has developed socially since starting primary school?
- What kind of play does Hanif now take part in with his friends?

Understanding Personal Development and Relationships

1 What kinds of physical skills do children develop during childhood?

2 How does a child's thinking change develop during childhood?

3 What does the term moral development refer to?

4 How can going to school influence a child's social development?

5 How can a child's self-confidence and independence be developed?

6 What does the term 'egocentric' mean?

7 What is cooperative play?

Adolescence (9–18 years)

Adolescence can begin from the age of 9 and typically ends at about 18 years of age. The process of maturation that happens in this life stage is called **puberty**. It is a process that results in a lot of physical growth and change as well as considerable intellectual, emotional and social development.

Physical growth and change

The growth spurt and physical changes that occur in puberty are caused by an increase in hormonal activity. **Hormones** are chemical secretions that pass directly into the blood from the endocrine glands. The thyroid gland and the pituitary gland are the two main glands that secrete growth and development hormones. Several different hormones are secreted by each of these glands (see figure 1.10).

The pituitary gland controls the production of hormones that affect growth and development. The pituitary gland is located at the base of the brain and is only the size of a pea. The thyroid gland is located in the neck. It influences our general growth rate, bone and muscle development and the functioning of our reproductive organs. During puberty the testes in boys produce the hormone testosterone and the ovaries in girls produce oestrogen and progesterone. These hormones control the development and function of the reproductive organs.

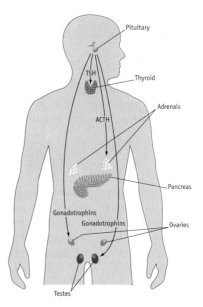

Figure 1.10 Hormones are released from endocrine glands.

Figure 1.11 Physical changes in puberty.

Physical changes in boys	Physical changes in girls
Grow taller and heavier	Grow taller and heavier
Grow pubic, facial and underarm hair	Menstruation (periods) start
Penis and testes grow larger	Develop breasts
Shoulders and chest broaden and muscles develop	Hips broaden and shape changes
Voice 'breaks' or deepens	Grow pubic and underarm hair

During puberty boys and girls develop the secondary sexual characteristics that enable them to produce children and which give them their adult body shape.

Intellectual development

The emergence of **abstract thinking** skills is the key feature of intellectual development during adolescence. A person who can think abstractly can think about things in a theoretical or hypothetical way. For example, mathematical equations involve abstract thinking as does thinking about what you would like to do in the future. Children do not have abstract thinking skills so they can't plan ahead in the same way as adolescents. Piaget called this the **formal operational** stage of intellectual development. It enables the person to use logic to think through and solve the problems they face in everyday life. Abstract thinking is considered to be the final stage of thought development. However, a person's intellectual development is not completed in adolescence because we gain and use experience during early, middle and later adulthood to improve our thinking, understanding and decision-making.

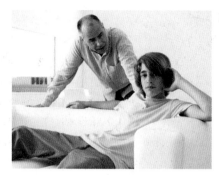

Emotions and relationships can feel intense and be difficult for many adolescents to manage

Emotional development

Adolescence can be an emotionally difficult but eventful time. The hormonal changes of puberty can cause mood swings and intense emotions that may at times be difficult for the adolescent, as well as their family and friends, to cope with. Developing a clear personal identity, making friendships and experiencing emotional support from peers and family members are all important concerns in this phase.

Adolescents often experiment with intimate personal relationships with members of the opposite sex, and sometimes the same sex, as they explore their sexuality and the positive and negative emotions that result from close relationships. This experimentation can include making decisions about whether or not to engage in sexual activity as part of a boyfriend/girlfriend relationship. In this phase of emotional development, individuals tend to gain greater understanding of their own emotions as well as the thoughts, feelings and motives of others.

Social development

Adolescents strive to achieve a personal identity that is distinctive and separate from that of their parents. As a result social relationships with people outside of the person's immediate family become more important. For example, peer groups and close friends become important influences and sources of advice and guidance in the quest for a new sense of 'who' the adolescent is. The questioning and sometimes rejection of parent's values and opinions that is often a part of this process can lead to conflict. Adolescents may also experiment with their clothes, appearance and behaviour to both try and find an identity for themselves and to fit in with others of the same age and background. Wearing the right clothes, listening to the right music and being seen in the right places with the right people become important issues for many adolescents. Because of their need to fit in and achieve a sense of belonging to a peer group, some adolescents experiment with alcohol, drugs and sexual relationships. **Peer group pressure** can lead some adolescents into

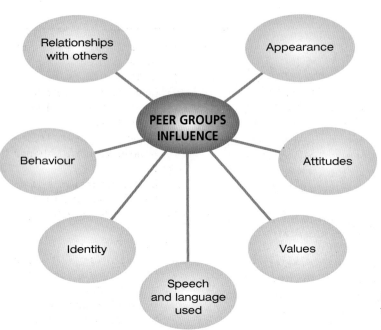

Figure 1.12 Peer groups affect various aspects of development.

activities and situations that they find difficult to resist or challenge despite them knowing that they shouldn't participate.

Moral development

During adolescence the way that people think about moral issues - such as the difference between 'right' and 'wrong' - changes. Adolescents typically base their judgements about what is 'right' and 'wrong' on the rules, or norms, of the social groups to which they belong. Family, friendship and peer groups and any churches or clubs to which we belong influence our moral judgements. In contrast to childhood when we believe that good behaviour is what pleases the important individuals in our lives, we tend to be guided by the more abstract laws and rules of society during adolescence. Adolescents are more likely to be guided by a sense of duty to conform to the general rules of the social groups to which they belong rather than obeying the specific things that their parents tell them. Being law abiding and a good citizen or accepted as one of the gang is now more important than being a 'good boy' or a 'good girl'.

Over to you!

How have you developed since you left primary school? Using the headings 'Physical development', 'Intellectual development', 'Emotional development' and 'Social development' list the ways in which you have changed and developed since this time.

Knowledge Check

1 What is the process of maturation that happens in adolescence called?

2 Describe three physical changes that girls experience during puberty.

3 Describe three physical changes that boys experience during puberty.

4 How do hormones influence growth and development during adolescence?

5 Which new type of thinking skill develops during adolescence?

6 How is a person's way of judging moral issues likely to change during adolescence?

7 What does the term 'peer group' mean?

8 Explain why conflict with parents is often a feature of adolescence.

Case study

Maddie is 14 years of age. She currently has a poor relationship with her mum who she says is 'too mean and always picking on me'. Maddie believes that she is 'grown up enough' to meet her friends from school in town on Saturday. Maddie's parents agreed until one of their neighbours told them that Maddie had been seen smoking and drinking alcohol with her friends and some older boys in the garden of a local pub. Maddie's parents were very annoyed about this and have since stopped her from going out at weekends unless they are with her. Maddie is equally annoyed with her parents. She claims their reaction is 'embarrassing' her and that they are ruining her friendships. Maddie refuses to accept that she has done anything wrong because 'no one got hurt, did they?' She becomes very angry when her mum says that she will 'get a reputation' if she carries on behaving like this. Maddie argues that as 'everyone else treats me like an adult, you should too'.

- What is the process of maturation that Maddie is currently experiencing called?
- Describe the main physical effects that Maddie's hormones will be having on her body.
- Explain why teenagers like Maddie often come into conflict with their parents.
- Are Maddie's parents right to be concerned about her behaviour or is this 'normal' for someone in her life stage?
- Do you think Maddie's social development is likely to be helped or hindered by close involvement with her peer group?
- Why do you think Maddie is unable to accept her parents view that her behaviour is wrong?

Early adulthood (19–45 years)

Early adulthood is when people commonly think of themselves as being 'grown up'. It is, in some ways, the high point of human development. Early adulthood is the developmental stage in which people achieve their maximum physical size and capacity and the stage at which a person's intellectual abilities are at their peak. Overall, adulthood is the longest human life stage though there are significant differences between early, middle and late adulthood.

Physical growth and development

Physical changes in adulthood are not like the changes that occur in childhood and adolescence, as they are not always about growth. Physical growth is largely complete by the end of adolescence. However, a lot of physical development does occur in early adulthood as people apply their physical potential and abilities. For example, most people are capable of achieving their maximum physical performance during early adulthood. You may have noticed that athletes and sports professionals tend to achieve their best performances while they are young adults. Early adulthood is also the life stage in which men and women usually produce their children.

Physical change is occurring gradually throughout early adulthood. A person's physique, their fitness and their physical abilities are all slowly declining as the person ages. For example, in the second half of early adulthood, from about 30 years to 45 years, the amount of fatty tissue in a person's body increases, they move more slowly and take longer to recover from their efforts. By the end of early adulthood, many people have begun to lose their hair or go grey and will begin to see wrinkles developing around their eyes as their skin becomes less supple.

Most women have their children during early adulthood.

Intellectual development

Adults are generally capable of abstract thought, have memories functioning at their peak and can think very quickly. Adults often improve their intellectual skills and abilities through education and training and by using them to solve problems at work and in everyday life situations. Acquiring new knowledge and skills is necessary during adulthood to cope with the changes that frequently occur in a person's personal life – such as having children – or at work or in the job they do. People who seek to progress in their jobs or gain promotion will need to undertake some additional learning to achieve their goals. Compared to older people, however, younger adults lack experience. As a result, they may not always make good decisions or have the same depth of knowledge.

Emotional development

It is difficult to generalise about emotional development in early adulthood because people have such a broad range of experiences. Achieving a stable and fulfilling relationship, perhaps also having children, is a life goal for many young adults. However, other young adults choose to live their life without a partner and may not wish to have children either. Adults are expected to be emotionally mature and to have more self-control and self-awareness than adolescents.

Figure 1.13 Factors influencing adult emotional development.

People can experience a number of transitions that have important emotional consequences during early adulthood. Marriage and divorce, parenthood and increasing work responsibility, and the loss of elderly parents for example, are life events that may be experienced during early adulthood and which influence emotional development.

Moral development

Many people find that they need to revise their ways of judging right and wrong and how they make other moral judgements during adulthood. This happens where people discover that the complexities of adult life mean the simple, clear-cut moral rules they used in adolescence are no longer helpful. As a result some adults develop what is known as **principled morality**. This means that they tend to make judgements on self-chosen principles. They discover situations where they feel that rules and laws need to be ignored or changed and try to use universal principles like truth, equality and social justice to make their decisions. This way of thinking about moral issues is clearly very different to that of children who apply simple rules to gain the approval of parents and other people.

Social development

People typically leave home to live independently of their family in early adulthood. Greater independence requires new relationships. Often young adults make new friendships through work and social life, focus quite strongly on finding a partner and sustaining an intimate relationship. New responsibilities and an extension of the person's social circle may also result from marriage or cohabitation. Much of adulthood is concerned with trying to find a balance between the competing demands of work, family and friends. Each of these types of relationship contributes to social development by giving the person a sense of connection and belonging to others.

Over to you!

What skills, qualities or abilities do you want to develop by the time you reach middle adulthood? Make some lists using these headings.

Case study

Richard Masters is 41 years of age. As an ambitious deputy head teacher, Richard has recently attended a course to prepare him for a headship. He is hoping to apply for jobs in the near future. However, other parts of Richard's life are less successful. Richard feels very disappointed that his 18-year marriage has failed. His wife and 11-year-old daughter Katy have moved away and he is missing them. Richard feels that he still has a responsibility to support Katy financially and wants to maintain his close parental relationship with her. Richard's mother Belinda, who is 82 years of age, recently moved to live in a residential home as she is no longer able to live on her own. Belinda now relies on Richard for practical and emotional support. She looks forward to visits from Richard and Katy as they usually have lots of news to tell her. Richard hasn't told his mum about his marital problems and he is feeling very stressed by this.

- Which aspect of Richard's development has been affected by his attendance at the recent headship training course?
- How would you expect Richard's body to have changed during the life stage he is currently in?
- Identify three experiences Richard has had during early adulthood that will have influenced his emotional development.
- How might Richard's personal development be affected by the failure of his marriage?
- In what ways might Richard's personal development be affected by his changing relationship with his mother?
- What could Richard do to improve his social development as he enters middle adulthood?

Knowledge Check

1 What kinds of physical changes happen in early adulthood?

2 Explain why intellectual development is important during early adulthood.

3 What kind of events can affect emotional during early adulthood?

4 Why are most athletics records set by people in early adulthood?

5 What does the term 'principled morality' mean?

6 Describe the kinds of factors that influence social development during early adulthood.

UNIT 1

Middle adulthood (46–65 years)

Some people view the middle phase of adulthood – or middle age – in a positive way, seeing it as a person's best years. Others view it with dread and associate it with the loss of youth and the onset of old age. The majority of people who reach middle adulthood can expect to live into later adulthood though they will experience significant physical, intellectual, emotional and social changes during this period of their life.

Physical development

Physical change becomes more obvious again during middle adulthood. During this phase of adulthood many people experience a reduction in their physical abilities and a decline in their physical performance compared to earlier stages of their life. These physical changes are often referred to as **ageing**. During middle adulthood a person is likely to experience some or all of the following physical changes:

Physical fitness maintains health in middle age.

- Increasing and more obvious hair loss
- Slower movement and reduced stamina
- Reduced hand-eye coordination
- Less muscle power
- Deteriorating eyesight
- Appearance of wrinkles as the skin loses elasticity
- Decline in fertility as sperm production diminishes (men)
- Loss of natural fertility following the onset of menopause (women)
- An increase in weight.

The role of hormones

Both men and women lose some or all of their ability to reproduce during middle adulthood. In men a gradual reduction in fertility occurs as their levels of testosterone decline throughout adulthood. A better-known physical change is the one which affects women. **Menopause**, or the ending of menstruation and the natural ability to produce children, occurs because a woman's ovaries produce less and less of the hormones oestrogen and progesterone until a point is reached at which the ovaries stop producing eggs.

Intellectual development

The highest position that a person achieves in their job or career is often reached during middle adulthood. This is the life stage where people are able to combine intellectual abilities developed during adolescence and early adulthood with the experience they have gained throughout their working life. Many people in this life stage also seek intellectual stimulation through their hobbies and social life or by extending their education through evening classes or other part-time courses. It is also not unusual for people to retrain for new careers or to pursue new directions in their personal life during their middle age. These kinds of changes often require the person to acquire further knowledge and learn new skills.

Emotional development

The nature of emotional development during middle adulthood is often determined by the emotional foundations laid by the person earlier in life. For some people, middle adulthood is a period of contentment and satisfaction. For others, it is a period of crisis. People who experience good health, financial stability and already have caring and supportive family and friends are more likely to enjoy their middle age than those who fear growing old, have health problems and lack support from others.

Social development

Social development during middle adulthood tends to revolve around people trying to achieve their position in society, their ambitions in life and adjustments to some of their existing relationships. During middle adulthood people often find that they need to review and adjust their social relationships as children leave home (the 'empty-nest syndrome'), parents become unwell or infirm and retirement from work becomes a reality. For many people, these changes in social relationships have a significant impact and result in changes to their self-concept. Adjusting to the 'empty-nest syndrome', retiring from work and finding a new role and purpose in life are social challenges faced by many people in this life stage.

Changing relationships with own (adult) children

Retirement from work

SOCIAL CHANGES

Changing relationships with ageing parents

Promotion and increased responsibilities at work

Figure 1.14 Social changes during middle age.

Case study

Elizabeth is 47 years of age. Recently she has been feeling as if she is both mentally and physically unwell. She has tried to explain this to her husband but can't properly express how she feels or explain how bad it can get some days. Elizabeth's husband said she should see her GP (family doctor) to get some help. Elizabeth is reluctant to do this in case she gets 'bad news'. She is now having trouble sleeping because of hot flushes. She has a lot of aches and pains and feels very irritable with her family and work colleagues. Elizabeth explained to her friend Jo that she feels lonely, unloved and that she 'might be suffering from a terrible disease or something'. Every day seems like a struggle for Elizabeth. She is worried because she knows something is happening to her but she doesn't understand what this is.

- What is the name of the physical change that is affecting Elizabeth?
- Explain why Elizabeth is experiencing this physical change.
- How might Elizabeth's emotional development be affected by this experience?
- What could Jo do or say that might be supportive for Elizabeth?

Knowledge Check

1 Describe three physical changes that affect people during middle adulthood.

2 What does the term 'menopause' refer to?

3 Why do women experience the menopause?

4 What can people do to promote their intellectual development during middle adulthood?

5 Describe how the 'empty-nest' syndrome might affect an individual's personal development during middle adulthood.

Understanding Personal Development and Relationships

Later adulthood (65+ years)

The process of physical ageing quickens for all people from about the age of 55 years. By the age of 75 years the physical effects of ageing are clearly evident. However, despite the reality of physical decline in later adulthood older people don't suddenly or always become unwell, infirm or need extra care. Many older people are physically healthy, robust and active enough to continue living without any special support in their own homes. While the stereotypes of older people are quite negative, the gradual decline in abilities that occur in later adulthood doesn't necessarily mean that older people have a poor quality of life or are unhappy.

Physical development

During later adulthood people experience a gradual physical decline in both the structure and functioning of their body. These changes are part of the normal ageing process and include:

Older people are often physically active.

- Reduced heart and lung function.

- Reduced mobility, often resulting from muscle wastage, brittle bones and stiff joints.

- Loss of elasticity in the skin and the development of wrinkles.

- Changes in hair colour (grey then white) and texture (finer and thinner). Many men, and a smaller proportion of women, lose hair from the top of the head.

- Changes to the nervous system may impair the person's sense of taste and smell and can mean that they are less sensitive to the cold. This increases the risk of hypothermia.

- Hearing tends to deteriorate slowly as people age. Quiet and high-pitched sounds (and voices!) become more difficult to hear.

- Sight is affected because the lens in the eye loses its elasticity. The result is that older people find it harder to focus on close objects.

- Weakening of bones, also known as **osteoporosis**, also affects some people in later adulthood. Calcium and protein are lost from the bones and older people can become physically frail and experience fractures as a result.

- Many people become shorter in later adulthood as their **intervertebral discs** in the spine become thinner and their posture becomes bent.

Intellectual development

Ageing doesn't necessarily reduce intellectual ability

Older people maintain and use their intellectual abilities in much the same ways as adults and middle-aged people. Both the young-old (60–75 years) and the old-old (75 years and over) need and enjoy intellectually stimulating activities in their lives. The speed at which older people are able to think and respond is generally reduced, but mental capacity and intelligence are not lost. Older people do not become any less intelligent as a result of ageing!

There are many negative ideas about older people's intellectual abilities. While it is true that a minority of older people do

Understanding Personal Development and Relationships

develop **dementia-related illnesses** and have memory problems, the majority of older people do not. People who develop dementia-related illnesses tend to have memory problems, especially in recalling recent information, and become confused more easily. These types of illnesses also result in sufferers gradually losing speech and other abilities that are controlled by the brain.

Emotional and social development

Social and emotional development takes on a new importance in the later stages of the life span. Many older people reflect on their achievements and past experiences as a way of making sense of their life. This may involve coming to terms with the changes that occur in their relationships as children move into early and middle adulthood, partners and friends may die and a range of previous life roles (work and personal) may end. However, older people do continue to develop and change emotionally as they experience new life events and transitions, such as becoming grandparents and retiring from work. They may also have more leisure time in which to build relationships with friends and family members. Despite this many older people also experience insecurity and loneliness if their social contacts are reduced and they become isolated.

Grandchildren can enhance later life.

Case study

Maureen Walker is 83 years of age, and very proud of it! She has one son who is now in his early sixties. Maureen's husband Gerald died ten years ago. Her only sister Stella died earlier this year. Maureen is still grieving for the loss of her sister. However, Maureen is very sociable and keen to make the most of each day. She enjoys driving her Mini around town, visiting friends and keeping appointments with the large number of people she knows. Maureen likes to go the local garden centre for her lunch. The staff at the garden centre expect her each day and keep a table by the counter so that she can chat to them during her lunch. Maureen is also well known to health care workers as she makes regular visits to see her GP, Dr Teddy. Maureen has been suffering from curvature of the spine since her late sixties and now walks with a stoop. She also complains of aches and pains in her joints and back and has had some problems with her right hip. Despite this, Maureen is proud of her advancing years and believes that she is very healthy for her age. She is a leading member of a local art group, though she says that her paintings aren't as good since she started having problems with her eyes a few years ago. Maureen visits her sons and her grandchildren, who are now adults, as often as she can and loves to talk to people talks about their achievements.

- Which aspects of Maureen's physical health may be the result of normal ageing?
- Which aspects of Maureen's life are likely to influence her intellectual development and wellbeing?
- Which events in Maureen's life may have had a significant effect on her emotional development?
- How might Maureen's relationships with others contribute to her social development and wellbeing?
- What effect might normal ageing have had on Maureen's intellectual abilities?

Knowledge Check

1 Is it true that some people get shorter in old age?

2 Explain why people develop wrinkles as they grow older.

3 What does the term 'osteoporosis' mean and why does it occur?

4 Do all people over the age of 70 suffer from dementia-type illnesses?

5 What kinds of events can affect a person's emotional and social development during later adulthood?

Investigate ...

Use your knowledge of human growth and development to produce a set of questions that you could use to interview an adult or older person about their pattern and experiences of growth and development. You will need to ensure that your interviewee is a willing volunteer and is happy for you to write about the things they tell you. Produce a timeline and a profile describing the key features of and influences on the person's growth and development.

Self-concept

A person's self-concept is their view of 'who' they are. Self-concept is a combination of self-image and self-esteem. An individual's self-concept is continually developing during each life stage and is closely linked to emotional and social development. It expresses what we think and feel about ourselves as individuals and gives us our sense of identity.

Self-esteem refers to the way a person values themselves. Self-esteem often results from the way we compare ourselves to other people. People who compare themselves negatively to others, thinking they are not as good, not as attractive or not as capable are more likely to have low self-esteem. People who are confident but not arrogant, who accept that they have both strengths and weaknesses, and who feel encouraged, loved and wanted, tend not to undervalue themselves so much. Their self-esteem is generally higher as a result.

Over to you!

Think about your main features and characteristics. For example, consider:

- your height
- your gender
- your eye colour
- where you live
- your personality

Using both words and pictures, produce a self-portrait that describes your own view of the 'essential you' at this point in your life

Figure 1.15 Aspects of self-concept.

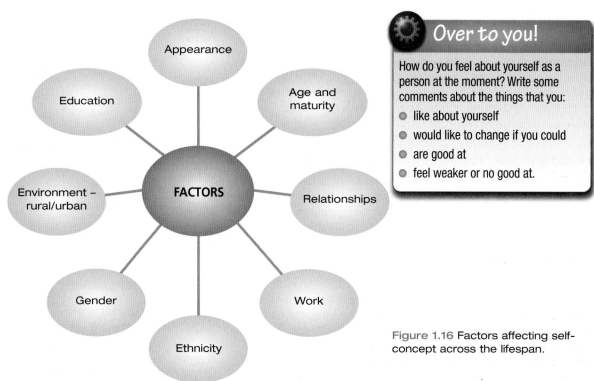

Over to you!

How do you feel about yourself as a person at the moment? Write some comments about the things that you:
- like about yourself
- would like to change if you could
- are good at
- feel weaker or no good at.

Figure 1.16 Factors affecting self-concept across the lifespan.

Having a clear, positive picture of who we are and how we feel about ourselves helps to make us feel secure and affects the way that we relate to other people. A number of factors influence the way an individual's self-concept develops and changes.

Age and maturity

The image that you have of yourself today will not be the same self-image that you reflect on when you are 40, 60 or 80 years old. The physical, intellectual, emotional and social changes that occur as you age and mature will affect your self-concept over time. For example, a person's self-image can be linked to the view that they have of their physical capabilities. Your physical capabilities will change as you experience health, fitness, illness and disability at different points in your life. The value that society attaches to you as an individual will also alter as you grow older. In Western societies old age is generally viewed negatively and older people seem to be less valued than younger people. This is sometimes different for members of minority ethnic groups who may value old age more. The way that people of different ages are portrayed in the media confirms this and inevitably affects the self-concepts of many older people.

An individual will generally become more emotionally mature as they age. Growing maturity allows a person to become more reflective and accepting of themselves. This can mean that as people age they come to recognise both their personal strengths and limitations. Emotional maturity and self-knowledge play an important part in an individual's ability to establish and maintain close personal relationships as well as working relationships with others.

Appearance

A person's physical features, their clothes and their non-verbal behaviour, all influence and express aspects of their self-concept. How we present ourselves and how we believe others see us are particularly important influences on self-concept when we are adolescents and young adults. As we get older, physical appearance and the way that we present ourselves tend to have a smaller impact on our self-concept.

Ethnicity

Ethnicity affects self-concept by influencing people's feelings of belonging and ideas about membership of different social groups. Culture and ethnic identity can, for example, give people a sense of shared values. However, it can also lead to people being treated differently, perhaps in an unfair and discriminatory way, and thereby affects their sense of self-worth and self-esteem.

Gender

Gender refers to the way ideas about masculinity and femininity are applied to men and women in our society. Wider social attitudes towards gender can shape a person's self-concept. In Western societies there are a number of **gender stereotypes** associated with male and female roles and behaviour. The images of men and women presented in the media express these stereotypes and the general social expectations of men and women.

Even though gender stereotypes do not reflect the reality of most people's lives in British society they can still shape self-image and self-esteem in a positive way, especially where an individual is able and wishes to conform to the roles and ways of looking and behaving that the stereotypes suggest. Gender stereotypes can also have a negative effect on self-concept. They can induce guilt, a sense of inadequacy and lack of self-confidence, especially where the person is unable or unwilling to match up to the stereotype of men or women in a particular situation.

Urban/rural environments

The type of environment into which we are born and develop can influence and shape our self-concept. Housing, the amount of money a family has and the quality of the physical surroundings in which they live are all important environmental features. Different types of environments give people different opportunities and expose people to different pressures and influences. For example, people growing up in an urban, inner-city environment have different experiences, pressures and opportunities to those of people who grow up in rural, village surroundings. These different experiences are likely to be reflected in individuals' self-concepts as they try to work out who they are in relation to the type of environment they live in.

Investigate ...

Use your knowledge and understanding of the influences on self-concept to write some survey questions about the way male and female teenagers think about themselves and develop their self-concepts. Conduct your survey by asking the questions to an equal number of boys and girls. Write a brief summary of your findings.

Education

Educational experiences can have a major impact on a person's self-concept. The things that teachers and fellow students say, and the way that they treat us, can affect our self-image and self-esteem during childhood and adolescence. We are very open to suggestions about who and what we are during these life stages. For some people, educational success helps to form a positive self-image and promotes high self-esteem. For others, school can be a more negative experience that leaves them feeling less capable than others, or with a negative view of themselves, their skills and their self-worth.

Relationships

The relationships that an individual has, especially within their family, during education and at work, will have a powerful effect on their self-concept. Family relationships play a critical role in shaping our self-concept. Early relationships are built on effective attachments to parents and close family members. The sense of security and feelings of being loved that can develop from these bonds are key ingredients in a positive self-concept. Poor family relationships, however, can do lasting damage to a person's self-concept.

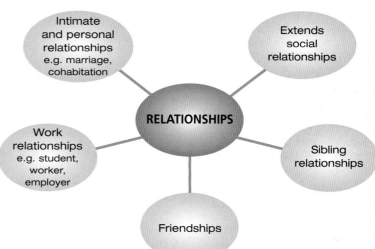

Figure 1.17 Relationships affecting self-concept.

We go through a number of phases of emotional and sexual development during adolescence and adulthood as we experience new friendships and more intimate relationships with non-family members. These experiences affect our self-concept. Simply because we grow older and become more emotionally mature, we also tend to adapt our outlook and behaviour towards others to take account of the thoughts and feelings that other people have. For example, a couple who may both have had a strong images of themselves as young, free and single individuals learn new things about themselves and have to adapt their self-concepts when they form an intimate, long-term partnership or get married.

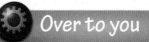

Over to you

Identify one way in which the following individuals have influenced your personal development:

- Your mum or dad
- Your brother(s) or sister(s)
- Another relative in your family
- A teacher
- A friend
- Neighbours.

Analyse which aspects of your development each person influenced and then explain who has had the most significant effect on the development of your self-concept.

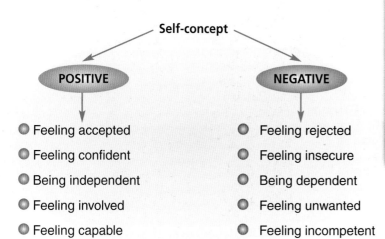

◀ Figure 1.18 Effects of positive and negative self-concepts.

Case study

Rachel Stein is 25 years old. She has been doing a lot of thinking about herself and her life recently. Rachel has worked in the same nursery since leaving school at 18. This is something Rachel now regrets. In particular, she felt left out and a bit of a failure when her friends all went off to university. Despite enjoying her job as a nursery team leader, Rachel feels she could – and should – have achieved more in life. Because she works long work hours, Rachel doesn't meet up with her friends very often. In fact, she rarely sees people outside of work. Many of Rachel's friends have also got married over the last few years. Rachel regrets not having found a partner but can't see why anyone would be attracted to her. Rachel thinks she looks 'plain and a bit overweight'. She has started to think that her life is not as good as that of other people her age. Rachel looks at herself in the mirror each morning, wondering how she got into this situation, wishing she could change the way that she feels about herself and her life.

- What image does Rachel have of herself?
- How would you describe Rachel's self-esteem?
- Using the information provided in the example, summarise Rachel's self-concept.
- What factors do you think have influenced the way Rachel's self-concept has developed?
- Explain why Rachel's self-concept is likely to change as she moves through adulthood.

Knowledge Check

1 What does the term 'self-concept' mean?

2 Why might a person have low self-esteem?

3 What are the characteristics of high self-esteem?

4 How can a person's educational experiences affect their self-concept?

5 What impact can family relationships have on an individual's self-concept?

6 During which life stage does physical appearance seem to have a strong influence on an individual's self-concept?

7 Explain how a person's ethnic ... ay have a positive effect on their self-concept.

8 Explain how being uncomfortable with your gender may affect a person's self-concept.

9 Describe how a person's self-concept changes as they get older.

Topic review

The box below provides a summary of the areas covered in
Topic 1.1. Tick the areas that you feel you understand and would
be confident answering exam questions about. If there are any
areas that you don't understand or are not confident about, you
will need to return to them before you begin your exam revision.

Life stages ☐
Developmental norms ☐
Infancy
  Physical growth ☐
  Physical development ☐
  Intellectual development ☐
  Emotional development ☐
  Social development ☐

Childhood
  Physical growth ☐
  Physical development ☐
  Intellectual development ☐
  Emotional development ☐
  Social development ☐

Adolescence
  Physical growth ☐
  Physical development ☐
  Intellectual development ☐
  Emotional development ☐
  Social development ☐

Early adulthood
  Physical growth ☐
  Physical development ☐
  Intellectual development ☐
  Emotional development ☐
  Social development ☐

Middle adulthood
  Physical growth ☐
  Physical development ☐
  Intellectual development ☐
  Emotional development ☐
  Social development ☐

Later adulthood
  Physical growth ☐
  Physical development ☐
  Intellectual development ☐
  Emotional development ☐
  Social development ☐

Self-concept
  Factors affecting self-concept ☐

Assessment Guide

Your learning in this unit will be assessed through a one hour
and fifteen minute written examination.

The examination will consist of multiple-choice questions and a
series of questions based on case studies and short scenarios.

You will need to show that you understand:

- The stages and patterns of human growth and
  development
- The different factors that can affect human growth and
  development
- The development of self-concept.

Understanding Personal Development and Relationships

Topic 1.2

Factors affecting human growth and development

Topic focus

What factors cause human beings to grow and develop? Human growth and development is a complex process that follows some predictable patterns and processes but which also results in people who are unique and individually different. Topic 1.2 focuses on the different types of factors that affect human growth and development, including:

● *Physical factors*, such as **genetic inheritance**, illness and disease, diet, exercise, alcohol and smoking

● *Social, cultural and emotional factors*, such as family, friends, educational experiences, employment / unemployment, community involvement, gender, **ethnicity, culture** and religion, **sexual orientation** and relationship formation

● *Economic factors*, including income and wealth, poverty and **material possessions**

● *Environmental factors*, such as air and noise pollution, housing conditions and rural / urban lifestyles

● *Psychological factors* such as stress, relationships with family, friends and partners.

This topic focuses on how these factors can influence an individual's pattern of growth and development and their self-concept.

Physical factors
e.g. genetic inheritance, diet, exercise

● **Growth**
● **Health**
● **Wellbeing**
● **Life opportunities**

Social and environmental factors
e.g. gender, family, friends, education, ethnicity, culture, religion, employment/ unemployment

Environmental factors
e.g. pollution, housing conditions

Economic factors
e.g. income/wealth, material possessions, property, social class

Figure 1.19 Factors affecting growth and development.

Physical factors

The genes we inherit, our diet, the amount and type of exercise we undertake, whether we smoke or consume alcohol to excess and the illnesses and diseases we experience are all examples of physical factors that can affect our growth and development.

Genetic inheritance

The genes that we inherit from our parents play a very important role in controlling our physical growth, appearance and the abilities we develop. Each cell in the human body contains two sets of 23 chromosomes – one set from each parent.

Each **chromosome** can contain up to 4,000 different genes. These are the 'instructions' or codes that tell our body's cells how to grow. The genes that control how we grow are a unique combination of our biological parents' genes. One consequence of this is that we can do very little to change the physical features and growth potential that we have. If both of your biological parents are over 6 feet tall, have large feet and are fast runners, you are also likely to grow tall, have large feet and be able to run fast! It also follows that if your parents aren't tall, you are very unlikely to grow tall. Because of your genetic inheritance, you will grow and develop to look like one or both of your parents as your body responds to the 'instructions' in your genes.

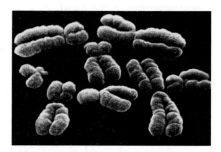
Human chromosomes magnified.

Genes also carry a lot of information that affects growth and development throughout life. A person's genes are often responsible for the illnesses and diseases that they develop during their lifetime. This is because the risk of getting conditions like heart disease, cancers and **strokes** can be inherited. A person born into a family with a history of heart disease is at greater risk of developing this condition if they have inherited 'heart disease genes'. Whether this person goes on to develop heart disease or not will depend on many non-genetic factors too. Lifestyle, for example, will be a key issue for a person in this position.

Illness and disease

Many of the illnesses that we experience are short-term and treatable. Coughs, colds and even broken limbs can all be cured with the right medicine and treatment and don't have any lasting impact on growth or development. However, some illnesses and diseases can have much more serious consequences. Genetic diseases, such as haemophilia, Down's syndrome and cystic fibrosis, are all lifelong conditions that cannot be cured and which have an impact on a person's growth and development. Infectious diseases, such as tuberculosis, meningitis and HIV, can also cause significant and permanent damage to a person's health and development and may prove fatal if left untreated. Degenerative conditions, such as Alzheimer's disease, multiple sclerosis and arthritis, tend to affect people's health and development opportunities in adulthood or later adulthood. As well as having a severe physical impact, degenerative conditions such as these can also have a major impact on a person's social relationships, result in emotional distress and destroy their intellectual abilities.

Diet

Food is essential for life and a balanced diet is the basis of good physical health. This is true in all life stages. However, the amount and types of food that a person requires to meet their physical needs will depend on factors such

Investigate ...

Use the Internet to research the following genetic conditions: PKU, cystic fibrosis, sickle cell anaemia and Friedrich's ataxia. Identify:

● What each condition is
● The main effects on the health and development needs of individuals who have the condition
● How the condition is treated.

Case study

Victor O'Brien is 72 years old. He was diagnosed with Alzheimer's disease three years ago. Victor first noticed problems with his memory when he was out shopping with his wife. He often had difficulty recalling what he wanted to buy and relied on his wife remembering where they had parked the car. Victor gave up driving when his memory problems and bouts of confusion increased. Victor's GP finally sent him to see a consultant psychiatrist at the local district general hospital when Victor got lost after popping out to get a newspaper from his local shop. Victor walked over 10 miles looking for his home and was eventually found, crying and frightened by the police. Victor still lives at home with his wife. She now helps him to wash, dress and eat. Victor says less and less but does like to sit listening to the radio. He has lost the ability to read and write though his wife believes that Victor does still recognise her and is able to understand most of what she says to him.

- How has Alzheimer's disease affected Victor's mental health?
- What impact has Victor's condition had on his intellectual development and wellbeing?
- What kind of care needs does Victor have as a result of having Alzheimer's disease?
- What could Victor's wife do to ensure that Victor is as physically healthy as he can be?

as their age, physical build and gender as well as how physically active they are.

An infant less than six months old can gain all the nutrients they require from breast milk or infant formula (specially made powdered milk). However, as they become more active they need to be weaned on to a balanced range of solid foods in order to grow and develop appropriately.

Children also need a balanced diet to maintain their physical growth and development and provide 'fuel' for their increasingly active lives and growing bodies. When a child consumes too much food, or an excessive amount of sugary or fatty food, they are likely to become overweight or even **obese**. This can harm the child's physical development as it may reduce their opportunities to exercise, limit mobility and hinder muscle development. Being overweight or obese can also lead to social and emotional problems for children. Being teased or bullied for being 'fat' may have a negative effect on a child's emotional development because it can lead to low self-esteem. An obese or overweight child may develop a negative self-image that also inhibits their self-confidence and their ability to make and maintain relationships with other children.

Diet can have both a positive and negative effect on health and development.

The onset of puberty during adolescence results in a physical growth spurt that has to be 'fuelled' by a diet of nutritionally balanced and regular meals. However, at the same time as needing to feed a growing and rapidly changing body, adolescents (particularly girls) become more conscious of how they look and may be less conscientious about eating either balanced or regular meals. In some instances this can result in the development of eating disorders such as **anorexia nervosa** and **bulimia nervosa**. Both of these conditions tend to develop in response to a fear of 'being fat'. However, whilst most sufferers have a distorted rather than a realistic body image, the consequences of starving themselves or making themselves sick can be serious and may cause long-term physical damage.

An adult's dietary needs will depend on how much energy they require for their work and everyday life. People who have very physically demanding jobs have high energy needs. They can safely consume more food than people who have much less physically demanding jobs or lifestyles. However, an adult's dietary needs may change if they become unwell, if they are pregnant or breastfeeding or if they raise or reduce their level of physical activity for some other reason. A person who does not have a balanced diet may develop health problems because they lack vital nutrients, such as vitamins and minerals, or may become obese, develop heart disease or even diabetes if they consume too much fatty or sugary food and are not active enough to burn off the calories in their diet.

Exercise

Undertaking an appropriate amount and type of exercise is important for physical growth and development in every life stage. Activity that exercises the different parts of the body is important in infancy and childhood because it builds up strength, stamina, suppleness and co-ordination. Failing to exercise may result in a person becoming unfit, overweight and even obese during any life stage. Lack of physical fitness, stiff joints, heart disease, osteoporosis, constipation and strokes may all be experienced by adults and older people who have not looked after their bodies well enough by taking regular physical exercise.

Over to you!

- Athletes often consume a diet that contains a large amount of carbohydrates. Why do you think this might be?
- What factors affect the choices you make about what you eat? Make a list of the range of factors that influence what you regularly consume.

Investigate ...

Dietary deficiencies can lead to the development of health problems. Investigate one or more of the following conditions and identify which nutrient deficiency is linked to it:
- Tooth decay
- Rickets
- Beri beri.

Figure 1.20 The benefits of exercise.

Exercise isn't just about physical health and development though. It can also be a good way of meeting a person's emotional and social needs. For example, exercise is a good way of managing and reducing stress, can be a good way of meeting people and making friendships and generally has a positive effect on a person's self-esteem and mood.

Alcohol

Alcohol consumption can be both a positive and a negative influence on human growth and development. Adults and young people who are over 18 years of age frequently use alcohol within their social life. In controlled and moderate amounts alcohol can be pleasurable to drink. Friendships and personal relationships are also often formed when people meet for a drink in a pub, club or restaurant. In this way, alcohol can indirectly help to promote social and emotional development.

However, there are also many situations where alcohol can have a negative effect on growth and development. These include consumption of alcohol whilst pregnant, drinking alcohol during childhood, binge-drinking and excessive drinking over a long period.

A child whose mother drinks alcohol whilst she is pregnant may develop foetal alcohol syndrome (FAS). FAS is associated with abnormal growth and mental retardation. Mental retardation occurs because the alcohol consumed by the child's mother disrupts the formation and survival of nerve cells in the foetus' brain. FAS is the most common cause of non-inherited mental retardation in the UK.

FAS is a preventable birth defect that has lifelong consequences. Most people who go on to experience developmental problems related to alcohol consumption begin life without alcohol problems. Drinking alcohol to excess in any life stage can inhibit physical development because it causes damage to a range of human body systems. Brain damage, damage to the cardio-vascular system, weight gain, high blood pressure and liver damage (cirrhosis) are all direct consequences of drinking excessive amounts of alcohol over a long period of time. Drinking large quantities of alcohol destroys a person's brain cells. This can have a significant effect on brain development in infancy, childhood and adolescence and may lead to a reduction in a person's thinking and memory abilities in adulthood and later life. Binge-drinking in adolescence and adulthood is also associated with an increased risk of being involved in accidents, experiencing violence and taking part in unsafe sex. A person's social and emotional development can be harmed by alcohol problems where damage is done to their workplace, family and personal relationships by binge-drinking or as a result of their longer-term alcohol dependency. The growth and development problems that can result from drinking excess alcohol can be prevented by moderate and sensible drinking or by abstaining from alcohol.

Smoking

Smoking can seriously damage a person's health and physical development. Tobacco smoke contains over 4,000 chemicals, including nicotine, carbon monoxide and tar. As much as 70% of the tar contained in cigarette smoke remains in the smoker's lungs. Tar also damages the smoker's respiratory system and can lead to the development of cancer and serious respiratory disorders such as **emphysema**. The nicotine in a cigarette raises a smoker's blood pressure and their heart rate.

Smoking is likely to reduce a person's life expectancy and will increase the likelihood of the smoker developing a chronic health problem, such as bronchitis or heart disease and significantly increase the risk of lung, mouth or throat cancer. It is clear that there are no physical health or development benefits associated with smoking. Children and adolescents who smoke are likely to be less physically active and substantially increase the risk of

Consequences of
Foetal Alcohol Syndrome

- Abnormal facial features
- Reduced growth
- Central nervous system abnormalities
- Impaired learning and memory skills
- Behaviour problems such as hyperactivity.

A child with FAS.

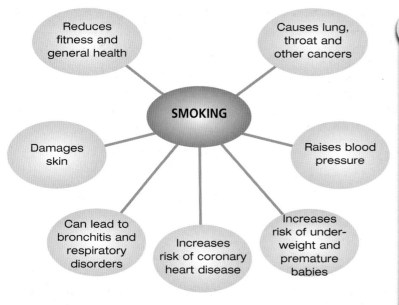

Figure 1.21 The effects of smoking.

damaging their developing respiratory systems. Adults who smoke are more likely to experience a range of health problems that will limit their involvement in work and leisure activities that require physical effort.

Social, cultural and emotional factors

Social, cultural and emotional factors are those things that influence our relationships with, attachments to and feelings about ourselves and other people in our life.

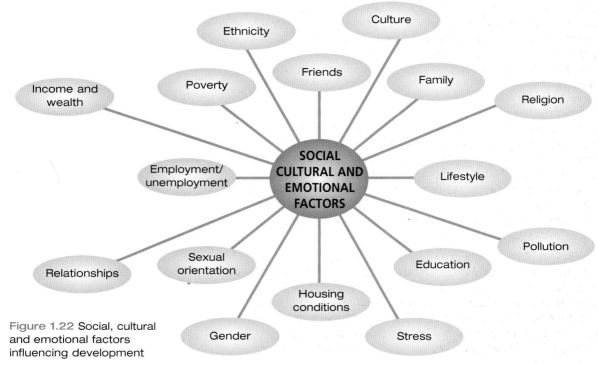

Figure 1.22 Social, cultural and emotional factors influencing development

Understanding Personal Development and Relationships

Family

Most people live as part of a family at some time in their life. The family is often seen as the foundation of society because of the key role it plays in human development. The family is said to carry out **primary socialisation**. This means that family members, especially parents, teach children the values, beliefs and skills that will prepare them for later life. The relationships we have with parents, brothers and sisters ensure that we are provided for, supported and protected as we grow and develop.

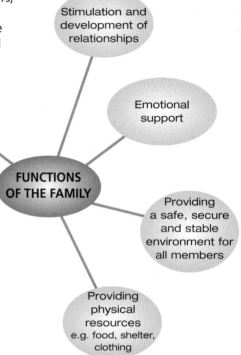

Providing

The family *provides* informal education and socialization for children. This teaches children attitudes, values and how to behave. The family also provides the physical resources needed for growth and intellectual development, such as food, toys and other stimulation.

Supporting

Families give emotional support from infancy through to adulthood. Early attachment and bonding (see page 000) are important sources of the stability and security we all need.

Protecting

Family members protect the health and wellbeing of other members by giving informal care, advice and guidance. Family relationships are often very deep and have a lifelong influence on human development.

Whether we live in an extended family, a nuclear family, a lone parent family or a blended family our physical, intellectual, emotional and social development will be strongly influenced by other family members.

Figure 1.23 Families provide an important way of meeting all our PIES needs.

Friends

Friendships play an important role in our social and emotional development. We first learn how to behave and relate to others through family relationships during infancy. As we move into early childhood, we begin meeting other children and increase our range of friendships. Friendships can feel especially important during adolescence when young people are trying to forge an identity separate from their parents and in adulthood where friendships form the basis of our social lives outside of the family. Friendships in later adulthood can be a vital source of companionship and connection to a person's past.

Throughout life, a person's personality, social skills and emotional development are all shaped by their friendships. Friendships play a role in helping people to feel they belong, are wanted and liked by others and that there are people they can turn to for support. However, the other side of childhood and adolescent relationships, such as bullying and rejection by peers, can have a negative effect on an individual's self-esteem and identity.

Bullying can damage personal development.

Educational experiences

In the United Kingdom most children go to school between the ages of 5 and 16 years to receive their formal education. People in the United Kingdom now have to spend a minimum of twelve years in primary and secondary education. Education promotes intellectual development because it is about learning. Intellectual development happens when a person increases their knowledge and thinking skills. However, education also has a powerful effect on a person's social and emotional development. Educational experiences are part of what is known as **secondary socialisation**. In this situation, friends, **peers** (people of the same age and social group) and teachers influence the attitudes, values and ways in which we behave. This builds on the primary socialisation that has already occurred within the family.

Some people learn a lot at school, succeed at exams and see education as a positive influence on their personal development. Educational success is very good for the self-esteem and self-image of these people. However, not everybody enjoys school and not everybody succeeds. Failure and bad experiences at school can lead some people to develop a negative self-image and low self-esteem.

Employment and unemployment

Employment also contributes to secondary socialisation because a person's values, beliefs and attitudes are often influenced by employers and work colleagues. Work is also an opportunity to develop new skills and extend physical, intellectual and social abilities. People often develop strong friendships at work, especially if they stay in the same job for a long time. As well as learning the social skills of co-operating with and supporting others, work-based relationships can lead to emotional development where colleagues care about each other and have a shared sense of belonging to a friendship group.

Being unemployed can also affect an individual's development because it is a stressful experience. People who become unemployed may feel angry about what they have lost, anxious about their future and can suffer a sense of rejection that affects their self-esteem and self-concept. The loss of income that unemployment brings may also mean that an unemployed individual is no longer able to participate in social and leisure activities with friends, such as going to the cinema, the pub or on holiday together. Over time this could affect social relationships and may even exclude the unemployed person from a friendship group. Long-term unemployment can reduce a person's self-esteem and limit their ability to use and develop their social skills and to provide a good quality of life for themselves and their family.

Over to you!

Make a list of all the current and past friendships that have influenced your personal development. Try to identify how each friend has influenced you. Who, out of all of your friends, would you say has been most influential?

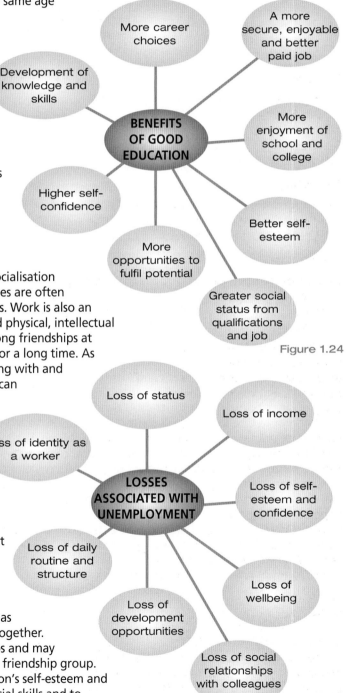

BENEFITS OF GOOD EDUCATION
- More career choices
- A more secure, enjoyable and better paid job
- Development of knowledge and skills
- More enjoyment of school and college
- Higher self-confidence
- Better self-esteem
- More opportunities to fulfil potential
- Greater social status from qualifications and job

Figure 1.24

LOSSES ASSOCIATED WITH UNEMPLOYMENT
- Loss of status
- Loss of income
- Loss of identity as a worker
- Loss of self-esteem and confidence
- Loss of daily routine and structure
- Loss of wellbeing
- Loss of development opportunities
- Loss of social relationships with colleagues

Figure 1.25

Understanding Personal Development and Relationships

Case study

Ken Brown, aged 56, has been employed in Bennett's Department Store since he left school at 16 years of age. Forty years and many promotions later, Ken is now operations manager for the whole store. Ken is very proud of his achievements and believes that he has played an important part in the success of Bennett's over the years. Recent financial problems, largely resulting from growing unemployment in the area, have led to a crisis situation at Bennett's. Ken and the rest of the employees have been told that the company is in a lot of difficulty and may go out of business if sales don't improve in the run-up to Christmas. This has come as a huge shock to Ken. He sees Bennett's as an extended family, a place where his colleagues are also his friends and where he has grown up. Ken met his wife, another employee, at Bennett's and still sees his job as a central part of his everyday life. He claims that he has learnt more during his time at Bennett's than he ever did at school or could have learnt at college. Ken feels very emotional when he looks around the store and talks to his colleagues about the prospect of Bennett's closing down.

- How has employment at Bennett's contributed to Ken's intellectual and social development?

- Identify how working at Bennett's has influenced Ken's emotional development.

- Which aspect(s) of Ken's development are likely to be affected if Bennett's closes down?

- What impact might unemployment have on Ken's self-concept?

Community involvement

A community is a group of people who live and interact with each other in a common location. As well as referring to both the group of people and the place in which they live, the idea of 'community' also refers to the supportive bonds, shared beliefs and the feelings of belonging that connect people to each other. Being involved in the activities and life of a local community, perhaps through sport, leisure or child care groups or just through regular contact and interaction with other local people, will affect a person's self-concept and identity and contribute to their social and emotional development. Community involvement can provide opportunities for friendships and other social relationships to develop and may contribute positively to a person's sense of who they are and where they belong. Feeling excluded, disconnected or isolated from the local community may, by contrast, have negative effect on a person's emotional wellbeing and self-concept. This might happen if the person feels they don't belong, don't know anyone or have nothing in common with others in the local community.

Summer events bring communities together.

Religion

People who are religious generally have a set of beliefs and take part in forms of worship that focus on the existence and importance of God. Religious beliefs of one sort or another are present in all societies. Many different religions are now practiced in the United Kingdom, including Christianity, Islam, Hinduism, Sikhism and Buddhism amongst others. People who are religious often develop particular moral beliefs (about right and wrong, good and bad) and behave in ways that are expected of members of their faith. For example, drinking alcohol, cohabiting with a partner and eating meat are all practices that followers of some religions would avoid. As a result religion can have a strong influence on an individual's intellectual, social and emotional development. Religious beliefs tend to have a positive effect on a person's mental health because they raise self-esteem and give an individual the sense of belonging to a larger community of people and of having a relationship with God. However, people who are not religious sometimes argue that religious beliefs limit a person's development because they impose rules and restrictions on how an individual ought to live. As a result, non-believers may see religion as restricting the range of social relationships an individual might develop and as being the cause of low self-esteem in those people who lose their faith or who cannot live up to or break the rules of their religion.

Culture

Culture refers to the way of life of a particular group of people. The United Kingdom is a multicultural society in which different ethnic, religious and other social groups live together. However, all these groups have differences in their attitudes, beliefs, language, diets and social activities. As a result, an adult whose cultural background is African-Caribbean is likely to have had different cultural experiences to an adult whose family has a white, working-class British cultural background. Culture can influence an individual's physical, intellectual, emotional and social development because of the way that it affects all aspects of an individual's lifestyle. An individual's self-concept, their dietary preferences and their attitudes towards factors such as education, alcohol and family relationships are all likely to be affected by the culture in which they grew up and now live. A person's ethnicity, religion and culture often combine and overlap to influence their personal development.

Ethnicity, religion and culture often combine in special festivals.

Ethnicity

People who have the same **ethnicity** have a shared way of life or **culture**, a common geographical origin, a particular skin colour or a common language or religion. Ethnicity can be an important feature of a person's identity, particularly where religion plays a part. It may affect personal development because it leads the individual to seek out and take part in particular activities or social groups. It may also be a label (e.g. 'Asian', 'Black', 'Welsh', 'Muslim' or 'Jewish') that influences how other people treat and respond to the person. This in itself can have a powerful effect on personal development.

Gender

A person's sex refers to whether they are biologically male or female. Gender on the other hand refers to the behaviour society expects from men and women. In Western societies girls are taught, or socialised, to express 'feminine' qualities such as being kind, caring and gentle. In contrast, boys are socialised to express 'masculine' characteristics such as being boisterous, aggressive and tough. Parents, schools, friends and the media all play a part in gender socialisation.

The gender expectations that we experience influence how we think about ourselves and how we relate to others. The idea that boys and men should experience better opportunities – especially in education and in employment – than girls and women because they are the 'superior sex' has a long history that is now being

Why do dolls and girls seem to go together?

challenged. Gender is still an important issue that affects personal development but it isn't as powerful as it once was. Girls and boys now have the same educational opportunities and there are similar numbers of men and women in employment. However, on average men still earn more than women and still occupy more of the higher paid and most powerful jobs. Girls on the other hand currently get better results than boys in public examinations, like GCSEs, and may change this situation in the future.

Sexual orientation

A person's sexual orientation refers to their preference for either a same-sex or opposite sex partner. Whilst some people identify themselves as heterosexual (attracted to the opposite sex), others identify themselves as lesbian, gay (attracted to the same sex) or bisexual (attracted to either sex). We tend to first become aware of our sexual orientation in adolescence though many people remain uncertain about, experiment with or change their sexual orientation during adulthood. A person's sexual orientation will have a significant impact on their self-concept and on their social and emotional development.

Male homosexuality was illegal in the United Kingdom until 1967. Lesbian relationships have never been illegal in the UK though social disapproval and unfair discrimination against people who had same-sex partners, whether male or female, was widespread until the late twentieth century. However, social attitudes have changed significantly so that a person's sexual orientation is now much less of an issue in most situations. This does not mean that prejudice and social disapproval about same-sex relationships has disappeared and many people still struggle to 'come out' about their homosexuality. Gay and lesbian adolescents and young people are particularly vulnerable to bullying and intimidation from peers if they declare their sexual

Case study

Angelo and Charisa are Year 12 pupils and best friends. They go out to parties and clubs together at weekends but have other partners. Angelo has a boyfriend who he has been seeing for 6 months. Charisa doesn't have a girlfriend at the moment but has had short relationships with older girls in the  past. Both Angelo and Charisa are open about their sexuality to close friends and members of their family. However, they are very concerned about other people, particularly other pupils at school, finding out about their sexual orientation. This is because they have seen how other pupils and teachers have been taunted and bullied for 'being gay'. Angelo has also been chased by a group of local teenagers on his way home from school. This frightened him a great deal so he now makes sure he doesn't walk home on his own or take shortcuts across the park. Charisa has recently reported two girls in her years at school who have been calling her 'sick' and who sent her threatening and pornographic text messages.

- Which aspects of personal development are likely to be affected by a person's sexual orientation?

- How might a person's development be affected if they were unable to express their preferred sexual orientation?

- How does sexual orientation affect Angelo and Charisa's relationships with members of their peer group?

- What impact might bullying have on Angelo and Charisa's self-concept?

orientation. Therefore many choose not to 'come out' until they are older and able to find support from a group or community of people who understand their interests, needs and concerns.

Relationship formation

Couples tend to form relationships with the intention of living together and caring for each other. Whilst most people who do form a relationship will marry or have a civil partnership to formalise their relationship, an increasing number of people are cohabiting. Living with another person in a monogamous relationship will have a significant impact on a person's social and emotional development. A close personal relationship involves an emotional commitment that is likely to have a major impact on a person's self-concept and sense of emotional security. The breakdown of a close personal relationship can also be a turning point in a person's life. Divorce is a very stressful life event for many people – including the children of the couple who are divorcing. Both the formation and the breakdown of a close personal relationship can result in a person having to reassess their identity and self-concept.

Knowledge Check

1 What does primary socialisation involve?

2 How can an infant's family influence their growth and development?

3 What does secondary socialisation involve?

4 How can friendships influence a person's development?

5 How can a person's sexual orientation affect their personal development?

6 Which aspects of personal development are promoted by involvement in local community activities?

7 What does the term 'ethnicity' refer to?

8 Explain how a person's gender can affect their personal development.

Economic factors

Personal development can be affected by a number of money-related or economic factors. Economic factors have a strong influence on the kinds of opportunities that a person is able to enjoy in each life stage.

Income and wealth

Income refers to the money that a household or individual receives. People receive money through working, pension payments, welfare benefits and other sources such as investments. The amount of income that an individual and their family have, and the things they spend it on, can have a big impact on their personal development because it affects the quality of life available to them. People with plenty of income are likely to have better educational and leisure opportunities and will live in better circumstances than people who have little income and who may be in poverty. Having better opportunities and little or no money-related stress puts some individuals and families in a position to make the most of their abilities and potential. The reverse is the case for poorer people.

Poverty and material possessions

People who have a very low income and who experience **poverty** are most likely to suffer illhealth and have their opportunities for personal development restricted. The following quotation explains this:

"Poverty means staying at home, often being bored, not seeing friends, not going to the cinema, not going out for a drink and not being able to take the children out for a trip or a treat or a holiday. It means coping with the stresses of managing on very little money, often for months or even years. It means having to withstand the onslaught of society's pressure to consume … Above all, poverty takes away the building blocks to create the tools for the future – your 'life chances'. It steals away the opportunity to have a life unmarked by sickness, a decent education, a secure home and a long retirement. It stops people being able to plan ahead. It stops people being able to take control of their lives." (C. Oppenheim and L. Harker (1996) *Poverty: The Facts*, 3rd edn, Child Poverty Action Group)

Because of the existence of welfare benefits it is rare for people in the UK not to have enough income for essential food, clothing and housing. Despite this, there are still situations in which some people fall through the welfare benefits 'safety net' and live for periods of time in **absolute poverty**. This means that they find themselves without the basic means to pay for essential items like food, clothing and housing.

Far more people in the UK live in **relative poverty**. This means that a person is poor when compared to most other people in society. People living in relative poverty often don't have access to the same services and can't afford the same material possessions as others in their local community. As a result many people living in poverty are said to experience social exclusion. Children who are born into families experiencing poverty may find this difficult to escape from. Poverty and social exclusion have such a powerful effect on personal development and life chances that people are often held back by the disadvantages and lack of opportunities that result from social exclusion.

Homeless people are usually living in poverty.

Employment status and occupation

Having paid employment is the way most adults in the UK gain their income. However, some jobs provide better incomes, better working conditions and higher status than others. A person's employment status partly determines their **social class**. People in higher status employment are allocated to higher social class groups and vice versa. As well as providing income, a person's job may influence their self-concept, their intellectual development and their social and emotional development. Having high status employment and stimulating work is likely to have a positive effect on personal development. Working in very difficult or stressful conditions, a low status job or in an environment where employers and colleagues are not supportive or friendly may have a negative effect on self-esteem and personal development.

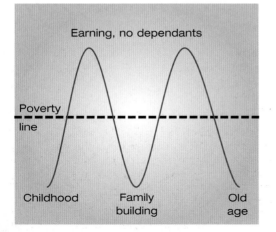

Figure 1.26 The poverty cycle.

Knowledge Check

1 What does the term 'income' refer to?

2 How might a family's income affect the personal development of its members?

3 Describe two forms of poverty and their impact on personal development.

4 What does the term 'social class' refer to?

5 How might a person's employment status influence their personal development?

Case study

Kieran Goff, aged 42, is a solicitor. He has never been unemployed. Kieran worked part-time in shops and on building sites whilst he was studying to become a solicitor. He is very proud of his employment record and of the high status that his job gives him. This is particularly important for Kieran because he comes from an estate where very few people went to college or university and where over half of the men are unemployed at any one time. Kieran was determined to escape from this situation. He believes that he has succeeded in life because he worked very hard and was very determined to achieve his goals. Kieran still sets himself challenges and says that he is 'driven to succeed'. He believes that he can do most things if he sets his mind to it.

- How would you describe Kieran's self-esteem?
- In what way does Kieran's job affect his self-concept?
- Which aspect of Kieran's personal development has been affected most by his determination to become a solicitor?
- Which social class is Kieran now a part of?

Environmental factors

A person's physical growth as well as other aspects of their personal development can be directly and indirectly affected by the physical conditions, or environment, in which they live. Important features of the physical environment that affect growth and development include the quality of a person's housing, pollution, noise and whether they live in a rural or urban area.

Air and noise pollution

Physical growth and development can be directly affected by the presence of pollution in the atmosphere. Carbon monoxide and other harmful gas emissions from vehicles, ships and factories are particularly damaging to a person's respiratory system. Babies and children can have their growth potential restricted, though people at all stages of life can have their physical health damaged by the effects of poor air quality. Noise pollution from vehicles, aircraft and busy crowded environments can damage a person's hearing and their psychological wellbeing. Unwanted noise is also associated with high stress levels, sleep disturbances and high blood pressure. Noise pollution is worst in built-up, urban environments.

Aircraft produce noise and air pollution.

Housing conditions

The quality of a person's housing is important because it can affect their physical health and development. Overcrowded and neglected properties provide the kinds of conditions that lead to respiratory disorders and infectious diseases, such as bronchitis and tuberculosis. Overcrowded and cramped housing can also have a damaging effect on the growth and physical development of babies, children and young people who need enough space to play and be active. The type and standard of housing that people live in is related to their income. People with low incomes are less able to afford a good standard of housing and are less able to maintain it and heat it adequately.

Over to you!

What is good housing? Identify the features that you feel are important in making a person's housing conditions 'healthy'. Alternatively, if you were looking for somewhere to live, what kind of conditions would put you off renting or buying a house or flat?

Urban and rural lifestyles

Urban lifestyles result from living in cities or large towns where there is a built-up environment, a relatively large, more diverse, population and a lot of hustle and bustle from everyday activities. Urban environments are associated with a higher level of stress and a faster pace of life. By contrast, **rural lifestyles** are associated with a calmer pace of life, a tranquil countryside environment and closer, more supportive communities. Both of these images may be a true reflection of some people's lives. However, for others they are just stereotypes that don't reflect reality. The slower pace of life in rural areas may be a source of stress for some people who are frustrated by lack of activities and lack of opportunity to develop their skills and potential. Similarly, busy city environments can be very stimulating and provide lots of opportunities for personal development for some people whilst others experience them as overwhelming, impersonal and oppressive. Urban and rural environments provide differing opportunities for personal development depending on how people adapt to and experience them.

Over to you!

Do you have an urban or a rural lifestyle or a mixture of the two? How have the places where you have lived affected your personal development?

Case study

Ian and David Edwards both grew up in a small village on the North Wales coast. Ian still lives in the village and, apart from when he left to go to university in London for three years, has never really lived anywhere else. Ian says he loves the pace of life, the closeness of the sea and the fact that he knows everyone who lives in the village. He runs a local café and bookshop and describes his life as 'perfect'. David left the village when he was 21 years of age. He joined the Royal Navy and travelled to different parts of the world. David now lives in New York where he works as a journalist. David says he loves the bustle, energy and noise of the city and wouldn't want to live anywhere else. He does visit his brother and the village he grew up in every few years but he says that after about a fortnight he becomes restless and bored.

- What is it about a rural lifestyle that Ian enjoys?
- Which characteristics of urban living appeal to David?
- Which aspects of rural living have a negative effect on David's wellbeing?
- Describe how Ian and David's personal development are likely to have been affected by their different choices of lifestyle.

Knowledge Check

1 Describe two sources of air pollution.

2 What effect might air pollution have on the health of a developing child?

3 How can a person's housing conditions affect their health and development?

4 Describe how living in an urban environment may have both a positive and a negative effect on an adolescent's development.

Psychological factors

Psychological factors are those things that influence a person's inner feelings about themselves and have an emotional effect on their relationships with others.

Stress

Stress is what we feel when we feel challenged or threatened by the demands that other people or situations place on us. The more we feel unable to cope, the more stressed we feel. Extreme stress can lead to a range of physical and mental health problems. These include eczema, asthma, high blood pressure and migraines as well as anxiety and depression.

Stress can be experienced during any life stage. Infants and children experience stress when they don't feel safe or secure and when they are put under too much pressure to achieve things that they don't believe they are capable of. Adolescents can experience a great deal of stress at school as a result of pressures to achieve good exam results and in their personal lives when they are trying to form and maintain friendships with their peers. Coping with the combined and perhaps conflicting demands of work, family life and relationships causes many adults to feel stressed. Similarly, older people who are finding everyday life harder to cope with as their abilities and energy levels diminish may experience stress as a result. High stress levels in any life stage will have an impact on a person's emotional development because of the negative, uncomfortable feelings that they cause. A person's social development may be affected if their stress levels cause difficulties in their relationships with others.

Relationship problems

Relationship problems are likely to have an impact on a person's social and emotional development. Relationships in the family can become stressful for a range of reasons. Stresses and tensions that arise in a couple's relationship may cause both partners a lot of stress and also have an impact on any children they have. Problems with the behaviour of children and teenagers can also cause tensions and difficulties that everyone in the family feels. Arguments, not eating or sleeping well and being unsupportive towards other family members can have a damaging effect on the emotional and social development and the self-concepts of those involved. Similarly, the breakdown of friendships can be very hurtful and cause people to question both themselves and the extent to which they are willing to risk becoming emotionally close to others in the future.

The impact that relationships can have on personal growth and development is covered in more detail in the next section.

Stress can damage health and wellbeing.

Over to you!

What are the most common sources of stress nowadays? List all the sources of stress that you can think of. What are the best ways of reducing stress? Identify as many stress-reduction strategies as you can think of.

Knowledge Check

1 What is stress?

2 Describe how stress can have a damaging effect on a person's health and development.

3 Which areas of PIES development might be affected by the breakdown of a close friendship?

4 How can relationship problems in a family affect the personal development of family members?

Case study

Matthew is sitting in a solicitor's office, explaining that he no longer loves his wife, Sarah. He has come to the conclusion that he is a very different person now compared to when he married Sarah 10 years ago. Matthew has told the solicitor about the regular arguments he and Sarah have about money and about how they should bring up their three-year-old son. He believes that Sarah is incapable of listening to his point of view and is unwilling to accept that their son has behaviour problems. Matthew explains that he is now taking anti-depressants and sleeping tablets because of the stress that his marital problems are causing him. He believes that his relationship with Sarah has broken down and is seeking legal advice on the best way to bring it to an end.

- Which aspects of Matthew's personal development are likely to be affected by the breakdown of his relationship with Sarah?
- How has Matthew's health and wellbeing been affected by the current situation?
- What impact might divorce have on Matthew's self-concept and self-esteem?
- What effect might a divorce have on the personal development of Matthew and Sarah's son?

Topic review

The box below provides a summary of the areas covered in Topic 1.2. Tick the areas that you feel you understand and would be confident answering exam questions about. If there are any areas that you don't understand or are not confident about, you will need to return to them before you begin your exam revision.

Physical factors
- Genetic inheritance ❑
- Illness and disease ❑
- Diet ❑
- Exercise ❑
- Alcohol ❑
- Smoking ❑

Social, cultural and emotional factors
- Family ❑
- Friends ❑
- Educational experiences ❑
- Employment / unemployment ❑
- Community involvement ❑
- Gender ❑
- Culture, ethnicity and religion ❑
- Sexual orientation ❑
- Relationship formation ❑

Economic factors
- Income and wealth ❑
- Employment status ❑
- Occupation / social class ❑
- Poverty and material possessions ❑

Physical environment factors
- Pollution ❑
- Noise ❑
- Housing conditions ❑
- Rural / urban lifestyles ❑

Psychological factors
- Stress ❑
- Relationships within the family, friends and partners ❑

Assessment Guide

Your learning in this unit will be assessed through a one hour and fifteen minute written examination.

The examination will consist of multiple-choice questions and a series of questions based on case studies and short scenarios.

You will need to show that you understand:

- The different factors that can affect human growth and development
- The development of self-concept.

Topic 1.3

Effects of relationships on personal growth and development

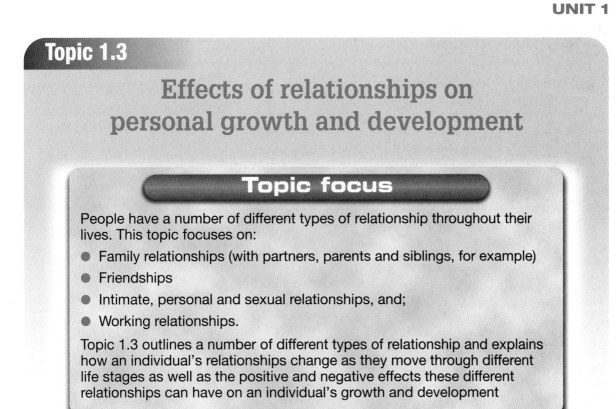

Topic focus

People have a number of different types of relationship throughout their lives. This topic focuses on:

- Family relationships (with partners, parents and siblings, for example)
- Friendships
- Intimate, personal and sexual relationships, and;
- Working relationships.

Topic 1.3 outlines a number of different types of relationship and explains how an individual's relationships change as they move through different life stages as well as the positive and negative effects these different relationships can have on an individual's growth and development

Types of relationship

People form different types of relationship at different stages of their life. Family relationships tend to be most important during infancy and childhood. There is a then a gradual shift in adolescence as friendships become more important, though emotional support from within family is also essential for adolescent development. A whole range of new personal and working relationships are formed as the individual progresses into adulthood.

Figure 1.27 Types of relationships.

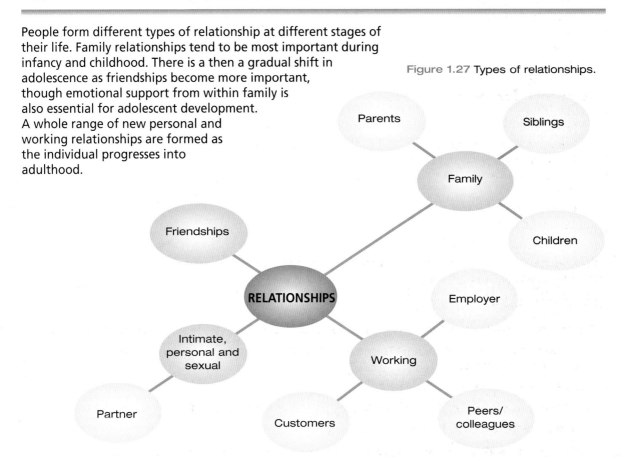

Understanding Personal Development and Relationships

Family relationships

You will know from previous learning that there are many different types of family structure. Whatever type of family structure a person lives in, their relationship with their parent(s) will play a big part in their personal development. Relationships with siblings (brothers and sisters in the family) are also important family relationships. An individual's feelings about their family and the skills they develop (or don't develop) in relating to others within the family will play an important part in the wider relationships they develop outside of the family during each life stage.

Investigate ...

Use sociology textbooks or the Internet to find out about the differences between the different types of families in figure 1.28. Which type(s) of family have you been a member of?

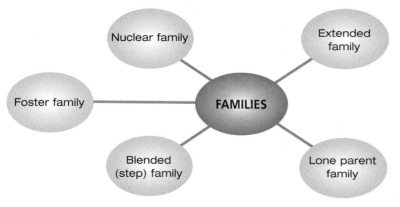

Figure 1.28 Types of families.

An individual's family relationships develop and change throughout life. Family relationships are usually seen as 'special' because of the biological connections and often very close emotional bonds between family members. However, whilst family relationships can be a source of love, protection and mutual support, negative family relationships that involve abuse, neglect or violence can also result in people being physically hurt or psychologically and emotionally damaged. Family relationships are often complex and many people have both good experiences of family relationships that support their personal development and some difficult times within their family relationships that they struggle to deal with.

Infancy

An infant generally forms their first relationship with one or both of their parents. Close physical contact, the provision of food and regular, reassuring care and communication between the child and their parents should result in an **attachment relationship** developing. This will provide the child with a sense of emotional security and basic self-confidence if they feel loved and learn to trust their parents. An infant's relationships with their **siblings** will vary depending on how close in age they are and whether their brother(s) or sister(s) were jealous about their arrival in the family. A new baby may cause jealousy and a hostile reaction if the older child feels they are no longer important or less loved by their parents. However, siblings can also provide role models for younger children and may also be very caring and interested in their infant brother or sister. Infants do show interest in other children of the same age when they meet them but are not able to form friendships until they have a clearer sense of their own identity. This tends to develop in early childhood.

Effects of relationships on personal growth and development

This is a stereotypical nuclear family.

Childhood

A child's parents continue to play an important role in their development as they get older and move into childhood. Parents become role models, socialising the child (see pp.xx), providing care and support and helping them to learn how they should behave towards others. During this stage of life parents have a strong influence on their child's self-concept and self-esteem. Siblings can form strong, supportive and very close friendships during childhood although there are often ups and downs in these relationships as brothers and sisters argue, fight and make up again.

Adolescence

By the time they reach adolescence, an individual is likely to have a much broader and more complicated network of personal relationships than when they were a child. Family relationships, particularly with parents, are still a vital part of this network. However, when a person moves into adolescence their relationship with their parents tends to change. In particular, there is less focus on socialisation and providing physical support and more focus on emotional support. Despite the growing desire for independence and the strains and tensions that this can bring to family relationships, an adolescent still needs affection, trust and approval from their parents. Adolescents who have a trusting, supportive and affectionate relationship with their parents will tend to have better self-esteem and be better equipped for the transition to adulthood than adolescents who lack this. Adolescents are often less confident about themselves and more uncertain in their relationships with other people than they let on. To support social and emotional development, parents need to remain open and approachable to their adolescent children during this life stage without being too controlling, judgemental or directive.

The pattern of sibling relationships in a family is often set within childhood. Teenage siblings may argue and fight whilst also being very caring and supportive of each other. It is important for parents to avoid favouring one sibling over others as the less favoured sibling may feel hurt or undervalued and may direct their upset or anger about this at the favoured sibling.

Friends become more important in adolescence.

Case study

Sharon McDonagh is 23 years old. She returned to live with her parents when she left the Royal Navy 6 months ago. Sharon is now keen to move into a flat with her boyfriend, Gareth. Sharon's parents have quite strong views about marriage and cohabitation. They believe that Sharon and Gareth should get married before they begin living together.

Sharon and Gareth disagree and have explained that they don't wish to get married as they have only known each other for a year. Sharon feels torn between living her life in the way she wants to and keeping her parents happy. She feels that although she still loves her parents a great deal, her relationship with them is changing. She has tried to explain this to her mum who has complained that 'Gareth seems to mean more to you than we do'.

- Which aspects of Sharon's personal development are currently undergoing change?

- What is happening to Sharon's relationship with her parents?

- How might Sharon's personal development be affected if she continued to live with her parents throughout early adulthood?

Disagreements and arguments between siblings can seem quite serious during adolescence. Even where there appears to be a fundamental dislike and breakdown of the relationship, it is often the case that siblings will resolve their differences and form good relationships again as they mature and become more self-confident during adulthood.

Adulthood

A person's family relationships may change significantly during adulthood. The majority of people leave home and begin new relationships with people outside of their birth family, perhaps getting married or living with a partner and starting a family of their own. As a result adults tend to readjust the relationship they have with their parents. Whilst still being their parent's child, an adult is also now independent, able to manage their own life and committed to relationships in their new family. Despite this parents can still play an important part in an adult's emotional life and may still be consulted about important decisions or issues that the person faces. Good relationships with parents and siblings can also cushion the impact of negative life events, such as divorce, **redundancy** or serious illness that may affect an individual during their adult life.

As people enter later adulthood their role within the family often changes. Their decision-making role is likely to change as their children become independent adults. They may take on the new role of grandparent as their children have children of their own. This new role enables many people to provide a useful range of practical help and emotional support and gives them a valued role within the family. Existing family relationships can also be the main source of support for people in later adulthood. However, the care and daily living needs of older people can become increasingly difficult for family members to meet. This is partly because caring for an older parent or other relative requires a change in a person's usual role and relationships within the family. Providing personal, intimate care, for example, may be something that both the older person and their adult is deeply uncomfortable with. The loss of work status, changing

Effects of relationships on personal growth and development

family roles and an increasing need for support can put pressure on the family relationships of older people. Whilst an older person may need more support they may be reluctant to acknowledge or accept this. Family relationships in later adulthood can make a positive contribution to an individual's social and emotional development, particularly their self-concept, where the person feels valued and supported. Where this isn't the case, difficulties in family relationships can lead to low self-esteem and poor emotional wellbeing.

Marriage and cohabitation

Statistics show that rates of marriage are declining in the UK whilst rates of **cohabitation** (living together) are increasing. However, both of these trends suggest that most people wish to have and seek a close personal relationship with a partner. Both marriage and cohabitation are seen as a source of emotional support. In many but not all cases being married or cohabiting with a partner has a positive effect on an individual's self-confidence and self-esteem and influences the development of an individual's self-concept.

Divorce and relationship breakdown

When problems occur in marital or partner relationships both people involved typically experience emotional distress and increased levels of anxiety, stress and mood problems. Divorce or relationship breakdown can lead to a person feeling angry, depressed and insecure about their self-worth. However, for many people, divorce and relationship breakdown are necessary experiences that allow them to end or leave unsatisfactory relationships in order to move on to new, more fulfilling relationships or move to new phases in their life where they experience better emotional and social wellbeing.

> **Over to you!**
>
> Look at the statistics in figure 1.29. Which two groups of men and women were most likely to be cohabiting in 2006? What percentage of single women were cohabiting in 2006?

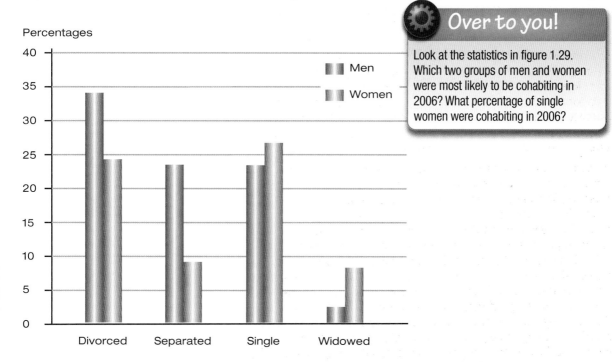

Figure 1.29 Percentage of people cohabiting by marital status, 2006. Great Britain, ONS

Understanding Personal Development and Relationships

Blended families

Blended families are also known as reconstructed, reconstituted or, more popularly, as step-families. What all of these ideas have in common is the notion of two families merging or being blended into a new family. The 'merger' that occurs when a blended family is created usually involves two partners bringing dependent children from a previous relationship into a new family situation. A blended family may also develop further when the new partners produce children themselves. Approximately 10% of children live with a step-parent in the UK and many enjoy a safe, happy and supportive family environment that contributes to their health, wellbeing and personal development. However, blended families are often poorer than other types of families and relationships between step-parents and step-children can be emotionally difficult and lead to problems. The self-concept of each member of a blended family is likely to be changed by the 'merger' and the new set of relationships that develop. For some individuals, life in a blended family can have a negative effect on their emotional development and wellbeing if they struggle to come to terms with the loss or ending of their original, birth family and reject opportunities to form new relationships with step-parents or step-children.

Parenthood

Becoming a parent is a very significant event in life. It is usually seen as a positive change in a person's life although it can also be seen as a point at which an individual 'lost' their individual freedom and sense of identity. New parents are faced with a challenging situation because they have to adapt their own roles and relationship to cope with the needs of a dependant child

Case study

Sameena and her husband Raj spent 10 years trying to produce their first child. Following a referral by her GP to the fertility clinic at her local General Hospital, both Sameena and Raj underwent several fertility investigations. The couple then had a course of invitro-fertilisation (IVF) in which two embryos were implanted in Sameena's womb. Nine months later Taleem and Younis were born. Sameena is now a devoted mother and very proud parent of 18-month-old twins. She finds caring for Taleem and Younis very tiring but also sees it as the best thing that has happened to her. Raj does his best to provide practical help when he is at home. He is also very proud of his new role as a dad but says that his relationship with Sameena is sometimes strained by the pressures of caring for their children. Sameena and Raj spend almost all their time with their children and now see a lot less of their friends and family. Raj hopes that this will change as their children get older as he misses spending time with his friends. Sameena says that she finds it hard to remember what her life was like before she had children. Sometimes she worries that she will get stuck being 'just a mum'.

- Which aspects of Raj and Sameena's personal development have been affected by them becoming parents?

- In what ways has parenthood affected Raj and Sameena's self-concepts?

- What concerns do Raj and Sameena have about the effects parenthood might be having on their personal development or relationships?

without any prior training or experience. This can feel overwhelming for some people, particularly where they have limited experience of young children. Many people cope by drawing on their own experiences of childhood and by relying on their parents and other relatives to provide practical and emotional support.

Parenthood can also be a major test of the new parents' relationship as both find themselves under increasing pressure. Some people are able to offer their partner the practical and emotional support needed and strengthen their partnership when they become parents. Other people find that they are unable or unwilling to do this and experience relationship difficulties and even the breakdown of their marriage or partnership as a result. Parenthood tends to result in a shift in a person's self-concept as they adapt to their new 'mum' or dad' role.

For many the birth of a child is a positive emotional milestone that results in them changing their lifestyle and life goals in order to be the best possible parent they can be. However, for others, parenthood can be an unwelcome burden that triggers personal mental health difficulties or leads them to neglect or abuse their child because they cannot cope with the pressures and demands that parenthood places on them.

Knowledge Check

1 Identify two different types of family relationship that affect personal development during infancy and childhood.
2 Explain why good family relationships are important for emotional development during infancy.
3 Briefly explain what the term 'sibling' means.
4 Explain how family relationships change during adolescence.
5 What do statistics reveal about the popularity of marriage in the UK?
6 How can marriage affect an individual's personal development?
7 Identify one positive and one negative effect that divorce can have on personal development.
8 How can parenthood affect an individual's emotional and social development?

Friendships

Friends are people whom we generally see as likeable, dependable and whom we can communicate easily with. People form friendships for a variety of reasons. Common attitudes, values and interests, a need for emotional support and companionship are a few of these reasons. Friendships tend to boost a person's self-esteem, self-confidence and help people to develop social skills. Overall friendships make an important contribution to an individual's emotional and social development and the formation of their self-concept.

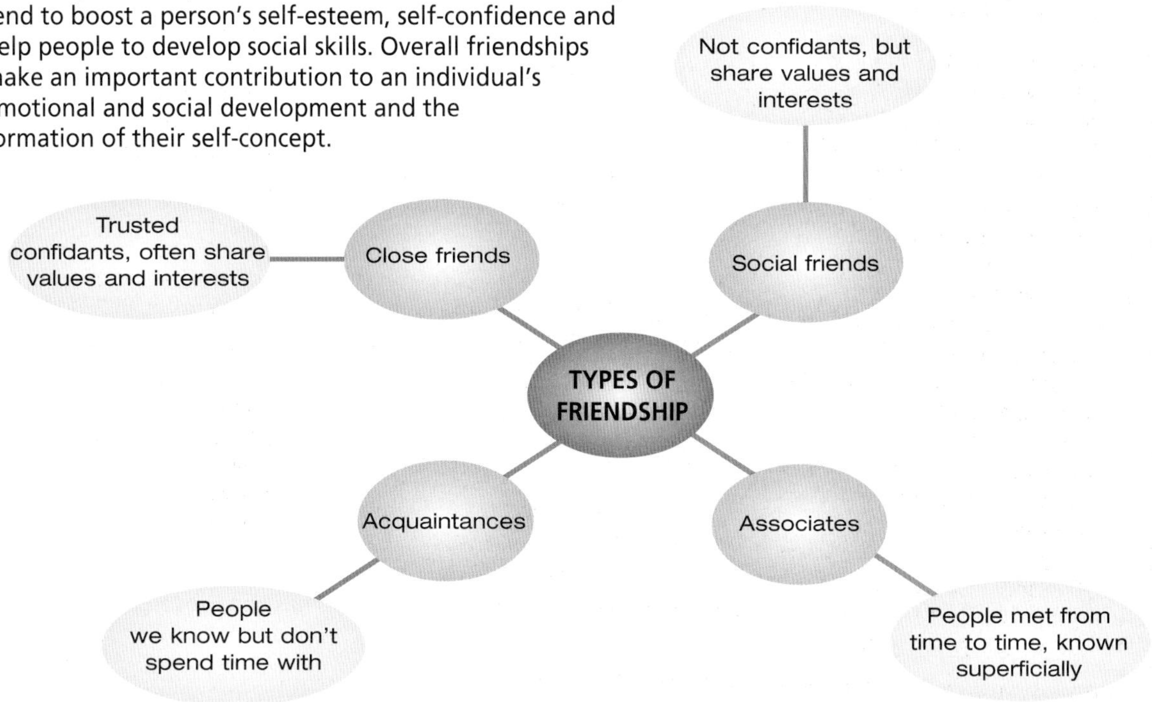

Figure 1.30

Understanding Personal Development and Relationships

Early friendships

Friendships start to affect an individual's development during childhood. Initially friendships are quite superficial and involve playing with other, familiar children. It is only at the end of childhood as the individual is preparing to move into adolescence that friendships come to be seen as a supportive two-way relationships. Throughout childhood, friendships play an important part in developing and supporting a child's self-esteem. Being liked and accepted by other children is very important for self-confidence and self-image. By contrast, children who struggle to make friends or who are rejected or bullied by other children are likely to suffer low self-confidence and have lower self-esteem because they become aware of this lack of social acceptance. This can damage the child's long-term social and emotional development if they develop a negative self-concept as a result.

Friendships become increasingly important, and are often more intense, during adolescence. Boys and girls now begin to form opposite sex friendships in contrast to childhood where friendships are mainly with members of the same sex. Girls tend to want to belong to smaller friendship groups and have more emotionally involving and intense friendship relationships whereas boys tend to form larger friendship groups in which members share common practical or sporting interests. Belonging to a friendship group provides an adolescent with an important sense of belonging and social acceptance outside their family. Some adolescents who lack social skills or who have significantly different values to their peers or who are physically different in some way can be ostracised or left out of friendship groups. This can be damaging to self-esteem and social and emotional development generally. Similarly, adolescents who lack self-confidence and self-esteem may find themselves vulnerable to

Over to you!

Can you remember your childhood friends? Did you have a 'best friend' during early childhood? Did any of your early friendships affect your self-image and self-confidence?

Case study

Ffion, Nia and Eleri are all 32 years of age. They have known each other since they started primary school together when they were 5 years old. The three women are all now married, have two children each and live in different parts of the UK. Living hundreds of miles from each other hasn't got in the way of their friendship. All three communicate regularly, sending text messages a couple of times a week and speaking quite frequently on the phone. Ffion still lives in the part of Wales where the three friends grew up. When Nia and Eleri visit their families at Christmas and in the summer, they also arrange to go out for a meal or have a barbeque at Ffion's house. Ffion, Nia and Eleri discuss quite personal feelings and seek advice from each other when they have personal or practical problems to deal with. Each trusts the other a great deal and believe they have an honest, supportive and genuine friendship that they can rely on whatever else is happening in their lives.

- Which aspects of their personal development is likely to have been affected by the friendship between Ffion, Nia and Eleri?

- Explain why the friendship between these three women is likely to have had a positive effect on each individual's self-concept.

- Using the information provided, identify possible reasons why the friendship between the three women has been so long-lasting and successful.

peer group pressure within friendship groups. This can lead them to take part in activities, such as drinking, petty crime, drug use or sex, that they are not comfortable with but which they go along with to remain a member of the group.

Adult friendships

Adult friendships tend to be carefully chosen and based on shared interests and values. Friendships in adulthood tend to be longer lasting than earlier friendships if both parties meet each other's emotional needs for support, loyalty and honesty in the relationship. Adult friends can be especially important for social and emotional development as they provide the basis for a supportive social network. They are particularly important when an individual experiences life events, such as divorce, unexpected illness or stress, which has a significant impact on them and requires people who will listen and offer emotional support. Adults can also experience emotional difficulties when they lose friends as a result of retirement from work, ill-health or death. The loss of friends can lead to loneliness, isolation and feelings of insecurity.

Intimate, personal and sexual relationships

People generally start to become interested in more personal relationships in their early teens. Adolescents tend to fall in and out of love quite frequently as they experience 'crushes' or infatuations during puberty. This can be emotionally painful but most teenagers use these experiences to learn more about the emotional aspects of relationships and to extend their understanding of their own needs and preferences. Girls tend to seek and engage in romantic, intimate and, to a lesser extent sexual, relationships at a younger age than boys. For many teenagers their first intimate relationship is an intense emotional experience rather than a sexual one.

Intimate relationships do develop out of sexual attraction although sexual intercourse is not necessarily a part of teenager's intimate relationships. Kissing, hand-holding and other forms of physical contact are more frequently used to express physical and emotional attraction during this life stage. Intimate personal relationships tend to be short-lived during early adolescence

but become longer and are more emotionally and physically involved in later adolescence. These longer term relationships are based on greater emotional maturity and a stronger sense of personal identity. They also help to prepare young people for future relationships with the partners they meet as adults.

Sexual relationships are a normal part of intimate personal relationships during all phases of adulthood. Engaging in sexual activity with a partner expresses both a physical and emotional need for most adults. Sexuality often becomes an feature of an individual's self-concept during adulthood. During adulthood people typically search for a partner and develop emotionally and physically intimate relationships with one or more individuals before they form a longer term, usually monogamous, relationship. Whilst some people avoid sexual relationships outside of marriage, many other people form intimate relationships before, or without, getting married. The physical and emotional intimacy of a close personal and sexual relationship contributes to an individual's social and emotional development. Unprotected sex, promiscuity and extramarital affairs may damage an individual's existing relationship and personal development because of the risk of unwanted pregnancy, sexually transmitted disease, and the emotional distress that this can cause to existing partners. Adults who find themselves in sexually abusive relationships may also experience significant emotional distress, physical injury, or low self-esteem until they find a way of ending the relationship or stopping the abuse.

Working relationships

Working relationships are different to other forms of relationship because the relationship serves a particular, non-personal purpose – it is about work or getting a particular job done. Most working relationships are also formed between individuals who are not of equal status. One person usually has more power or authority in the relationship than the other. Relationships between students and teachers, between employers and employees and between work mates are examples of working relationships.

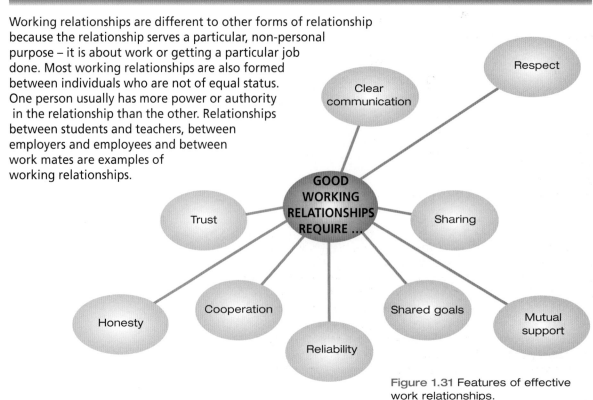

Figure 1.31 Features of effective work relationships.

Effective work relationships tend to be based on good communication, trust and respect between the people involved. Figure 1.31 identifies some other qualities of good working relationships.

Effective, positive working relationships contribute to social, emotional and intellectual development because they can lead to:

- Higher self-esteem
- Positive self-image
- Development of new skills and understanding
- A positive sense of self-worth
- A clear sense of personal identity.

Student / teacher relationships

Learning is the specific focus of student-teacher relationships at any age. Children typically begin attending primary school at 5 years of age in the UK, though many attend nurseries and other pre-school day care provision before this age. Relationships with class teachers and nursery workers become important in children's lives from this point. A child needs to trust their teacher or nursery worker to establish the kind of relationship that enables them to develop their communication skills, self-confidence and self-esteem. A lack of trust or a negative, unsupportive relationship is likely to hamper the child's social, emotional and intellectual development.

Relationships with teachers are vital for intellectual development during adolescence. The relationship between a student and teacher becomes more of a partnership during adolescence. Both parties have an interest in promoting and experiencing learning and general intellectual development. The teacher may still have more authority in the relationship but learning cannot occur without the student's willing and active participation. A good working relationship between student and teacher is likely to contribute positively to the self-esteem, self-confidence and self-concept of both individuals and provides the basis for the student's intellectual development.

Over to you!

Think about a working relationship of your own (with a teacher or employer perhaps) that has had a positive effect on you. Did any of the relationship features listed in figure 1.31 play a part in the success of this relationship? Try to identify reasons why the relationship had a positive effect on you.

UNIT 1

Employer/employee relationships

Relationships between employers and employees can be an important influence on personal – especially social and intellectual – development. The employer-employee relationship is an example of a **formal relationship**. This means it is based on a set of rules and expectations about how people should relate to each other because of their employment relationship. The employer has the most power and authority to direct the activities of the employee in these situations. Employment relationships can affect an individual's self-image, their social skills and their intellectual development – depending on the type of work they do and the development opportunities they are given. A person's relationship with their employers may also influence their attitudes, values and behaviour as well as their self-concept.

Peers and work mates

Some work colleagues are peers. That is, they are people of equal status and similar background. People involved in these types of working relationships may also be friends and tend to have equal status within the relationship. Effective relationships with peers and work mates are important because people often need to learn to cooperate and work together in work situations. Being liked and valued by work mates also increases an individual's self-confidence and self-esteem.

Topic review

The box below provides a summary of the areas covered in Topic 1.3. Tick the areas that you feel you understand and would be confident answering exam questions about. If there are any areas that you don't understand or are not confident about, you will need to return to them before you begin your exam revision.

Types of relationship

Family relationships
- Marriage ❑
- Divorce ❑
- Parenthood ❑
- Sibling relationships ❑

Friendships ❑

Intimate, personal and sexual relationships ❑

Working relationships ❑

Knowledge Check

1 Identify three reasons why people form friendships.
2 Which aspects of personal development are promoted by relationships with friends?
3 What effects can a lack of friendships have on an individual's development?
4 How do relationships with friends tend to change during adolescence?
5 Explain why friendships become more important for personal development during adolescence.
6 Identify two distinctive characteristics of an intimate relationship.
7 How can an intimate sexual relationship have a positive effect on an adult's personal development?
8 What impact might an abusive sexual relationship have on an individual's emotional development?
9 Identify three types of working relationship.
10 Using examples, explain how effective working relationships can contribute to personal development.

Assessment Guide

Your learning in this unit will be assessed through a one hour and fifteen minute written examination.

The examination will consist of multiple-choice questions and a series of questions based on case studies and short scenarios.

You will need to show that you understand:
- The development of self-concept. and personal relationships
- The role of relationships in personal development.

Topic 1.4

The effect of life events on personal development

Topic focus

The events that a person experiences in their life will influence how they develop and change in each life stage. Having different life experiences is part of the reason for individual differences between people. The important life events that people experience include:

- Relationship changes – such as marriage, divorce, living with a partner or **bereavement**
- Physical changes – such as puberty, menopause, accidents or illness
- Changes in life circumstances, such as starting school or further education, redundancy or retirement.

This topic will enable you to identify and describe different types of life event and the effects that they can have on personal development. You will also learn how people use sources of support to cope with the effects of life events. These sources of support include:

- partners, family and friends
- professional carers and services
- voluntary and faith-based services.

Life events and change

A **life event** is an experience that changes the direction of a person's life and affects their personal development. Every person's life changes as a result of the significant events that happen and the experiences they have at each stage of their life.

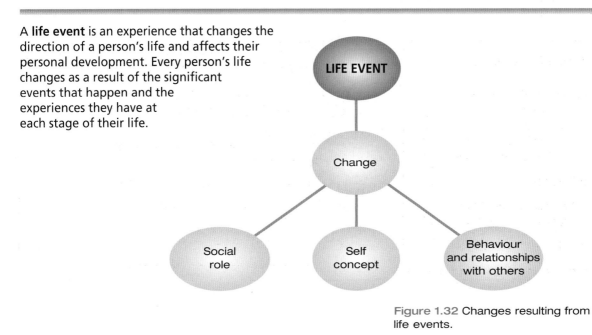

Figure 1.32 Changes resulting from life events.

Expected life events, such as starting school, going through puberty and retiring from work, are predictable and act as milestones in our personal development. Expected life events often mark a transition from one stage of life or status to another. **Unexpected life events**, such as sudden illness or injury, redundancy and the death of a friend or relative, occur in an unpredictable way and are often associated with loss. However, unexpected life events can sometimes result in positive changes occurring in a person's life. For example, illness or disability may force someone to give up a certain kind of work which might allow them to move into a new career, have more time for a hobby or interest, or even return to education or training again.

Relationships changes

People have different types of relationship in each of the main life stages. These include family relationships with parents, **siblings** (brothers and sisters) and other relatives, friendships, work relationships and intimate and sexual relationships with partners in late adolescence, adulthood and old age. Changes in our relationships can occur for many reasons. They often have a big impact on our emotional and social development.

Marriage

Marriage is a life event that is generally viewed positively and which is celebrated by hundreds of thousands of people each year (see figure 1.33). It can involve a major adaptation in personal relationships and behaviour for both the couple involved and their close relatives and friends. Ideally, the couple will establish a deeper emotional and psychological commitment to each other. Marriages also alter family relationships. The roles

Investigate ...

Interview an adult or older person about significant events in their life. Draw a timeline highlighting:

- Expected life events that have happened to them
- Unexpected life events that have happened to them.

Using the information you obtain, and being careful about confidentiality, describe the impact of these life events on the person's personal development, particularly their self-concept.

Over to you!

What does the graph tell you about the general trend in marriages? In which year (approximately) was marriage most popular? How many people got remarried in 2007?

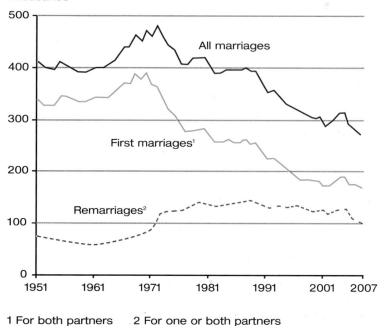

Thousands

All marriages

First marriages[1]

Remarriages[2]

1 For both partners   2 For one or both partners

Figure 1.33 Marriages, United Kingdom, 1951–2007, ONS

of family members change and new members are introduced into family groups. For example, in-laws become part of a wider family network and relationships between original family members may weaken because of the practicalities of a son or daughter moving away to live with their new partner. This can cause a sense of loss for the parents of the new couple and for the couple themselves as they move away from their birth family to begin a family of their own.

Divorce

People do not marry intending to get divorced, but divorce is now relatively common in the UK. One in three marriages are likely to end in divorce. Despite being relatively common, divorce is an unexpected life event that often has a major emotional impact on the couple involved and on those who are part of any family that has resulted from the couple's marriage. Marriage breakdown and the process of going through a divorce usually have major financial and practical consequences too. Separation will probably mean having to find different accommodation and independent sources of income. Where the couple has children, the impact of their divorce will be felt by the children because of new living arrangements, changing relationships and sometimes the need to adapt to step-parents. Though divorce can have a negative impact on the lives of those affected, it may still be preferable to being in a stressful and unsatisfactory relationship.

Living with a partner

Cohabitation or 'living together' is increasingly common in the UK. Many people live with a partner before getting married or forming a civil partnership. Between 1996 and 2006 the proportion of cohabiting couple families increased from 9 per cent to 14 per cent. Younger adults are most likely to cohabit with 33 per cent of men aged 25 to 29 years of age and 29 per cent of women aged 25 to 29 years of age cohabiting. People may choose to live together because they do not wish to marry or because they have been married and don't wish to risk getting divorced again.

Living with a partner may be an alternative to marriage but often involves the couple having to make a very similar commitment to share financial resources and provide emotional and practical support for each other as happens in a marriage. The partners in a cohabiting relationship are also likely to experience the same distress and feelings of loss that a married couple will feel if their relationship breaks down. Practical and emotional issues relating to any children and other relatives closely involved in the cohabiting couple's life will also need to be taken into account if the couple separate.

Death of a partner, relative or friend

Bereavement is the term given to the deep feelings of loss that people experience when someone to whom they are emotionally attached, such as a partner, relative or friend, dies. Bereavement can cause a major change in a person's life, affecting their social and emotional development as well as impacting on their self-concept. Sometimes a person's death may be anticipated and prepared for because of old age or because they have a terminal illness. In other cases, however, a person's death can be sudden and unexpected. Even when a person's death is anticipated because of illness, the sense of loss that follows can be very hard to accept and the powerful emotions of disbelief, sadness, anger and guilt that can follow the death of someone close may be very difficult to deal with. Bereavement can be even more traumatic and psychologically difficult when a person's death occurs suddenly or dramatically because of an accident, serious injury or suicide, for example. A sense of bereavement can cause both short-term and long-term problems in accepting and adjusting to the loss of the person concerned.

Case study

Eric, the drummer in Positive Peace, a reggae band, was 25 years old when he developed leukaemia. Eric's fellow band members and close friends were all shocked when he told them his diagnosis and that he would be having chemotherapy. Eric's friends and family were all very hopeful that the doctors who were treating Eric would be proved right and that he would survive the leukaemia. Eric was in hospital for several weeks, receiving treatment and being monitored. Robbie, Eric's closest friend in the band, was present with Eric's family when he died after an unexpected deterioration in his condition. Robbie was deeply affected by the loss of his friend and by being present when he passed away. He said he felt numb for weeks and cried a lot when he was on his own. Robbie now thinks about how long he might have left to live and says it taught him that nobody lives forever. A year later he still can't believe that Eric has gone. Robbie has now lost interest in playing music and says that he still finds it hard to listen to his reggae albums because it brings back the feelings he had when Eric died.

Knowledge Check

1 What is a life event?

2 Describe a life event that can be expected to occur during early adulthood.

3 How can marriage influence personal development?

4 Explain why an unexpected life event like divorce can have a negative effect on a person's social development

5 How might the death of a partner affect a person's emotional development?

● Which aspects of Robbie's experiences following the death of his friend suggest he has suffered a bereavement?

● Explain how Eric's death has affected Robbie's emotional wellbeing.

● What impact might Eric's death have on the development of Robbie's self-concept?

Physical changes

Physical changes related to human growth, development and ageing, as well as the experience of illness, can also have a major effect on the way we develop in each life stage. Puberty and the menopause are two of the most notable physical changes that occur in adolescence and middle adulthood. Accidents and illnesses can occur in any life stage.

Puberty

Puberty is a physical process that occurs during a person's adolescent or teenage years. Puberty is a major life event because of the major physical changes that occur but also because of the emotional impact that it can have. The physical changes that occur in puberty involve growth and the development of sexual or reproductive capability. These physical changes, and the way that other people relate to the person who experiences them, can affect the development of self-image and self-concept. For example, adolescents often become concerned about their appearance and their attractiveness to others during puberty. A person's beliefs about these issues will contribute to the development of their self-concept. Boys and girls who experience puberty either later or earlier than average may experience particular difficulties. This can happen if the person feels uncomfortable and self-conscious about the onset or absence of changes to their body or if their peers respond to this by teasing, bullying or harassing them.

Menopause

Menopause is a naturally occurring physical change that affects women in early middle age, typically between 45 and 55 years of age. It is the time when a woman stops menstruating and loses the ability to conceive children. Menopause is a major life event because of the sometimes unpleasant physical changes that occur and because of the psychological impact that the loss of reproductive ability can have on some women. The menopause is seen by some women as a signal that they are moving from young adulthood into middle age and that their (re)productive years are over. This in turn can cause some women to reflect deeply on their past experiences, their role in life as well as on their future. Hormone Replacement Therapy (HRT) is used by some women to control the physical symptoms of the menopause.

Accidents and illnesses

Accidents and illness can affect a person's development at any stage of their life. Where an accident or illness is serious it may cause either a temporary problem that the person can recover fully from or have a permanent effect on the person. For example, accidents and some types of illness can result in a disability, such as the loss of a person's sight or hearing or the loss of a limb. A person who acquires a disability in this way will need to adapt their skills and lifestyle to cope with the everyday situations that they face. For example, a disability can cause practical problems, such as not being able to move, pick up and hold things or manage personal hygiene and toilet needs without assistance.

Investigate ...

Use biology textbooks or the Internet to find out more about the causes and effects of the menopause. Find out about the biological changes that occur and the psychological and emotional impact that this can have.

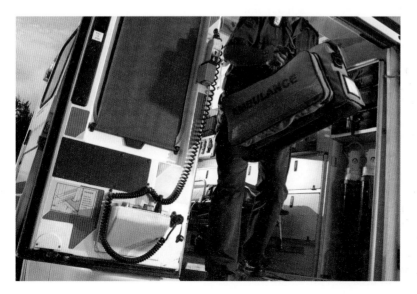

It may also result in psychological stress, change a person's self-concept and affect their personal relationships. Friends, family and colleagues will need to adjust their relationship with the person to take account of the disabled person's new situation.

Serious illness can be a major but unexpected event in an individual's life. It can result in massive changes to the person's whole lifestyle as he or she tries to cope with the effects of the illness. People who experience serious illnesses, such as heart attacks, multiple sclerosis or cancer, may find they are no longer able to carry out their usual daily routines, and they may lose their independence. They can also find that their relationships with others change because of their illness. This might be because they need additional practical help or emotional support from close relatives or their friends. For partners and close relatives, the person's illness may be the central factor around which they now have to organize their own time, lifestyle and relationship with the person.

Knowledge Check

1 Why is puberty a significant life event for an adolescent?

2 How can puberty affect a person's self-concept?

3 Explain the impact that the menopause can have on a woman's development and wellbeing during middle adulthood.

4 Describe the ways in which being involved in a serious car accident might affect a child's PIES development.

5 How can acquiring a physical disability as a result of accident or illness affect a person's close relationships?

Case study

Valerie Fitzharris, aged 66 years, had two operations on her spine last year. Her problems started with a nagging pain in her lower back. Despite painkillers and massage, these pains just got worse until she began experiencing intensely painful stabs of sharp pain that left her unable to move and often in tears. Valerie's GP referred her to a specialist centre for spinal injuries. After several scans they diagnosed that one of the discs in Valerie's spine was crumbling and a piece of it was sticking into her spinal cord. They decided to operate straight away. The operation was successful and Valerie quickly regained her mobility.

Valerie was very keen to get back to her old routines and activities following the operation. In fact, she made the mistake of going on a five-day coach trip to France with some friends a month after her operation. When she returned, she knew something was wrong. The pain in her back gradually returned and Valerie had to have a second operation to remove another piece of the broken disc. Valerie is now much more careful about not overstretching herself each day. She says the experience has made her think differently about her needs and abilities. As someone who had never really been unwell before, this episode has changed the way she thinks about herself and her future. She also said that she found out who her real friends were as they gave her a lot of practical and emotional support when she was at her lowest point.

● Which aspects of Valerie's personal development and wellbeing have been affected by her recent health problems?

● How might long-term spinal problems affect the way that Valerie is able to live her life?

● What impact might Valerie's experiences of illness have had on her self-concept?

Changes in life circumstances

A change in a person's life circumstances will usually involve some kind of social transition. Some of these transitions, like starting work, are expected; others, like redundancy, are unexpected. A change in life circumstances can have a big impact

Case study

Michelle is 11 years old. She lives in a small village with her parents and two younger brothers: Tim, aged 8, and David, aged 6. Her grandparents live 10 miles away and are regular visitors. Michelle is about to finish at primary school and move to a secondary school in September. She knows everyone at her primary school. All the children come from the same village and the same teachers have worked at the school since she started. Michelle doesn't want to leave her primary school and admits to being scared of going to secondary school 8 miles away. Michelle's best friend at school is Natalie. They go to swimming club together and belong to the same church group. Michelle is upset that Natalie will be going to a different school in September.

- How might moving from primary to secondary school affect Michelle's development and wellbeing in the next few months?

- What type of help and support might Michelle need as she experiences this change in her life?

- If you were one of Michelle's parents, what would you tell her about the possible impact of changing schools on her friendship with Natalie?

on a person's development because it affects the opportunities open to them or disrupts the way they currently live their life or their future plans.

Starting school

Going to school for the first time is a big event for most children. Families and schools often try hard to prepare children for this life transition. Talking about what happens at school, going for short visits and then for morning or afternoon play sessions can all help a child get used to the idea of starting school. However, even the most well prepared child may still feel frightened and reluctant to be left at school by their parents on their first day. Teachers and other school staff who are used to this situation can usually provide enough support and reassurance to help young children settle at school.

Starting secondary school can also have a significant impact on a child's personal development. The case study about Michelle illustrates some of the issues that children face when making this transition.

Starting further education

The transition from secondary school to a further education college or sixth form is an expected event that most people look forward to. The increase in freedom that college students enjoy and the more relaxed, less formal atmosphere (no school uniform, jewellery and make-up allowed!) means that students are treated more like adults. However, with this change come new responsibilities to organise and motivate yourself and cope with less guidance and direction from teachers. Some young people take this in their stride whilst others struggle to adjust.

Relocation

A person may relocate their life from one place to another for a variety of reasons. For some people, relocation is a positive choice. An adult may choose to move from one part of the UK to another to be nearer to relatives, to live with their partner or to take up work or educational opportunities. A great deal of this kind of internal migration occurs within the UK each year. In these cases people frequently make choices that have a positive effect on their personal development. However, where a person experiences a bereavement, redundancy or is unable for some reason to stay in the place they would like to live, relocation may be a forced choice and may have a disruptive and negative effect on their personal development. This can be the case for children and adolescents who are required to move, leaving friends and school mates behind, when their parents decide to relocate. Social relationships and emotional attachments may be lost as a result of relocation and the individual may feel isolated and unsupported in their new location. This can also happen when an older person moves, perhaps reluctantly, from living in their own home to living in a care home. A fundamental change in self-concept can occur in this situation as the older person loses their independence and their social and emotional connections with friends, neighbours and the community more generally.

Retirement

Retirement is the point at which people end their working career. For many people this happens between the ages of 60 and 65 years. Recent changes in legislation and the date at which people will become eligible for a state pension mean that people will have to work longer and will retire at a later age in future. At the same time, it is also not unusual for people who have the financial resources to take early retirement before they reach the point at which they can receive a state pension. Whenever it happens, retirement is a major predictable change that requires an adjustment in an individual's daily routine. It also means an alteration in status and has an impact on people's social relationships and financial situation. Retirement can have both positive and negative effects on development and wellbeing.

For people who have been very committed to their work, and whose work provided their social life, retirement can result in too much time to fill and the loss of contact with work friends. Retirement can also cause financial problems. State and occupational pensions usually provide less money than a salary. For many older people retirement can be the beginning of financial hardship. For other people who have planned for their retirement and who have other interests and friendships, retirement can offer new opportunities, provide more time to

Over to you!

Which of the following life events are expected and which are unexpected? Make a list of each type of life event.

- Becoming a parent
- Starting school
- Getting married
- Getting your first job
- Being promoted
- Moving to a new house
- Leaving home
- Getting divorced
- Retiring from work
- Going bankrupt
- Taking exams
- The death of a loved one
- Losing your job
- Learning to read
- Going into care
- Winning the Lottery
- Getting a nursing qualification.

Retirement can provide more time for family relationships.

The effect of life events on personal development

enjoy hobbies and more time to enjoy the company of friends and family. For these people retirement is welcomed as a positive life event.

Redundancy

Redundancy happens when an employer decides that a job is no longer required and ends the contract of employment of the person who does that job. It is different to dismissal or sacking, as people who are made redundant lose their jobs through no fault of their own. However, being made 'redundant' can have a significant effect on a person's self-esteem and emotional wellbeing.

Because of rapid changes in the way that businesses are run and recent economic recessions, redundancy has become a much more common experience. Sometimes workers are unaware of the financial problems that their employer is facing so redundancy is unexpected and may happen suddenly. Even when redundancy is anticipated, it can still be upsetting or unwelcome. Redundancy can have a major impact on a person's wellbeing and lifestyle as the loss of salary can lead to financial problems and emotional insecurity. Redundancy can also break up firm friendships and leave people feeling as though they have no clear or valued role in life. This can affect a person's self-esteem and self-concept.

There can be a positive outcome to redundancy for some people. The loss of a job may motivate them to learn new skills, to start a small business or to change their lifestyle in a way that leads to them feeling happier and more satisfied in the long term.

Case study

Jimmy Davis is 49 years of age. He was made redundant from his job in a car factory nine months ago. He has applied for over a hundred jobs since then but still hasn't been able to get work. Jimmy has recently started to feel depressed, thinking that he will never get another job and that he is 'no good' because he can't find work. He has started an Open University course, which he enjoys, in order to fill his time whilst he looks for work. However, Jimmy's wife has started to worry about the way he is feeling and has suggested that he should go to see his GP to talk about it. Jimmy says he'd be too embarrassed to talk about 'being a failure'.

- Which aspects of Jimmy's personal development are likely to be affected by his redundancy?
- Using the information in the case study, identify some of the effects that redundancy has had on Jimmy's self-concept.
- Suggest reasons why Jimmy's experience of redundancy might actually have a positive impact on his personal development in the long-term.

Knowledge Check

1 What type of life event is starting primary school?

2 How might a person's development benefit from starting further education?

3 What is the difference between retirement and redundancy?

4 Which PIES areas of development are likely to be affected by the experience of redundancy?

Sources of support

Support from other people can help us to cope with the unsettling effects of major life events such as going to school, starting work, marriage, divorce and bereavement. Different sources of support, including partners, family and friends, professional carers and services and voluntary and faith-based services can be used to obtain help.

Partners, family and friends

Family support is often the first form of help that people seek when they experience a major life event. Partners, relatives and close friends may be able to provide practical and emotional support in times of stress, change or crisis. Providing a person with somewhere to stay, transport or a shoulder to cry on can help them to overcome problems that they face. People need support from their partner and family at different stages in their lives. For example, marriage and the birth of children are major life events in which adults are often supported emotionally, financially and practically by their partners, relatives and close friends. Similarly, divorce, bereavement and redundancy are life events that may require family members to support each other emotionally and financially.

Professional carers and services

In some situations people who need support do not have a partner, family or friends whom they can ask for help. In other situations the problems a person faces are too involved or too time-consuming for partners, family and friends to deal with. For example, a woman whose partner has died unexpectedly may need help with child care, financial assistance and considerable emotional support to cope with everyday life. When a person faces difficulties like this they can draw on the support of professional carers and services. Health, social care and early years workers are trained and qualified to deal with the complex difficulties that families and friends are unable to help with. Where people need financial help and advice, support is available from professionally qualified advisers, banks, building societies and government departments such as the Department

Over to you!

Can you think of any times or events when your family or friends were an important source of support, advice or help to you?

of Work and Pensions. General Practitioners, the Citizens Advice Bureau (CAB) and Local Authorities (Councils) are the main sources of information on where to obtain health, social care and welfare support.

Voluntary and faith-based services

Voluntary services are provided by charities and local groups of people who wish to offer support to people experiencing particular problems. For example, MIND provides services for individuals and families affected by mental illness, MENCAP provides services for people affected by learning disability and Relate provides support and counselling services to couples who needs marriage guidance. Faith-based organisations, such as Churches, Mosques, Synagogues and other religious groups, also provide support to members of their local community who are experiencing social and emotional problems.

The services of voluntary and faith-based groups are usually free or low-cost. The services offered are wide-ranging and include advice and guidance, information-giving, counselling as well as a range of practical help to meet specific needs.

NSPCC
Cruelty to children must stop. FULL STOP.

Dogs for the Disabled
Reg. Charity No. 700454

Barnardo's
GIVING CHILDREN BACK THEIR FUTURE

Case study

Julie is a member of Christ the King Pentecostal Church. Together with a couple of friends she runs a playgroup for under-fives on a Monday morning. The playgroup is quite informal, offering a range of play activities and a mid-morning snack for young children. Julie also ensures that tea, coffee and cakes are available for the parents who bring their children along to the group. Many of the parents who bring their children to the group come because it offers them a chance to meet other parents and to have a break from providing child care at home. The children who use the group enjoy playing with the various dolls, toys and pieces of play equipment. Most will also sit in small groups when Julie or one of the parents reads a story or provides them with a 'picnic snack' midway through the two-hour playgroup session.

- What kind of organisation provides the playgroup described in the case study?

- What kinds of services are provided by playgroup?

- How might going to the playgroup affect the personal development of the children who attend?

- How might going to the playgroup be beneficial for the personal development of the parents who attend?

Understanding Personal Development and Relationships

Knowledge Check

1 Describe a life event or problem for which the support of family, friends or partners would be the most suitable.

2 When is it appropriate to seek support from professional carers and services?

3 Which organisation offers support to people who are experiencing marital or relationship problems?

4 What kinds of problems do faith-based organisations provide support for?

5 What kinds of help do faith-based organisations offer?

Over to you!

How we react to a change in life circumstances is important as it can affect our health, wellbeing and development. Identify ways of coping with the changes that may result from each of the major life events listed below. Write down examples of the types of support that you think would help a person to cope with each situation.

- The break up of a marriage or long-term relationship.
- Leaving school or college with no job to go to.
- Moving to a new area of the country with your family.
- Being involved in a car crash.
- Losing your sight.
- Being promoted to a very responsible position at work.
- Leaving home to go to university or to live with friends.
- The birth of your first child.
- Being made redundant.
- Failing to get the exam grades that are needed for a job.
- The death of a close relative or friend.
- Being diagnosed with a serious illness.
- The onset of puberty.
- Winning the National Lottery jackpot.
- Being sent to prison.
- Starting employment.
- Moving from primary to secondary school.
- Getting married.
- Getting into serious debt.
- One of your parents developing Alzheimer's disease.
- Retiring from work after forty years in the same job.

Discuss your ideas with a class colleague, explaining the reasons for your decisions.

Topic review

The box below provides a summary of the areas covered in Topic 1.4. Tick the areas that you feel you understand and would be confident answering exam questions about. If there are any areas that you don't understand or are not confident about, you will need to return to them before you begin your exam revision.

Expected and unexpected life events ☐

Relationship changes
    Marriage / cohabitation ☐
    Birth of children ☐
    Death (of partner, relative or friend ☐

Physical changes
    Puberty ☐
    Menopause ☐
    Accidents and injury ☐

Changes in life circumstances
    Starting school ☐
    Starting further education ☐
    Beginning work ☐
    Retirement ☐
    Redundancy ☐

Sources of support
    Partners, family and friends ☐
    Professional carers and services ☐
    Voluntary and faith-based services ☐

Assessment Guide

Your learning in this unit will be assessed through a one hour and fifteen minute written examination.

The examination will consist of multiple-choice questions and a series of questions based on case studies and short scenarios.

You will need to show that you understand:

● Major life changes and how people manage the effects of these.

Exploring Health, Social Care and Early Years Provision

Introduction

This unit is about the range of care needs individuals have and the care services that are provided to meet these needs. You will learn about:

- The range of care needs of different service user groups

- The types of services that are provided to meet service user needs

- The ways services have developed and how they are organised

- Ways of obtaining care services

- Reasons people sometimes don't get the care services that they need

- The jobs and skills of people who work in health, social care and early years services

- The principles of care and values that care workers put into practice through their work with service users.

If you are thinking about working in the health, social care or early years field, this unit will help you to understand how the care system works and the different jobs that are available within it. Understanding what care services are available and how they work will also help should you or a member of your family need to use services in the future.

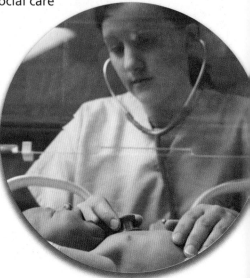

Topic 2.1

The range of care needs of major client groups

Topic focus

Health, social care and early years services are provided to meet the **care needs** of major **client groups**. Topic 2.1 outlines the health, development and social care needs of the following major client groups:

- Infants
- Children
- Adolescents
- Individuals in early adulthood
- Individuals in middle adulthood
- Individuals in later adulthood
- Individuals with specific needs.

You will learn about the physical, intellectual, emotional and social needs that members of these client groups have. Topic 2.1 will also explain how health, social care and early years services respond to these needs and demands of these client groups. By the end of the unit you should understand why individuals may need to use health, social care and early years services.

Client groups

Care services are planned for groups of people who have the same type of problems or similar unmet needs. These groups of people are known as **client groups**. A **service user** is a member of a client group who actually receives a care service. Care organisations in the United Kingdom provide health care, social care and early education services that meet the physical, intellectual, social and emotional needs of major client groups. Some of the services that are provided for a client group are **universal services**, such as general health care provided by GPs (family doctors). These services are suitable for all members of the client group. However, care organisations like the NHS also develop **targeted services**, such as child and adolescent mental health services and adult spinal rehabilitation services, for members of client groups who have particular care and development needs. The groups of service users you need to know about are:

- Infants (0–2 years)
- Children (3–8 years)

- Adolescents (9–18 years)
- Adults (19–65 years)
- Older people (65+ years)
- Individuals with specific needs.

As you can see, these groups cover the whole of the human life span – from newborn babies to very old people. The general needs of human beings of all ages are described below (see Figure 2.1). A person whose physical, intellectual, emotional and social needs are satisfied is likely to experience positive health, wellbeing and personal development.

Figure 2.1 Examples of PIES needs.

Type of needs	Examples of needs
Physical needs	<ul><li>A balanced diet and sufficient fluids</li><li>Warmth</li><li>Shelter</li><li>Exercise</li><li>Sleep and rest</li><li>Good hygiene</li><li>Protection from harm, illness and injury</li></ul>
Intellectual needs	<ul><li>Interesting and purposeful activities</li><li>Learning opportunities</li><li>Mental challenges and new experiences</li></ul>
Emotional needs	<ul><li>Love, support and care</li><li>A sense of safety and security</li><li>Self-confidence and self-esteem</li></ul>
Social needs	<ul><li>Attachment to a trusted carer</li><li>Relationships with other people</li><li>A sense of identity and belonging within a community</li></ul>

A person's **physical needs** must be satisfied for them to be physically healthy. A person's **intellectual needs** are those things they require to develop their knowledge, skills and abilities. A person's **emotional and social needs** are the things they require to develop relationships and experience emotional wellbeing and good mental health.

The hierarchy of needs

Whilst all human beings have a common range of physical, intellectual, emotional and social needs, the precise nature of these needs vary across the different client groups. This is because a person's needs, and their ability to meet them, change as they move from one life stage to another. Care organisations recognise this and tailor their services to meet the particular health care, social care and developmental needs of each client group.

Abraham Maslow (1908 – 1970), an American psychologist, developed a way of thinking about human needs that is still very influential in care work. He suggested that a person's needs are best understood as a pyramid or hierarchy, arranged in levels of importance (see figure 2.2). He believed that physical needs were the most important because a person must meet these, or have help from other people to meet them, to survive. Maslow suggested that human beings of any age are motivated to have to meet needs higher up the pyramid only when they have meet lower level needs. As you study and understand the different stages of human development, you will notice that as people become more capable of meeting certain needs, the focus of their personal development shifts to other levels of need. For example, during infancy parents and care practitioners prioritise physical and safety needs as these are essential for an infant's development. During childhood, physical and safety needs are still important but are usually being met quite successfully. As a result, a child's social needs become more of a priority.

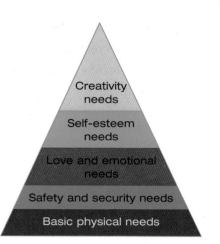

Figure 2.2 Maslow's hierarchy of needs.

Infants (0–2 years)

A newborn baby is dependent on others, usually their parents, to provide them with the things they need for health, wellbeing and development. To be healthy and to develop normally, infants require a lot of practical, hands-on care from their parents and from care professionals during the early stages of infancy. A lot of the care needs of babies result from their physical dependence and vulnerability to harm. Infants become less dependent in some ways as they grow and develop into toddlers. However, a 2-year-old toddler still depends on their parents to meet most of their physical, intellectual, emotional and social needs.

Figure 2.3 Care needs of infants.

Case study

Luke is 2 months old. He had a normal birth. After a range of checks by the midwife and doctor at the hospital, his parents took him home the day after his birth. As a young baby, Luke is totally dependent on others for basic care and protection from harm. Luke's mum breastfeeds him several times during the day and night. She and his dad take it in turns to change his nappy, wash him and comfort him when he starts crying. Luke's parents have to make sure that he is fed properly, that he is kept warm but that he doesn't get too hot and that he is kept clean and comfortable. Luke won't be able to meet these needs on his own until he is several years older.

- List any other basic needs that are not mentioned in the case study that you think Luke has. (Hint – what else does he need to be a healthy baby?)
- Identify two things that Luke's mum or dad do to meet his physical needs.
- Which care worker usually visits a mother and baby at home shortly after the birth to check that the baby is healthy and growing well?

Children (3–8 years)

Children need less basic care from their parents than infants as they learn how to meet some of their own basic needs. For example, children learn how to feed, wash and dress themselves in early childhood. Even so, children still need a lot of help and support from parents and care practitioners to develop:

- self-care skills (washing, dressing, going to the toilet)
- physical strength and stamina (play and outdoor activities)
- intellectual skills (basic reading, writing and numeracy)
- language skills (talking, reading and writing)
- social skills (friendships and relationships with other children and adults)
- emotional control and appropriate behaviour (at home and with others).

A range of health, social care and early years services are available for children who experience ill-health, social or emotional difficulties, developmental problems or who have disabilities. These services provide specialist forms of care that are targeted at the particular needs of children.

Over to you!

How might the basic care needs of a child be different to those of an adult and an older person?

Case study

Anna is three and a half years old. She has recently begun attending a playgroup two mornings a week. Anna's mum helps to run the playgroup. She thinks that attending playgroup is good for Anna's development. When she's at the playgroup, Anna meets and plays with up to ten other children. Anna enjoys playing with sand and water, climbing and using the trampoline. She now joins in games with other children. Her mum says that Anna has learnt how to make new friends and is much less shy than she was before she started going to playgroup.

- Give an example of one physical, one intellectual, one emotional and one social need that a child could meet through going to playgroup.
- What new skills or abilities might playgroup help Anna to develop?
- Explain how play might help Anna to develop intellectual skills.

Adolescents (9–18 years)

Adolescents have care needs that are different to those of children and adults. During adolescence young people go through **puberty**. This involves major physical growth and development but doesn't normally involve teenagers experiencing major health problems as a result of it. However, some teenagers do develop additional health needs that require specialist care and treatment. For example, teenage girls may require health care services for problems related to **menstruation** and many adolescents seek help for skin problems, such as acne, that often occur during puberty. Adolescents can also benefit from receiving information, advice and guidance from health promotion workers. This helps them make informed choices about aspects of their lifestyle and health behaviour such as smoking, exercise, contraception, drugs, alcohol and unprotected sex.

During adolescence young people often require support to help them with their rapidly changing social and emotional development. For example, young people may require:

- Support to help manage relationships with parents and other adults
- Experiences that build up confidence, self-esteem and assertiveness
- Opportunities to express opinions and explore feelings
- The chance to make personal decisions about the future
- Opportunities to develop knowledge and skills useful for adult life and work
- Opportunities to socialise, develop and express personal identity
- Advice and guidance about relationships, sex and sexuality.

Services to meet the particular health, social care and development needs of adolescents are less common than similar services for children or adults. Adolescents are often required to use children's services until they are 16 years old and then services for adults after their 16th birthday. However, some local areas do now provide specialist targeted services as awareness has grown about the specific needs of adolescents.

Case study

Gina is fifteen years old. She says that can't wait to leave school and get a job. Gina currently has a difficult relationship with her parents. She complains that they treat her like a child and are too strict with her. Gina believes that she is mature enough to make decisions for herself. Gina's parents complain that she has become 'very difficult' and that she no longer listens to what they tell her. They insist that she doesn't go out after school during the week and won't let her stay at friend's house at the weekend. Gina feels too angry with her parents to talk to them about any of these things at the moment.

- Who could help Gina to express how she feels?
- What kind of physical care needs do adolescents like Gina have?
- Why do you think parents have difficult relationships with their children during adolescence?

Individuals in early and middle adulthood

Adulthood is a life stage where people are expected to be able to meet their own physical, intellectual, emotional and social needs. However, there are always situations where people need help in meeting their needs, such as when they experience problems with their physical or mental health or social problems as a result of changes to their circumstances.

Over to you!

Look at figure 2.4. This is a graph showing the percentage of different age groups who experience long-term illness. Which group is most likely to experience limiting long-term illness? What percentage of people are affected by limiting long-term illness in early adulthood?

Percentages

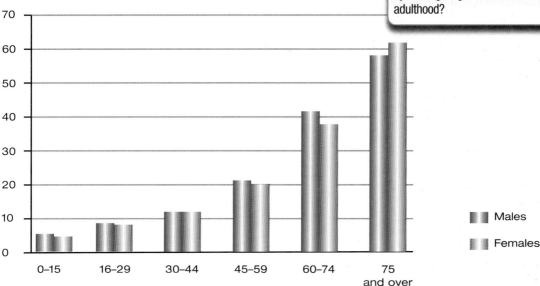

Figure 2.4 – Prevalence of limiting long-term illness by age and sex, UK 2001. Source ONS.

Adults may require health care services for much the same reasons as children and adolescents. However, adults are more likely than children and adolescents to experience serious diseases and disorders, such as cancers and mental health problems, which require a broader range of specialist medical treatment and care. Some health problems, like heart disease,

Case study

"My name is Nadine Burton. I'm twenty-six years old and have one child, Leon, who is now nine months old. I've used care services quite a lot recently, mainly because of stress, and for Leon. I saw my GP (family doctor) when I felt under pressure and I wasn't sleeping well. I thought that he could give me something to help me sleep. Leon was waking up in the night and I had to get up to feed him all the time. I was tired all day and I wasn't coping very well. My neighbours then started complaining about Leon's crying. It made me feel depressed. The GP got me some help from social services. They arranged for me to go to a mother and baby group. I now get to meet other new mums and we chat. I find it helps me to relax a bit. The GP also arranged for the Health Visitor to keep coming to see me. She gives me advice about feeding and caring for Leon and she's friendly. Things are getting easier now. Well, the neighbours have stopped complaining, anyway!"

- Which client group is Nadine a member of now?
- Which client group is Leon a member of?
- Give two reasons why Nadine needed help from care services.
- Explain how the care and support provided to Nadine helps to meet her social and emotional needs.

respiratory disorders or arthritis, may develop into chronic conditions and require the person to use care services throughout their adult life. The same situation is also true of social care services. Some adults may require help and support, such as temporary housing, for a short period, whilst other more vulnerable people need ongoing support to help them to cope with the stresses and difficulties in their life or with a permanent disability.

A wide range of health and social care services are available for adults who experience ill-health, social or emotional difficulties. These services provide specialist forms of care that are targeted at the diverse health, social care and development needs of adults.

Individuals in later adulthood

Older people aged 65+ are a major client group for health and social care services. This isn't because all older people are frail, incapable or unwell. However, the gradual effects of the ageing process do mean that many older people tend to experience a reduction in their ability to cope with the demands of daily life and become more vulnerable to ill-health, social isolation and loneliness. Individuals in later adulthood are more likely than younger adults to experience physical health problems that affect their **daily living skills**. Older people may require health services because they develop a condition or illness that reduces their ability to perform everyday tasks such as washing, dressing or shopping for food. Many older people also struggle to live on a reduced income once they retire and

stop earning an income. This again can reduce their quality of life by restricting what food they can buy, how much they are able to socialise and even whether they can afford to heat their homes in the winter. As a result, later adulthood is a life stage when many individuals become more vulnerable and require the support of health and social care services to help them to meet their physical, intellectual, emotional and social needs.

Over to you!

Can you think of any care services that are targeted at older people? What needs are these services aiming to meet?

Case study

Mrs Jean Baker is 78 years of age. Until a year ago she spent most of her time looking after her house and her husband Peter, aged 80. Peter Baker had a severe heart attack a year ago and has been in hospital ever since. Mrs Baker tries to visit him whenever she can but is finding life on her own very difficult. She feels that she needs help to cope with her housework and general chores like shopping. Mrs Baker has also been feeling unwell recently and has been lonely since her husband was admitted to hospital.

- What do you think Mrs Baker's care needs are?
- How could Mrs Baker be given more emotional support?
- Name two types of care service which are provided to meet the needs of older people.

Individuals with specific needs

Some forms of health, social care and early years services are developed and provided to meet the needs of people with specific conditions or problems. These include:

- People with learning disabilities
- People with mental health problems
- People with physical disabilities
- People with sensory impairments (visual or hearing).

Whilst these groups of service users have many of the same universal care needs as other people of a similar age, their particular problems require specialist care provision because of the need to also take account of the individual's disability or mental health problem. Learning and physical disabilities, mental health problems and sensory impairments can affect the personal development of people in all life stages. For example, an individual's particular disability or impairment may result in specific care needs because it disrupts, slows down or limits some aspect of their personal development so that the individual requires additional, specialist forms of help and support, such as medication, psychological therapy, special education or equipment or residential care services, to enable them to function to the best of their ability.

Over to you!

What kinds of specific care needs do you think an adult might have if they lost their eyesight in an accident?

Investigate ...

Use the Internet to find the websites of the RNID (www.rnid.org.uk) and the RNIB (www.rnib.org.uk). Find out what help is available for visually and hearing impaired people.

Specific needs	Targeted services	
Learning difficulties	● Day centres ● Supported housing	● Employment support ● Specialist education and training
Sensory impairments	● Adapted housing ● Hearing/guide dogs	● Adapted daily living equipment ● Occupational therapy
Mental health problems	● In-patient units ● Community nurses ● Day centres	● Supported employment ● Psychotherapy
Physical disability	● Residential care ● Transport services	● Occupational therapy ● Community support workers

Figure 2.5 Targeted services for individuals with special needs.

Case study

Richard is thirty-two years old and has Down's Syndrome. He lives at home with his parents and attends a day centre where he has made some friends. Richard has learnt to wash, dress and feed himself but requires help and support to adapt to new people and changes in his routine. Richard's parents and carers say that he is not able to make decisions for himself or live independently at the moment. Even so, Richard says that he'd like to be a bus driver and get married one day.

- What kinds of care needs do you think Richard has at the moment?
- Explain how going to the day centre could help to meet Richard's needs.
- How do you think Richard could be helped to become more independent?

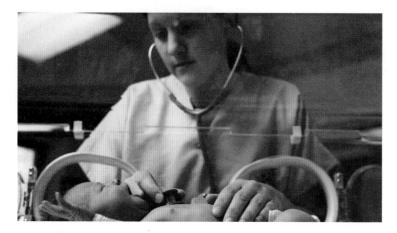

Premature babies have a range of specific care needs.

Permanent and temporary needs

We have seen that people have care needs in every life stage. However, it is important to distinguish between the temporary care needs that a person has and the more permanent, ongoing needs that can also develop.

A person may have **temporary care needs** because they become unwell or experience some social or developmental problems at a particular point in their life. This is usually the case where a person develops an **acute** (short term) **illness** or has an accident that requires treatment. When the person recovers or gets over their problems, their need for care will end. The same is true during infancy, childhood and early adolescence. Parents and other adults may provide forms of physical care and social, emotional and intellectual support for an individual until they are able to meet their needs independently. In this sense, we all have temporary care needs during the early parts of life.

An individual can develop, or be born with, **permanent care needs** because they have a **chronic** (ongoing) health problem or condition that affects their ability to function independently. For example, a person with chronic kidney disease may need regular **dialysis** (removal of waste products from the blood) for the rest of their life unless they receive a kidney transplant. Similarly, a child born with Down's syndrome is likely to need specialist health and social care support throughout their life because their learning difficulties will limit their social and intellectual development and prevent them from developing the skills needed for independent living.

Social policy goals

The government is responsible for funding, and in many cases providing, a range of health, social care, education and welfare services for the population of the United Kingdom. The main purpose of these services is to provide help for people 'in need'. One of the key challenges for any government is to identify the main health and social problems facing society (such as child protection, obesity and substance misuse, for example). They do this by commissioning research studies and reports into a wide range of health and social care issues and also by collecting and

Over to you!

Identify the last time you needed others to provide you with care. How temporary were your care needs?

Focus	Social policy goal	Government action
Early years	• To reduce child poverty • To improve early learning opportunities for all	• Development of Sure Start Children's centres • Employment and child care support for lone parent and low income families. • Employment of a range of family and child care support workers • Increased nursery places for children under 4 years of age
Health care	• To reduce deaths and illness from heart disease, cancers, strokes, accidents and suicide • To tackle inequalities in health experience between different groups in the population	• Reduction in waiting times for hospital appointments • Employment of more health care staff in the NHS • Development of more primary care and walk-in services to improve access to health care • A change in focus to preventative health care services

Figure 2.6 Social policies on health care and early years.

analysing data to identify which groups are most 'in need'. Once reports and data are available, the government produce social policies which set out how they intend to tackle the problems that have been identified. The social policies that are produced will include a range of targets or goals that need to be achieved in order to deal with the problems faced by those who are 'in need'.

Since 1997, the New Labour government has produced a range of social policies relating to health care and early years services. Some of these are described in figure 2.6.

There are a wide range of social policy goals that affect all areas of health, social care and early years service provision. The NHS, local authorities and voluntary organisations typically develop and adapt the services they provide in order to try and achieve the targets or goals set by each of the government's social policies.

Assessing population care needs

Social policies are one of the factors that influence the development of health, social care and early years services. Another factor, closely related to the development of social policies, is the range of care, development and support needs that exist within a local population. NHS Strategic Health Authorities are regional organisations that are responsible for implementing the government's social policies in specified local areas. They work directly with Primary Care Trusts and alongside Local Authorities to assess the health care, social care and early years support needs of the local population so that they can provide an appropriate range of care services. When the range of care needs within a local population are known the local NHS Primary Care Trust will commission health care services for all service user groups whilst the Local Authority has the responsibility for commissioning social care and early years services for vulnerable people and young children. The data required to assess health needs is generally obtained from hospital and GP records and from surveys carried out in local communities.

 **Over to you!**

Find out the name and website address of your local Primary Care Trust. Have a look on their website for information about the Joint Strategic Needs Assessment. This will tell you about population care needs in your local area.

Knowledge Check

1 What is a client group?

2 Why are care services planned for client groups?

3 What are the four types of need?

4 What can happen when a person has unmet needs?

5 What is a 'chronic' health problem?

6 Name two client groups that have non-adult members.

7 Why do babies need a lot of care?

8 Name two skills that babies develop before their first birthday.

9 Can you think of any other basic or specialist types of care a child might need to be healthy and happy?

10 How are the care needs of an adolescent different to those of an adult?

11 Which age range are 'adult' care services aimed at?

12 Why do some older people require help from care services?

Topic review

The box below summarises the areas covered in Topic 2.1. Tick the areas that you feel you understand and would be confident about when writing your assignment for this unit. If there are any areas that you don't understand or are not confident about, you will need to return to them before you begin to plan or write your assignment.

Client groups ☐

Types of need
Physical ☐
Intellectual ☐
Emotional ☐
Social ☐
Permanent ☐
Temporary ☐

Client group care needs
Infants ☐
Children ☐
Adolescents ☐
Adults (early / middle) ☐
Later adulthood ☐
Individuals with specific needs ☐

Assessing population health needs ☐

Social policy goals ☐

Assessment Guide

Your learning in this unit will be assessed through a controlled assignment. This will be set by Edexcel and marked by your tutor.

The assignment will require you to produce a report based on an investigation of the needs of one service user. Your report should also show how these needs are met by service providers and care practitioners.

You will need to show evidence of:

● The range of needs of major service user (client) groups

The needs of each major service user or client group have been explained in Topic 2.1. Your assignment report should demonstrate that you can apply your knowledge and understanding of care needs to the service user you have chosen to focus on in your assignment.

Topic 2.2

Access and barriers to health, social care and early years services

Topic focus

People who have care needs generally need to obtain appropriate services or forms of support to meet these needs. But how can people gain access to care services when they require them? Topic 2.2 focuses on the different ways of obtaining health, social care and early years services. You will learn about different methods of referral, including:

- Self-referral
- Professional referral
- Third party referral.

Topic 2.2 also outlines the different barriers that can prevent people from accessing the care services they need. These include:

- Physical barriers, including stairs, lack of lifts and lack of adaptations
- Psychological barriers, including social stigma and fears about loss of independence
- Financial barriers, including means-testing, charges and fees
- Geographical barriers, including poor transport links and distance
- Cultural and language barriers, including different cultural beliefs and different first language
- Resource barriers, including staff shortages, postcode lottery, lack of funding and heavy local demand for services.

By the end of the topic you should have a good understanding of the different ways of gaining access to care services and some of the barriers that service users can face in trying to obtain the care they need.

Access to care services

An individual may need to access health, social care or early years services because they are at a point in their life where they require:

- Care
- Practical or developmental support
- Advice or guidance
- Treatment or therapy.

People use care services when they have health problems, require social support or have unmet development needs. National and local care services are provided to meet the needs of the different client groups.

Local care organisations try to plan and develop services that meet local care needs. To do this, care organisations need to know who lives in their area and what kinds of health, social care

Exploring Health, Social Care and Early Years Provision

and development needs they have. For example, to provide maternity services, local health care organisations need to know how many women of childbearing age live in their area and how many children are likely to be born in a year.

The referral system

Service users can access health, social care and early years services in a number of ways. All types of care services use a **referral** system to manage the process of providing their care services. There are three different forms of referral:

- **Self-referral** occurs when a person applies for a care service themselves. Making an appointment to see your GP (family doctor), phoning **NHS Direct** for advice and information or going to an opticians for an eye-test are all ways of making a self-referral to health care services.

- **Professional referral** occurs when a care worker puts someone who has come to see them in touch with another care professional. An example of a professional referral occurs where a GP refers a patient to a counsellor for therapy.

- **Third party referral** occurs when a person who is not a care professional applies for a care service on behalf of someone else. For example, if a woman telephoned the local social services department to request home care services for her mother, this would be a third-party referral.

Referral to health care services

Primary health care services are the front-line 'family doctor' or health centre services that are available in all local areas. People usually obtain primary health care services by self-referring or through a third party referral. Everyone has a right to register with a GP and obtain primary health care services. If someone does not have a GP, their local health authority is expected to find them one within two working days.

Secondary health care services are more specialist hospital-based services. Some secondary health care services, such as accident and emergency (A&E) and genito-urinary medicine (GUM) clinics, can be obtained by self-referral. However, most secondary health care services are obtained through a GP's professional referral. This applies to both **in-patient** care (the patient stays in hospital) and out-patient services (the patient lives at home and comes to a hospital clinic occasionally).

To make a professional referral, a GP will contact a hospital consultant requesting an appointment or an admission for their patient. There is usually a waiting list system. The GP will tell the hospital consultant how urgent the referral is. In cases of serious emergency the patient will be admitted to hospital on the same day.

Referral to social care services

Access to social care can be by self, third-party or professional referral. Referrals to statutory organisations, like social services departments, will usually be dealt with by a duty social worker. It's their job to find out what exactly the situation is and what is needed.

An assessment of need is carried out on everyone who is referred to social services. An individual will receive social care services if a need is identified and they also meet the **eligibility criteria** to

Over to you!

For each of the following examples identify:

- the client group involved
- the type of referral(s) involved in each situation.

1 Mrs Arkwright is 78 years old and is frail. Her home carer noticed that she has a bad cough. The home carer rang Mrs Arkwright's GP, asking him to make a home visit.

2 Rosie Abdi, a social worker, has received a phone call about a three-year-old child who is being left alone during the day. The call came from a neighbour of the child's parents. Rosie has asked the family's GP to accompany her on a visit to the child's home.

3 Mr Ghupta, aged 35, has a long-term mental health problem. He takes himself to his local health centre or to the local hospital's accident and emergency department when he feels unwell and needs treatment.

4 Ellisha, aged 29, is five months pregnant. Her GP has made an appointment for her to have an ultrasound scan at the local hospital.

5 Jim has had a bad back for three days. His wife has made him an appointment with a private sector osteopath.

obtain services. The person carrying out the assessment will usually be a care co-ordinator or social worker. If the person referred to social services is a child, a special assessment would be carried out to see if the child is 'at risk' and in need of child protection services. If this isn't the case, an assessment will be carried out to establish whether the child is 'in need'. Appropriate services and support will then be provided.

Voluntary and private sector social care services

A lot of domiciliary, day and residential care is available directly from voluntary and private agencies. A self or third party referral can be used to gain access to these services. Most agencies carry out their own assessments. The only eligibility criteria are that:

a the person has the ability to pay, and

b the agency have the staff to supply the service.

Referral to early years services

For the most part access is by parents applying direct to a private or voluntary sector service provider, such as a private nursery or childminder. A child will usually be offered a place if they are considered suitable, the parents are able to afford the fees and there is a space available. The availability of spaces is usually the main issue affecting access to voluntary sector early years services. Affording the cost of services is usually the main issue affecting access to private sector early years services.

Barriers to accessing services

There are occasions where people have a need for a care service, but they are unable to get it. Some of the most common 'barriers' to obtaining health care services are described below.

Physical barriers

Physical barriers to healthcare services generally involve problems with the 'built environment'. That is, some people can't get into the places where care services are provided whilst others are unable to leave their own homes to go to the places where care is available. Physical 'barriers' within buildings, such as outside steps or narrow doorways, may prevent an individual from entering or leaving. For example, a wheelchair user would be unable to get care services at a health centre that only had steps up to the front door. A parent pushing a child in a pram would also struggle and may be put off from using this health centre. Other physical barriers, such as internal stairs, narrow corridors and doorways and a lack of lifts or adapted toilet facilities, sometimes occur within buildings and can prevent disabled and older people from using services.

Psychological barriers

Not everyone has a positive attitude towards managing their personal health and wellbeing or using care services. Some people avoid going to see their doctor because they are embarrassed, lack concern about their personal health or are frightened to find out what might be wrong with them. For example, the incidence of testicular cancer is higher than it should

Over to you!

How do you think these physical barriers could be overcome to allow wheelchair users to gain access to care services?

be partly because men are often reluctant to conduct self-examinations or seek help early if they find anything unusual. You may also know someone who is too scared to go to their doctor or dentist. Problems such as alcoholism, drug misuse, eating disorders, obesity, sexually transmitted diseases and mental health difficulties are sometimes seen as embarrassing or shameful. These negative feelings and beliefs may lead to people suffering from these problems not seeking help as early as they should.

Older people and disabled people with health and social care problems may also be frightened that they will lose their independence if they reveal a health problem or tell a care practitioner that they are finding it hard to cope at home. Similar psychological barriers can prevent people from accessing social services when they need them. In particular, some people feel that there is a stigma (or sense of shame) attached to using social service departments, so they will avoid doing so, even if they have a clear need. Accepting help from voluntary organisations or informal support groups can also be a problem for people who see these services as a form of 'charity'.

Financial barriers

Health, social care and early years services are sometimes only available to people if they pay some or all of the cost involved in providing them. For example, unless you fall into an exempt group you will have to pay **charges** for NHS prescriptions, eye tests and dental services. The financial cost of these and other services can act as a barrier to care for some people. For example, when free eye testing for people over 65 was withdrawn in 1989 there was a dramatic fall in the number of older people having eye tests. The British Medical Association claimed that this led to serious eye diseases and potential blindness going undetected. These free eye tests have now been reintroduced.

The range of health, social care and early years services provided by companies and individual practitioners who make up the private sector are only available to people who can afford to pay the fees for these services. Some people pay into insurance schemes or are given health insurance by their employers to cover these costs. However, many of the people who would otherwise have to pay out of their own pocket are put off by the cost of private sector fees. As a result financial barriers do prevent some people from obtaining some forms of health, social care and early years services that they would otherwise benefit from.

In social care, adult services are **means-tested**. This means that service users have their income and savings assessed before services are provided. Those who fall below the financial limit imposed by social services are eligible for services. People who have more money or savings than the limit have to pay some or all of the cost of the service they want. As a result, some people can be put off applying for social care services by the costs involved or by having to disclose financial information.

The health, social care and early years services provided by the private sector are only available to those people who can afford to pay for them. Some people have health insurance or employers who pay for or subsidise medical and child care costs. Those who don't have the money or an employer to subsidise them are likely to see the costs of private sector services as a financial barrier to them gaining the services they require.

Over to you

Why do you think there is a stigma attached to receiving help or support from local authority social services departments?

Investigate ...

How much are prescriptions and eye test charges for adults now? Find out how much adults have to pay for these services and who is eligible for free or reduced cost prescriptions and eye-tests.

Geographical barriers

Health, social care or early years services may be difficult to obtain if they are located several miles away from where a potential service user lives. This is a particular problem for people who live in rural (country) areas. The problem is made even worse for people who rely on public transport. Sometimes people have to travel very long distances to obtain specialist health care treatment that isn't available in their own health district. As a result the geographical location of services may act as a barrier to people getting the care they need. Health facilities, social care provision and early years services that are difficult to get to are not likely to be used by people who do not have easy access to their own transport.

Cultural and language barriers

The UK is a multicultural country in which people, particularly recent immigrants, speak a variety of languages. In areas where there are large numbers of people from minority ethnic communities, health and social care authorities try to ensure that language barriers are overcome by providing multi-lingual signs, interpreters and bilingual staff. However, health and care information is not always available in the languages that some people speak or in the formats needed by people who have eyesight or hearing problems. People who are unable to speak, or have limited understanding of English, or who have hearing or visual impairments can therefore struggle to find care that meets their cultural, language and communication needs. People will not use care services where they are unable to make themselves understood or which lack sensitivity to their cultural needs.

Resource barriers

The resources that organisations require before they can provide care services include:

● skilled staff

● buildings (including in-patient beds) and equipment

● money to pay for running costs and staff wages.

Service users sometimes find that care organisations have staff shortages or don't have enough money to provide the care services that they need when they need it. As a result, lack of human or financial resources can mean service users have to go on a waiting list for treatment. The area where a service user lives can also affect their ability to access care services. If a person lives in an area that has staffing shortages or a lack of funding for care services, they may have to wait longer or may even find that a particular service isn't available to them. By contrast, another person living nearby but in a different health authority area may get the treatment or services they require. This situation is known as the **postcode lottery**.

As the main providers of social care services, local authorities have to manage their resources carefully. When their budget is cut or restricted, a local authority may increase the eligibility criteria for services. For example, in the past many local authorities would help someone who was quite independent but who needed a home help to do some cleaning and shopping for them. Nowadays, these services are not available in many areas and someone must require personal care on a daily basis before they became eligible for a home help.

In many areas of the UK, there is a shortage of early years nursery education and day nursery places. Although there is no charge for state-run services in most cases, few people are eligible for them. As a result there is often great local demand for voluntary and private sector places. The limited number of places combined with the high demand for them is another example of a resource barrier that may prevent people from accessing the services they require.

Knowledge Check

1 What kind of referral is used most often to obtain primary health care services?

2 Who does a GP need to contact to make a professional referral for specialist hospital services?

3 Explain how language barriers can prevent some people from gaining the care services they need.

4 How do you think physical barriers could be overcome to allow wheelchair users to gain access to care services?

5 Why do you think there is a stigma attached to receiving help or support local authority social services departments?

6 What is a means-test?

7 Which type of care worker usually deals with a referral to a social services department?

8 Explain what has to happen before an adult can receive social care services from the local authority.

9 Describe two ways in which a person living in a rural area may face geographical barriers when they require health care services.

Topic review

The box below provides a summary of the areas covered in Topic 2.2. Tick the areas that you feel you understand and would be confident about when writing your assignment. If there are any areas that you don't understand or are not confident about, you will need to return to them before you begin planning or writing your assignment.

Methods of referral
Self-referral ☐
Professional referral ☐
Third-party referral ☐

Barriers to accessing services
Physical barriers ☐
Psychological barriers ☐
Financial barriers ☐
Geographical barriers ☐
Cultural/language barriers ☐
Resource barriers ☐

Assessment Guide

Your learning in this unit will be assessed through a controlled assignment. This will be set by Edexcel and marked by your tutor.

The assignment will require you to produce a report based on an investigation of the needs of one service user and how these needs are met by service providers and care practitioners.

You will need to show evidence of:

● The ways in which people can obtain care services and the barriers which could prevent service users gaining access to these services.

The different methods of referral used by health, social care and early years services and the barriers to accessing care servives have been explained in Topic 2.2.

Your assignment report should demonstrate that you can identify the methods of referral used by your chosen service user to access they services they require. You should also be able to describe any barriers faced by the person in gaining access to these services.

Topic 2.3

Health, social care and early years provision

Topic focus

A range of care services are available to meet the health, social care and development needs of people in each of the major client groups. Topic 2.3 will describe the types of services that are available and the way they are organised. You will learn about different types of care service providers, including:

● Statutory services (NHS Trusts and Local Authorities)

● Private services (companies and self-employed practitioners)

● Voluntary services (charities, local support groups and non-profit organisations)

● Informal services (family, friends and neighbours)

Care service providers often work together in order to meet the complex care needs of some service users. Topic 2.3 will explain how partnerships and multi-agency working are used to achieve this. By the end of the unit you should have a good understanding of the range of health, social care and early years services that are provided in the United Kingdom.

How are care services organised?

You probably know about a number of health, social care and early years services in your local area. There may be a hospital, health centre, family doctor service, nursery or residential home near to where you live, for example. You or members of your family may have used some of these services recently. Local care services like those mentioned are provided by a range of different organisations and self-employed care workers. One way of understanding how care services are provided is to look at how they are organised into statutory, voluntary, private and informal care sectors.

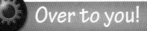

Over to you!

Make a list of all the health and social care services you have received. Divide your list into health, social care and early years services.

The statutory care sector

The government is responsible for controlling and running the part of the care system known as the **statutory sector**. This part of the care system includes organisations such as the **National Health Service** (NHS) and **Local Authorities** (local councils). These organisations provide a lot of health, social care and early years services throughout the United Kingdom. By law the government has to provide some types of care services. The laws that set out these duties are also called 'statutes' – this is where 'statutory' comes from.

Accident & Emergency

The voluntary care sector

The care system in the United Kingdom includes a large voluntary sector. The **voluntary care sector** is made up of organisations that provide their care services because they see a need for them. Voluntary sector care organisations are independent of government. They don't have a legal (or 'statutory') duty to provide care service but do it voluntarily. The sector is also called 'voluntary' because many of the organisations have workers who are unpaid volunteers. *MENCAP* is an example of a voluntary sector organisation that recruits volunteers to work with people who have learning disabilities. Voluntary organisations provide a large range of social care and early years services in the UK that are non-profit making as well as independent from government.

Origins of the voluntary sector

The voluntary care sector began in the nineteenth century when there were very few care services for ordinary people. At the time most care services had to be paid for and were too expensive for all but the rich. Charities and voluntary organisations grew out of the campaigns and donations of a few rich **philanthropists**. These were wealthy individuals, like Joseph Rowntree, who wanted to help their local communities and reduce the poverty and suffering they saw around them.

Joseph Rowntree 1836–1925

The voluntary sector now consists of large, national organisations, like MENCAP, Help the Aged and National Society for the Prevention of Cruelty to Children (NSPCC), and a large number of much smaller groups that work for a cause in their local area. An example would be a support group for single parents or a playgroup that aims to meet the developmental needs of local toddlers.

Most voluntary sector organisations are **registered charities**. This means that they obtain money for their services through donations and fund-raising. Some voluntary organisations also receive government grants and small payments from service users, but they put this income back into running their services and don't try to make a profit. Voluntary organisations usually

Case study

The Acorns Outdoor Gym is made up of a group of older people who meet regularly for country walks and other outdoor activities. All of the group members are either carers or are being cared for at home by a partner or other relative. The group go on organised walks around local beauty spots. There is usually a picnic or café stop in the middle of each walk. The people who take part in the group use it to maintain their fitness, to meet and socialise with other carers and to give and receive support from others in a similar situation. The Acorns Outdoor Gym is free to attend and relies on volunteers to plan and organise its activities.

- What make the Acorns Outdoor Gym part of the voluntary sector?

- What is the main purpose of a group like this?

- Who provides the services that this group offers?

Many early years groups are run by volunteers.

recruit unpaid volunteers who provide their time and skills for free. However, larger voluntary organisations also employ and pay some people to work as care practitioners, managers and administrative staff.

The private sector

The **private sector** is made up of care businesses, such as private hospitals, high street pharmacists and nurseries, and self-employed care practitioners, such as childminders, counsellors and osteopaths, for example. Private sector organisations and self-employed practitioners usually charge people a fee for the health, social care or early years services that they provide. Private sector care providers work to make a profit as well as to meet service users care needs.

In the UK, the private sector offers fewer services and has fewer organisations and service users than either the statutory or voluntary sectors. Private sector organisations focus more on health and early years services than on social care. Many of the services that are provided in the private sector cannot easily be obtained in the statutory system and are specialist, non-emergency services. Day care nurseries and osteopathy services are examples.

The informal sector

The informal sector consists of the very large number of unpaid people who look after members of their own family, their friends or their neighbours who have care needs. Because these people are not trained, employed or paid to provide care, they are known as informal carers. Informal carers provide a lot of care for infants and children, older people and people with disabilities.

Care providers in each of the four sectors make an important contribution to the overall delivery of care services in the UK. A care provider will usually focus on providing either health care, social care or early years services. However, there are overlaps between these types of care service and in practice different care organisations and self-employed practitioners often work together to provide a range of care services for clients who have complex needs.

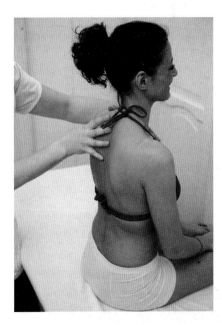

Osteopaths usually work in the private sector.

Exploring Health, Social Care and Early Years Provision

Case study

Sophie is 17 years of age and has Down's syndrome. Sophie's condition has affected her health and personal development throughout her life and will mean that she has lifelong care and support needs. Sophie currently receives care and support from a range of care practitioners who work together to meet her complex needs. Dr Hill is Sophie's GP. He works at a local health centre that is funded and run by the National Health Service (NHS). Alison Rasheed is a specialist learning disability social worker, employed by the local authority, who organises and monitors the special education and social care services that Sophie uses. Sophie attends the Stepping Stones day centre three days each week where she takes part in a range of education and leisure activities. The centre was established and is still managed MENCAP. Sophie's parents pay for her to attend a riding school that provides specialist classes for people with learning disabilities on Thursdays. Sophie is still very reliant on her parents for day-to-day care and support. They provide practical and emotional support in a variety of ways to help Sophie to develop her daily living skills.

- Which of the care practitioners working with Sophie are employed by the statutory sector?

- Identify the voluntary sector care service that Sophie uses.

- Which of the services mentioned is part of the private sector?

- What type of care do Sophie's parents provide for her?

Knowledge Check

1 Name the four main care sectors.

2 Which care sector is funded and run by the government?

3 What is distinctive about the voluntary sector?

4 Explain why voluntary organisations developed in the late nineteenth century.

5 Do voluntary groups only employ volunteers?

6 How do private sector organisations differ from voluntary sector organisations?

7 Describe two examples of private sector care services.

8 Who provides care in the informal sector?

Providers of health care services

Most health care services in the United Kingdom are now provided by the **statutory sector**. Private sector organisations and private practitioners also provide a significant range of health cares services. The voluntary and informal sectors provide very few health care services.

Statutory health care services

Statutory health care services first became available in 1948. This is when the Labour government at the time founded the National Health Service (NHS). The NHS was launched to tackle widespread problems of ill-health and to provide free services for all in the UK. Before this health services were not available to all people. Some voluntary services existed but most people had to pay a doctor privately or join an insurance scheme if they wanted

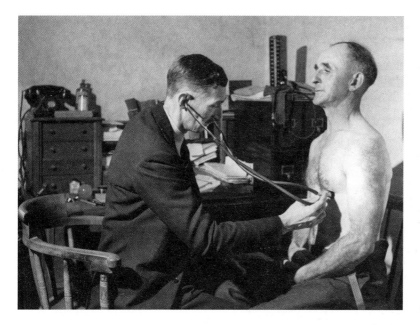

An early NHS consultation.

health care services. This meant that most people didn't receive good health care because they couldn't afford to pay.

National and local structures

The government of the UK is made up of politicians who are members of the political party that has won the last general election. Making sure that health care services are provided is one of the main tasks that every government has. Government politicians and civil servants make decisions about how statutory health care services should be organised and paid for throughout the country. The politician who has overall responsibility for this is called the **Secretary of State for Health**. England, Wales, Scotland and Northern Ireland each have different Secretaries of State for Health. They are each responsible for planning and making decisions about NHS services in their country.

The government is the main provider of the money for statutory health care services. This government money (also called

Organisation level	England	Wales	Scotland	N. Ireland
National	Parliament – Department of Health	National Assembly	Scottish Parliament – Scottish Health Department	Northern Ireland Assembly – DHSSPS
Regional	Strategic Health Authority	Regional Offices	NHS Unified Board	Health and Social Care Board
Local	NHS Trust/ Primary Care Trusts	NHS Trust/ Local Health Partnerships	Community Health Local Health and Social Care Group	Health and Social Services Trusts/

Figure 2.7 National and local health care structures in the UK.

'funding') is used to employ thousands of people in a wide variety of care jobs, buy equipment and keep the statutory health care system running. The government funds most hospitals, GP practices and community health services in the United Kingdom. The actual planning and monitoring of local statutory health care services is carried out by regional bodies. These are called Strategic Health Authorities in England and Wales, Local Health Boards in Scotland and Unified Health and Social Services Boards in Northern Ireland.

Types of NHS provider

Most of us will use statutory health care services at some point in our lives. We might need emergency hospital care or more likely we will have a less severe illness and go to our GP (family doctor) for help. The statutory health care services that we use will be provided by an **NHS Trust** organisation. Every area of the UK has an NHS Trust that takes responsibility for providing statutory health care in their locality. NHS Trust organisations provide two main types of health care service for people of all ages:

● primary health care services

● secondary health care services.

Primary health care services

Primary health care involves assessment, diagnosis and non-emergency treatment services. Primary health care is provided for all client groups in community settings, such as health centres, clinics and service user's homes. Primary health care providers offer general health assessment, diagnosis and treatment services as well as specialist care services aimed at tackling health problems like smoking, obesity and stress reduction. Some people need to use primary health care services regularly because they have a **chronic** health problem or a disability that requires continuing treatment or monitoring. However, most people use primary health care services on an occasional basis for minor illnesses.

Primary care services are usually provided by a **primary health care team** (PHCT). A GP (or family doctor) is often the leader or co-ordinator of the team. Other team members include practice nurses, district nurses, community psychiatric nurses and health visitors. Team members meet regularly to discuss patients and co-ordinate their work with them.

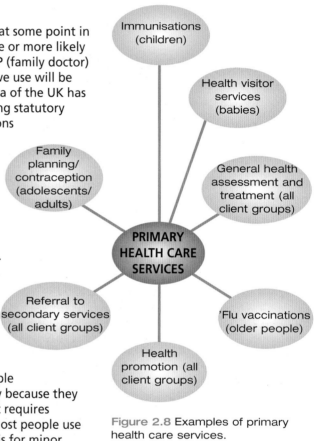

Figure 2.8 Examples of primary health care services.

Over to you!

Teenagers often feel that their health needs should be taken more seriously. Suggest two services that you think primary health care workers should offer to teenagers at your local health centre. Briefly explain your reasons.

Secondary health care services

Figure 2.9 Examples of secondary health care services.

The specialist types of care and treatment that are provided in a hospital or a specialist clinic are known as **secondary care**. Hospital care services focus on very specific, and often complex, health problems rather than on general, everyday problems. For example, large general hospitals usually have an accident and emergency (A&E) department that deals with life-threatening as well as minor injuries, a theatre or surgical department that deals with operations and a maternity unit that deals with childbirth. All of these departments provide specialised health care services.

As well as providing complex care and treatment services, hospitals often have specialist services such as laboratories and radiography (x-ray) departments that are used to diagnose (identify) health problems that GPs and other primary care workers are unable to identify because they don't have the specialist facilities or knowledge.

Most secondary health care is provided by **NHS Trust hospitals**. These are government-funded organisations that have a legal responsibility to provide health care services locally. There are a number of different kinds of hospital:

- District General Hospitals provide a wide range of secondary health care services for the whole population of an area. For example, they provide services for seriously ill adults and children who need an operation or treatment that involves contact with specially trained doctors and nurses.

- Local community hospitals usually provide a more limited range of treatments for a smaller number of people in an area. They often have facilities for people to be seen as out-patients and have far fewer beds than district general hospitals.

Over to you!

Make a list of the types of events or situations that can result in people needing urgent care or treatment from secondary health care services.

Investigate ...

Using information available through the Internet, leaflets or booklets produced by your local NHS Trust, investigate the services offered by your nearest NHS Trust hospital. What kinds of specialist care and treatment are provided for children? Does the hospital specialise in any other kinds of health care service? Summarise your findings in either a poster or a leaflet.

Exploring Health, Social Care and Early Years Provision

- National Teaching Hospitals and Specialist Units provide highly specialist medical, surgical and psychiatric treatment for patients who come from all over the country. Their expertise is available to both in-patients and out-patients. Two examples of this kind of hospital are Great Ormond Street Hospital for Sick Children and the Royal Homeopathic Hospital in central London.

Integrated children's services

Integrated children's services are a new feature of statutory services that have been developed throughout the UK since the Children Act (2004) was passed. This piece of legislation is the result of a government policy called *Every Child Matters*. The *Every Child Matters* policy put forward the idea of linking together (integrating) all of the services that children come into contact with. The importance of integrating children's services became very clear following the death of Victoria Climbie, an 8-year-old girl, in 2000. Victoria died as a result of severe physical abuse that was caused by her aunt and her aunt's boyfriend who were supposed to be caring for her. Victoria's death occurred despite the fact that care professionals from several different care organizations had come into contact with her. The fact that the different care professionals who had concerns about Victoria didn't communicate with each other or take responsibility for stopping what was happening occurred because of a lack of **multi-agency** and **partnership working**.

Integrated children's services now offer joined-up health, social care and education services to vulnerable children and their families through children's centres, extended schools, youth clubs and health care clinics. A local integrated children's service will typically:

- Be the first point of contact for all enquiries from children, families and professionals
- Receive and make referrals for services for children
- Identify, refer and monitor vulnerable children.

The care practitioners who are employed by an integrated children's service:

- Assess service user's needs
- Give information and advice
- Receive and make referrals for emergency and preventive services

Over to you

Identify the location of your nearest Sure Start Children's Centre. Find out:

- What services are available at the centre
- Who the services are provided for
- Which health, social care and early years professionals work at the centre
- What the aims and objectives of the centre are
- What the benefits of using the centre are to service users.

Case study

Ashok is nine years old. Last Christmas Ashok was admitted to a children's hospital when he fell over on his new rollerblades. Ashok broke his ankle and banged his head hard against the pavement. He stayed in the children's hospital for three days whilst tests were done and his ankle was put in plaster. Ashok felt frightened and lonely in hospital and was glad to go home after his short stay.

- What care needs did Ashok have a result of his accident?
- What effect did being in hospital have on Ashok's emotional wellbeing?
- List as many childhood illnesses as you can think of and try to identify the kinds of care or treatment that are provided to deal with them.

- Complete and manage information about a child and their family.

Integrating children's services is seen as a way of protecting vulnerable children and of improving the opportunities and life experiences of the poorest and most disadvantaged children. Examples of integrated children's services include:

- **Sure Start Children's Centres** (0–5 years) that offer child care, health and family welfare services.

- **Extended schools** (primary and secondary) that offer out-of-hours activities, parenting support, child care, community health services, adult learning and recreational activities.

- **Multi-agency disability** teams that provide a single point of referral, assessment and treatment for children and young people with physical, learning or sensory disabilities.

Integrated children's services are a new form of statutory care provision that combines health, social care and early years provision in order to target the needs of vulnerable children and families. As a result these services break down the traditional organisational barriers between health, social care and early years services.

Private health care services

Private sector health care organisations include a number of large care businesses, such as *BUPA* and *Nuffield Hospitals*. These organisations provide complex health care services, including surgery, in their own private hospitals. It is also possible to pay for care as a private patient in a ward or unit of some NHS hospitals. The private sector also includes a wide range of self-employed private practitioners who offer specialist forms of health care through a private practice. Many dentists, physiotherapists and counsellors work as private practitioners, for example. Sometimes a private practitioner offers clients an alternative service to those freely available from local statutory or voluntary sector organisations. In other circumstances they offer specialist services that are not available in the statutory or voluntary sector. An example might be osteopathy or acupuncture. Private sector health care clients pay for their care through health insurance or pay the costs directly from their own finances.

Investigate …

Use the Internet, your local library or other sources of information to identify five examples of private practitioners who offer different types of care service. Produce a leaflet containing a rough map of the area that shows where the practitioners are located and briefly describes the services each offers.

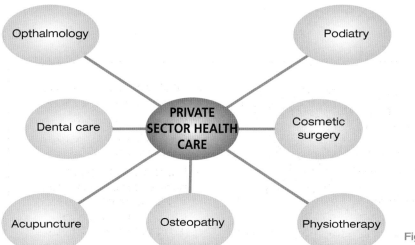

Figure 2.10 Examples of private health care services.

Exploring Health, Social Care and Early Years Provision

Outsourcing of indirect care services

Until the mid-1980s, statutory health and social care organisations like the NHS and local authorities were the direct employers of all of their staff. This meant that organisational services like cleaning, catering and security were provided from within the care organisation. However, towards the end of the 1980s financial pressures and a new attitude in government led to care organisations sub-contracting these services to specialist private sector organisations. In practice this meant, for example, that a private sector catering firm was contracted to provide all of the catering services for a care organisation. Similarly, indirect care services, like cleaning and laundry services were gradually sub-contracted, or outsourced, from private companies who competed to obtain these contracts. The purpose of outsourcing was to reduce costs and improve efficiency. Statutory sector care organisations throughout the United Kingdom now outsource many of the indirect care services that they require. As well as catering and cleaning, these services increasingly include large parts of the secretarial, administrative and financial functions as well as security, maintenance and non-emergency transport services.

Informal health care provision

Relatives, friends and neighbours may provide straightforward, usually non-technical health care services to an individual. For example, informal carers often give non-prescription medicines, like cough mixture or paracetamol, for minor ailments and treat small cuts and bruises without going to a doctor or other health care worker. Where a person has a chronic (long-term) health condition, the care team looking after them may instruct or train a relative to give more complex health care. For example, giving insulin injections to a diabetic relative or changing the dressing on a healing wound are examples of this. Informal health care provision is generally limited to the kinds of everyday care that people can provide without specialist training.

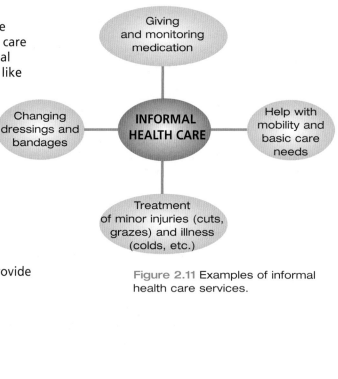

Figure 2.11 Examples of informal health care services.

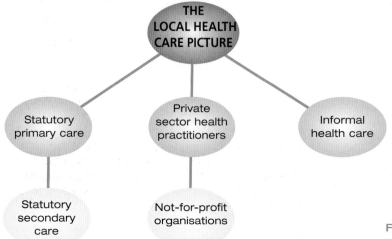

Figure 2.12 The local health care picture.

Knowledge Check

1 Name the two types of health care service provided by statutory health care organisations

2 When did statutory health care services become freely available in the UK?

3 What kinds of events or situations can result in adults needing urgent care or treatment from secondary health care services?

4 What is a primary health care team?

5 What are integrated children's services?

6 Identify three health promotion or prevention services primary health workers offer to clients.

7 Give two examples of specialist care services that are available in the private health care sector.

8 Why do you think some people choose to pay for health care services?

9 Describe two examples of informal health care provision.

Providers of social care services

Social care is a general term used to describe non-medical support and social care services for people who have personal, emotional or financial problems. Service users require social care because they are unable to meet their personal and social needs independently.

National and local social care structures

The **Secretary of State for Health** is the government minister (a politician) who has overall responsibility for making sure that statutory social care services are provided. The **Department of Health**, which includes the **Social Services Inspectorate** (SSI), is the part of government that plans and manages statutory social

Level	England	Wales	Scotland	N. Ireland
National (planners and purchasers)	UK Parliament ↓ Department of Children, Schools and Families	Welsh Assembly ↓ Health and Social Services Department	Scottish Government ↓ Scottish Government Health Directorates	Northern Ireland Assembly ↓ Department of Health, Social Services and Public Safety ↓ Health and Social Services Boards
Local (providers)	• Local authorities • Voluntary agencies • Private agencies	• Unitary authorities (social services departments) • Voluntary agencies • Private agencies	• Local authorities • Voluntary agencies • Private agencies	• Health and Social Care Trusts • Private agencies • Voluntary agencies

Figure 2.13 National and local social care structures.

care services. The government provides the funding for statutory social care services. The SSI also provide guidance to local authorities about social care and monitor and inspect the performance of social services departments.

Statutory social care services

Local Authorities (local councils) have a long history of providing statutory social care services in local areas throughout the United Kingdom. Local authorities provide social care, housing and education services for people of all ages in their local area.

The social services departments of local authorities (local councils) have responsibility for statutory social care services in the UK. The purchasing section of a social services department is involved in buying care services for adult clients whose social care needs have been assessed. The services that are purchased are known as a care package. The provider section of a social services department delivers some of the care services local people need, especially social work services. However, the purchasing section can also pay other voluntary and private sector organisations to provide the care services that their clients need. Even though they are not providing these services directly, this allows them to fulfil their legal responsibilities to provide certain types of care.

Local authorities also provide statutory social care services for children. The Children Act 1989 makes social services departments legally responsible for the welfare of children in need. For example, social services departments must provide child protection services, services for children under five and accommodation for children who are unable to live with their families.

Integrated children's services

Integrated children's services are a source of social care support for vulnerable children and their families. These services are provided through Sure Start Children's Centres, extended schools and specialist children and families teams employed by local authority social services departments.

Figure 2.14 Statutory social care services.

Investigate ...

Foster care is a form of social care that is provided for children and adolescents. Use the Internet to find out more about what foster care involves. You could start with the Fostering Network site (www.fostering-network.org.uk) and the National Foster Care Association (www.nfca.org.uk).

Case study

When Jenny was 10 years old, her mum, a lone parent, was admitted to hospital with a serious illness. Jenny, her mum and a social worker decided together that the best option was for Jenny to live with foster carers. Jenny lived with the Wilson family for three months until she returned to live at home with her mum. Jenny said she missed her mum a lot at first and felt like she didn't fit in, but she grew to like the Wilsons. She still receives a birthday card from them.

- Why did Jenny need care at this point in her life?
- What kinds of care and support do you think a foster carer would provide for a child like Jenny?
- When Jenny was missing her Mum, which of her needs were unmet?

Voluntary social care services

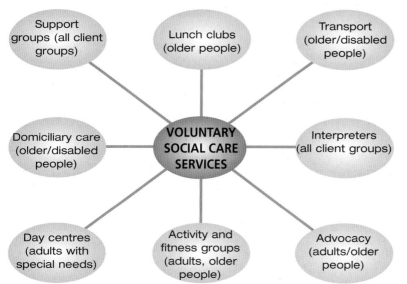

Figure 2.15 Examples of voluntary social care services.

There are a large number of voluntary organisations in the United Kingdom. The voluntary sector has its roots in the Victorian era and originated as a way of tackling major social problems such as poverty, unemployment and poor housing. Voluntary social care services are available for all client groups in the United Kingdom. However, unlike statutory social care services, they are not always available in every part of the country. This is because voluntary organisations differ considerably in the size and scope of their work. Some organisations, like the NSPCC or MIND, offer social care services to children and people with mental health problems throughout the country. Other organisations are smaller, focus on specific local issues and have very small budgets. However, when taken as a whole, the voluntary social care sector is a major provider of social care services in the United Kingdom. The services that are provided by organisations in this sector often fill the gaps left by the statutory sector and play a vital part in supporting vulnerable members of all client groups.

Private social care services

Compared to the statutory and voluntary sector, the private social care sector is small. There are relatively few social care organisations in the private sector. Those that do exist tend to provide specialised residential care services for older people or for disabled people or **domiciliary** (home care) services.

Over to you!

Find out about services that are provided for children by your local authority. They may provide leaflets or brochure describing the services they offer or have a site on the Internet that you can look at.

Investigate ...

Find out about the voluntary organisations that provide social care services for people in your local area. Try to identify at least one organisation that works on behalf of children, disabled people and older people. Add a brief summary of your findings to those of your class colleagues to make a directory of services provided by local voluntary organisations.

Figure 2.16 Examples of private social care services.

People who use private sector social care services either have to pay for the cost of the services themselves or, if they meet the **eligibility criteria**, they may have their fees paid by their local authority social services department.

Informal social care provision

Many people who need social care and support are not catered for by the statutory or voluntary sectors and cannot afford to buy services from the private sector. These people tend to receive informal social care and support from relatives, friends and neighbours. Basic services such as housing, financial assistance and emotional support are often provided this way. In fact, most of the social care provided for sick and vulnerable people in the United Kingdom is delivered in this way. Children, older people and those with long-term care needs receive most informal care services. It's very common for people to provide care for their elderly relatives and children at home.

Informal social care is also provided through support groups in some areas of the United Kingdom. The many thousands of local informal support groups that exist are usually run by informal carers and people who have special health and social care needs themselves. The purpose of informal support groups is to provide practical and emotional support to informal carers and the people they care for. An informal support group might consist, for example, of neighbours who share child care arrangements, people in a local area who all look after a relative alone at home, or a group of people who have got together to raise money to help an individual to finance his or her social care needs.

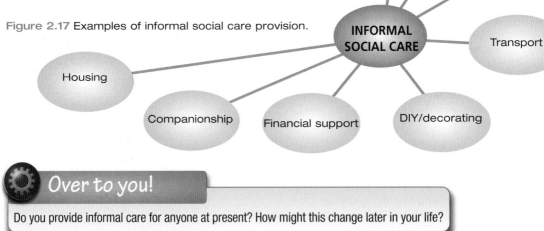

Figure 2.17 Examples of informal social care provision.

> ## Over to you!
>
> Find out about the range of private social care services available to people in your local area. Try to identify at least one service each for children, adults and older people.

> ## Over to you!
>
> Do you provide informal care for anyone at present? How might this change later in your life?

Case study

Mrs Bell is 79 years old and lives alone. She has some memory impairment and forgets what time of the day it is, whether she has eaten, and also the names of all but her closest relatives and her neighbour, Mrs Scott. Mrs Bell is unable to walk far due to her arthritis, very rarely goes out alone, and feels frightened of using her bath as she has difficulty getting in and out.

- What forms of informal care would Mrs Bell benefit from?
- Who might be able to provide each form of informal care for Mrs Bell?
- If you were a relative or neighbour of Mrs Bell's, how would you feel about giving up some of your time to offer Mrs Bell informal care and support?

Knowledge Check

1 Identify two examples of social care services.
2 Give two reasons why some people may need social care services.
3 Which government department is responsible for planning statutory social care services?
4 Who are the main providers of statutory social care services?
5 What part does the voluntary sector play in providing social care services in the UK?
6 Give an example of a social care service available in the private sector.
7 Explain what domiciliary care involves.
8 What is an informal support group?

Over to you!

What kinds of informal support groups exist in your local area? Find out by looking for posters and leaflets in places like the local library, sports centre, church halls, mosques or synagogues and in local day centres.

Providers of early years services

Early years organisations and self-employed practitioners like childminders provide education and child care services for children under the age of eight. The aim of these services is to help young children to meet their developmental needs. Play activities that help children to learn and develop their physical, intellectual, emotional and social skills are a common part of all early years services.

There are very few statutory child care services in the UK. This is because child care in the UK is generally seen as the responsibility of parents and other relatives. However, the government and local authority organisations are involved in providing some early years services and there is a lot of voluntary and private sector provision for young children throughout the UK.

Statutory early years services

Local authorities are responsible for purchasing (buying) early years care for children in need in their area. Early years care and education services are usually provided by the social services and education departments of a local authority. However, statutory early years services are only provided for families where a child is 'at risk' or where family pressures and problems can be reduced

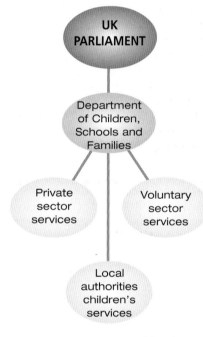

Figure 2.18 National and local early years structures.

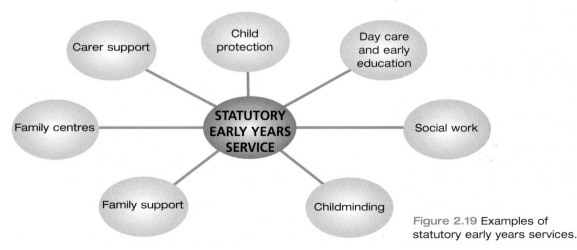

Figure 2.19 Examples of statutory early years services.

by child care support. Children with disabilities and children who have health or developmental problems are also eligible for these statutory services. Examples of early years services for children include playgroups, nurseries, childminders and family centres. Children and families who use these services must have unmet care and development needs that have been identified by a social worker or other early years professional.

The main legal duties that local authorities have for early years services are contained in the Children Acts 1989 and 2004. These laws, for example, make it a requirement that all childminders, and the premises in which they care for children, must be assessed by and registered with the social services department of their local authority.

Integrated Children's Services

Integrated children's services, particularly Sure Start Children's Centres are the main source of statutory early years provision for children and families. Sure Start nurseries offer high quality child care and early learning support for young children who, for a variety of reasons, have fallen behind other children in their language and learning development.

Voluntary early years services

The voluntary early years sector consists of some large national organisations, such as MENCAP, and a larger number of small, local voluntary groups who provide playgroups, nurseries and other support groups for both children under the age of 8 and their parents. The voluntary early years sector is a major provider of early years services. In a very similar way to the voluntary social care sector, these services fill the gaps in statutory and private sector services. Many services and informal support groups are developed and run by parents with children who are not eligible for statutory services and cannot afford or don't wish to pay for private early years care.

Private early years services

Early years services available from the private sector include nursery schools, playgroups, crèches and childminding services. These organisations provide child care and early education services to young children who have needs that are not met by the limited range of statutory sector services. As a child's parents must be able to afford to pay the fees charged, private sector child care services are not available to everyone who might need or benefit from them.

Some child carers also work in their own homes on a self-employed basis. Registered childminders are the largest group of self-employed carers working in this way. Like all self-employed carers, they charge the people who use their services a fee for their time and expertise.

Figure 2.20 Examples of voluntary early years services.

Figure 2.21 Examples of private early years services.

Informal early years provision

The majority of child care is provided by parents and other relatives at home. Caring for children is widely seen as a family responsibility in the UK. Parents who provide informal early years care for their children may also use statutory, voluntary or private services as well to supplement their own child care with additional or specialist input from trained child care and early learning practitioners.

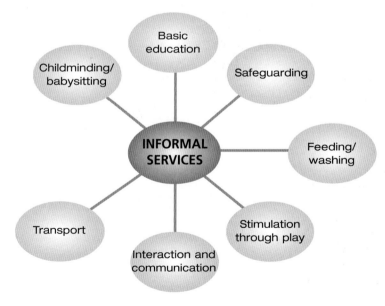

Figure 2.22 Examples of informal early years services.

Partnership and multi-agency working

So far we've looked at how the care system in the UK is organised into four different sectors. We've also considered the types of care services that are provided by local care organisations. This may have given you the impression that practitioners with health, social care or early years backgrounds work separately from each other. You might also be forgiven for thinking that care practitioners work within a particular care sector (statutory, private or voluntary, for example). Both of these situations may have been true in the past. However, there is an increasing emphasis within the health, social care and early years field on care practitioners and care organisations working in multi-disciplinary, **multi-agency teams** that break down the traditional health, social care and early years boundaries.

As a result of government social policies, health authorities, NHS Trusts and local authority social services departments are now working together to 'modernise' local care services. In some areas this involves developing new Health and Social Care Trust organisations.

It is likely that care practitioners with different professional backgrounds and care organisations from different care sectors are working together to provide services for clients in your local area. Partnership and multi-agency working can be organised in different ways. The three main ways of doing this are:

- **Multi-agency panels** in which practitioners employed by a variety of different care organisations meet regularly as a panel or network to discuss service users with complex needs who would benefit from multi-agency input. Child protection panels are an example of this type of multi-agency service.

- **Multi-agency teams** in which a group of care practitioners with different backgrounds are recruited to form a team that provides assessment, intervention and monitoring for groups of service users with specific needs. Multi-agency disability teams and virtual wards are an example of this type of multi-agency service.

- Integrated services in which a range of separate services merge together and work in a collaborative way to meet the broad but closely related needs of a particular client group. Sure Start children's centres and extended schools are an example of this kind of integrated multi-agency service.

The aims of **partnership** and **multi-agency working** are to:

- Improve access to services not previously available to service users

- Make access to services and care practitioner expertise easier and quicker

- Encourage early identification of and intervention in health, social care and developmental problems

- Reduce replication of services

- Provide better links between service providers

- Provide better quality services

- Reduce the costs of providing care

- Improve the efficiency and effectiveness of local care services.

Knowledge Check

1 Which age group are early years services targeted at?

2 Identify two examples of statutory early years services.

3 Explain why there are relatively few statutory child care services in the United Kingdom.

4 Identify two types of services that voluntary early years organisations provide.

5 Why are private early years services not available to everyone who could benefit from them?

6 Which care sector does a self-employed childminder belong to?

7 Who provides early years care in the informal sector?

8 What does multi-agency working refer to?

9 Describe the main benefits of multi-agency working.

Topic review

The box below summarises the areas covered in Topic 2.3. Tick the areas that you feel you understand and would be confident about when writing your assignment for this unit. If there are any areas that you don't understand or are not confident about, you will need to return to them before you begin planning or writing your assignment.

Types of service provider
Statutory providers ❑
Private providers ❑
Voluntary providers ❑
Informal carers ❑

The development of statutory, voluntary, private and informal service provision ❑

Organisation of health care services
Statutory health care services
– primary health care ❑
– secondary health care ❑
– integrated children's services ❑
Private health care services ❑
Informal health care provision ❑

The range of health care services provided for each service user group ❑

Organisation of social care services
Statutory social care services ❑
Voluntary social care services ❑
Private social care services ❑
Informal social care provision ❑

The range of social care services provided for each service user group ❑

Organisation of early years services
Statutory early years services ❑
Voluntary early years services ❑
Private early years services ❑
Informal early years provision ❑

The range of early years services provided for children ❑

Multi-agency and partnership working ❑

Assessment Guide

Your learning in this unit will be assessed through a controlled assignment. This will be set by Edexcel and marked by your tutor.

The assignment will require you to produce a report based on an investigation of the needs of one service user and how these needs are met by service providers and care practitioners.

You will need to show evidence of:

● The types of services that exist to meet service user needs.

● How services have developed and are organised.

The different types of health, social care and early years services have been explained in Topic 2.3. Your assignment report should demonstrate that you can identify and describe the types of care services that your chosen service user receives and explain how they developed and are organised.

Topic 2.4

Workers in health, social care and early years

Topic focus

There is a wide range of work roles in the health, social care and early years services. Topic 2.4 describes the work roles of:

- Direct care workers – including doctors, nurses, community nurses, health visitors, midwives, health care assistants, portage workers, child development workers, early years practitioners, family support workers, occupational therapists and teachers, for example.

- Indirect care workers – including practice managers, medical receptionists, school reception staff and catering staff, for example.

- Indirect services - provided through private company outsourcing by cleaners, caterers and security, portering and waste management workers, for example.

You will learn about the day-to-day activities of direct and indirect care staff who work in health, social care and early years services and develop your knowledge of the skills and qualifications that are needed for different types of care work. By the end of this topic you will have a good understanding of the main work roles of care practitioners and support staff in health, social care and early years services.

Working in care

Health, social care and early years organisations employ a large number of people. The NHS, for example, employs more people than any other organisation in Europe. As a result, there are a wide range of different work roles in health, social care and early years workplaces.

To simplify the range of care roles it is useful to consider the similarities and differences between:

- health care, social care and early years roles
- direct care workers and indirect care workers.

Health, social care and early years roles

People employed in **health care** roles usually deal with individuals who have physical, medical-related problems such as a disease, injury or acute illness. People employed in **social care** roles usually deal with people who are vulnerable and who have care needs that are mainly social, emotional or financial rather than physical. People working in **early years** roles are usually employed in child care and early education services for children under the age of eight.

Some care service users have a combination of health, social care or early developmental problems. This can mean that a care practitioner has to provide more than one type of care for that person. For example, a community psychiatric nurse who works with people experiencing mental health problems may need to offer their clients both health and social care.

Direct and indirect care workers

People who work in health, social care and early years services may have either a direct or an indirect care role. **Direct care** jobs involve providing one-to-one, or face-to-face care to service users in a 'hands-on', practical way. Examples of direct care workers include:

- Nursery nurses
- Occupational therapists
- Nurses
- Dentists.

Indirect care jobs involve providing support services. For example, people who work as receptionists, cleaners and porters have indirect care roles in health organisations. Direct care workers such as nurses, doctors, dentists and social workers are the people we are most likely to remember coming into contact with. We are less likely to notice the support and indirect care workers who operate behind the scenes.

Outsourced indirect services

Health, social care and early years organisations make use of a range of indirect services, such as catering, cleaning and security, that are necessary for the safe and effective provision of care services. Care organisations usually obtain these services from specialist private companies. This is known as outsourcing. The people who provide the outsourced services are usually trained and employed by the private company.

Figure 2.23 Examples of indirect service workers.

UNIT 2

Areas of care work

Jobs in health, social care and early can also be grouped into a number of different areas of work. Some of the more familiar work areas are:

Areas of health care work	Areas of social care work	Areas of early years work
Medicine	Social work	Child care – such as childminding
Midwifery	Community social care	Pre-school play and early learning
Nursing – in-patient and community	Residential social care	Early years education
Professions allied to medicine – such as occupational therapy	Family support	Developmental support – such as speech and language therapy
Managerial and administrative work	Managerial and administrative work	Managerial and administrative work

Within each area of work there are many specialist roles. Care workers tend to become more specialist as their careers progress. For example, within child care a person could begin their career as a nursery assistant, then qualify and work as a nursery nurse and, with further experience and training, go on to become a classroom teacher in primary education, or a nursery manager or early years practitioner for a local authority.

Over to you!

1 Write a sentence that briefly describes what you believe is involved in each of the care roles listed below. You could use careers booklets and the Internet to find out about occupational roles.

2 Reorganise the current list into three new lists headed 'health roles', 'social care roles' and 'early years roles'.

- District nurse
- Community psychiatric nurse
- Care manager
- Social worker
- Nursery nurse
- Paramedic
- Health visitor
- Residential social worker
- Hospital manager
- Gynaecologist
- Chiropodist
- Dentist
- Childminder
- Dental technician
- Pharmacist
- Surgeon

Knowledge Check

1 According to official statistics, which care profession employs more care workers than any other?

2 Name four different areas of care work.

3 Give two examples of indirect care roles in health care.

4 Give two examples of direct care roles in the early years field.

5 Explain the difference between a direct care job and an indirect care job.

Working in health care

Health care is a very broad area that covers a variety of different care professions. These include medicine, nursing, midwifery, health visiting and a variety of professions allied to medicine such as occupational therapy and physiotherapy.

Medicine

People who work in the medical field have some form of direct or indirect care role that involves dealing with individuals who are physically or mentally unwell and in need of diagnosis and treatment. Doctors, working either in hospitals or in general practice (GPs) are perhaps the most well known group of health care practitioners. All doctors of medicine have at least one degree in medicine. Many doctors obtain further qualifications to enable them to work in specialist areas of medicine, such as anaesthetics (pain control), cardiology (heart-related), paediatrics (children's medicine) or psychiatry (mental health) for example. Doctors work in both the NHS and in the private sector. In general, doctors:

- Assess and diagnose physical and mental health problems
- Carry out physical and psychological investigations and examinations
- Prescribe medication and other forms of treatment for health problems
- Monitor and support patients who are receiving treatment for health problems.

Doctors who are General Practitioners (GPs) tend to work as part of a primary health care team whilst hospital doctors work as part of multi-disciplinary teams alongside other health care practitioners such as nurses and physiotherapists, for example.

Nursing

Nurses make up the largest group of care staff in the United Kingdom. There are approximately 345,000 qualified nurses working in a range of areas of health care. There are four main branches of nursing - adult (also called general) nursing, children's nursing, learning disability nursing and mental health nursing. There are important differences in the type of training and work that these different groups of nurses do. Qualified nurses can work in in-patient settings (hospitals, clinics) or in community settings (GP surgeries, patient's homes).

Case study

Dr Sandra Saunders has worked as an anaesthetist at St Joseph's Hospital for the last three years. Her job is to anaesthetise patients and then to manage their airway and respiratory system safely while they are being treated or operated on. She works shifts to cover the 24-hour needs of the hospital and its patients. She works in the accident and emergency department and in the hospital's operating theatres. Dr Saunders works closely with other doctors and nursing staff as part of the team on call.

"You have got to be up to date with medical knowledge, careful, alert and confident to do my job"

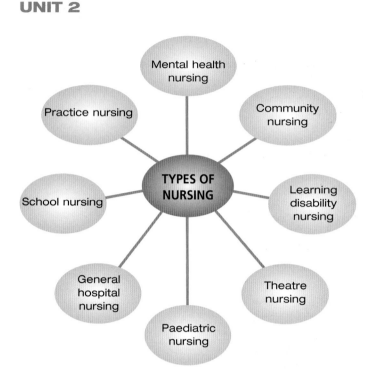

Figure 2.24 Different types of nursing in the UK.

When qualified, a registered nurse generally works as a staff nurse to gain experience and improve their practical skills. The day-to-day work that nurses do depends on the specialist area of care that they work in. For example, mental health nurses spend a lot of time talking with service users and providing emotional support, whereas general nurses working in accident and emergency spend more time treating people's wounds and injuries.

Nurses spend a lot of time in very close contact with patients, providing a wide range of direct care and support. Nursing is often a physically and emotionally tiring job. Caring for people who are sick and dependent can also involves carrying out tasks that may be unpleasant or physically demanding, such as changing soiled beds. As well as carrying out their care role, nurses have to complete administrative work relating to patients and often have a role in training student nurses.

Over to you!

Find out about the real day-to-day work that nurses do by carrying out an interview with somebody who works as a nurse. You could invite the school or college nurse to talk to your class or arrange to meet and talk with a nurse who works in a local care organisation. Remember to prepare plenty of questions before your interview.

Case study

Katie is ward manager in the children's unit of a teaching hospital. After qualifying as a registered general nurse fifteen years ago, she worked her way up to become ward manager. She has also worked in operating theatres and gained her BSc degree in nursing five years ago. Katie's work involves a lot of day-to-day management of the unit. For example, she has to plan the work rota to make sure enough staff are on duty and attend a variety of meetings about the running of the unit, like catering and cleaning. She also spends time supervising the nursing care of the children, meets their parents to provide information and support and talks to a range of other health care practitioners about the needs and treatment of children on her ward.

"I have to be very well organised and need to be able to decide which tasks are a priority every day. Management skills are just as important as nursing skills in my job"

Midwifery

Midwives work with women in all stages of pregnancy, when they are in labour and shortly after they have delivered their baby. Many midwives work in hospital services, especially the delivery suite where babies are born, though an increasing number are also working in the community visiting women at home, at GP practices and at children's centres. It is now necessary to have a degree to become a midwife. Many people now do midwifery degrees though some people take shorter courses in midwifery after they have obtained a degree and some experience in nursing. Once qualified, midwives develop their practical skills, knowledge and experience by working in hospital and community settings. Providing antenatal (pre-birth) and postnatal (following birth) care, support and education and delivering babies are all part of the day-to-day work of a midwife.

Health Visiting

Health visitors work with families, particularly mothers and young children, at home and in community settings. The role of the health visitor is to monitor and promote the health and development of young children. A health visitor will usually visit a mother and newborn baby at home a few days after the birth. They provide advice on a wide range of areas such as feeding, sleep, physical and emotional development and other general child care issues. People who work as health visitors are also qualified nurses or midwives (and often both).

Health care assistant

People who are interested in direct care work can gain some vocational training and experience as a health care assistant or support worker. Many health care assistants take an NVQ (National Vocational Qualification) course and are employed in all areas of health care. They often have a lot of direct patient contact, assisting registered nurses and other staff in providing care.

The role of a health care assistant is different to that of a registered nurse in a number of important ways:

- Health care assistants carry out most of the domestic tasks in a care setting, such as making beds.

Over to you!

Which organizations employ health care assistants in your local area?

Case study

Rob Fitzgerald is 22 years old. He has worked as a health care support worker in a learning disabilities unit for the last five years. He works day and night shifts and provides direct care and support for the ten residents of the bungalow where he works. Rob helps the residents in different ways depending on their individual needs. Some people need help with personal care, such as going to the toilet, washing and dressing, while others need assistance when travelling to college or on social outings. All of the residents benefit from the relationships that they have developed with Rob. He is currently taking an NVQ Level 2 in direct care and plans to go on to develop his care and managerial skills. He hopes to work in day centres and progress to social work training later in his career.

'Most of the time I really like working in the bungalow and going out with the residents. It can be fun and it's practical work, which I like. It's all about the relationships you have with people and the way that you communicate with them really.'

- The physical care that health care assistants provide relates to routine procedures such as lifting, bathing and dressing patients.
- Health care assistants carry out care planned by registered nurses.

Like nurses, health care assistants work day and night shifts and may also work at weekends. There is no minimum age requirement for health care assistants. Personal maturity is one of the key factors that employers take into account when recruiting people to these posts.

Professions allied to medicine

Physiotherapists and occupational therapists are examples of professions allied to medicine. Both of these professions focus on particular aspects of health and wellbeing, though each has its own specialist training programme and set of professional skills.

Physiotherapists work with people of all ages who have physical problems, particularly movement problems caused by accidents, illness or ageing. Physiotherapists diagnose and treat movement and other physical health problems using specialist physiotherapy techniques, massage and therapeutic exercises. They also provide a lot of health promotion and illness prevention information and guidance. Physiotherapists work in both the NHS and in private sector organisations and as private practitioners. Physiotherapists work in a variety of health care areas, including out-patient departments, intensive care units, women's health (especially labour) units, stroke rehabilitation units, children's services and in a variety of specialist services for people with mental health problems, learning disabilities or physical disabilities. Qualified physiotherapists have a degree in physiotherapy and then gain plenty of 'hands on' experience to improve their knowledge and practical skills. They tend to work in multi-disciplinary teams with other health care workers in both community and hospital settings.

Occupational therapy is a wide-ranging profession. Occupational therapists (OTs) work in hospital, community or specialist educational or care home settings with people of all ages who may have physical or mental health problems or learning disabilities. OTs usually work alongside other practitioners such as doctors, nurses, physiotherapists and social workers as part of a multi-disciplinary care team. Occupational therapists assess

Investigate ...

Find out more about the work of health care support workers by arranging to talk to a member of staff at a local hospital or nursing home. You might be able to find information by looking at careers websites or by obtaining a job description when a vacancy for this kind of role is advertised in your local newspaper.

Exploring Health, Social Care and Early Years Provision

people who are having difficulties with some aspect of daily living. They then develop treatment plans that involve the person taking part in forms of purposeful activity that will prevent their problems becoming worse and which will enable them to live as independently as they would like. At the end of a course of occupational therapy the service user and OT will evaluate how effective the treatment has been.

Management, administration and ancillary services

Health care organisations employ a wide range of support staff to carry out the administrative, management and ancillary jobs that are essential for both the organisation and the direct care workers to work efficiently.

Administrative work covers secretarial and clerical jobs such as typing, filing, record-keeping and calculating wages. People who work as receptionists, ward clerks and medical secretaries have roles that provide administrative support for direct care workers and for managers who run health care organisations.

Management work involves taking responsibility for the effective and efficient running of various aspects of a care organisation. People who work as managers may have specialist qualifications in the area in which they are working, such as medical laboratory science, catering or accountancy, for example. Managers have more authority and responsibility than administrative staff and are often responsible for a group of staff and a department.

Ancillary work covers a broad range of occupations that are required to keep a care organisation running smoothly, such as catering, cleaning and maintenance. Porters who move patients around hospitals, electricians and domestic assistants who clean in-patient areas and change beds are examples of ancillary workers employed in hospitals. People who are employed as ancillary staff may have vocational qualifications appropriate to the area in which they work, such as catering or electrical work. Many obtain their jobs because of their previous experience and the practical skills that they have.

Detailed information on a wide range of health care roles can be found on the NHS Careers website (www.nhscareers.nhs.uk).

Case study

Julia Benn is the practice manager at St Joseph's Health Centre. She is responsible for the safe and efficient running of the health centre and for managing the budgets. Julia has day-to-day responsibility for managing the administrative staff, including the secretaries and receptionists at the health centre. She also has overall responsibility for payroll, practice finance and personnel issues and she plays an important role in planning and developing the services of the health centre. Julia doesn't directly manage the health care practitioners at the health centre but she works closely with them to ensure that they are well supported and that they have the resources to provide high quality medical and psychological care to service users.

"My working day is very busy. I have a lot of meetings to attend and need to make sure that I see the support staff regularly. My job requires a range of business and management skills but I think that being a good communicator and problem-solver is the key to it."

Exploring Health, Social Care and Early Years Provision

Knowledge Check

1 What qualifications are needed to work as a doctor?

2 Name three tasks that doctors perform as part of their work.

3 What name is given to a highly qualified and experienced doctor who specialises in a particular area of hospital medicine?

4 Describe the health care role of a physiotherapist.

5 Which health care professional specialises in the use of purposeful activity?

6 Describe the care role of a midwife.

7 Explain how the work of a health care assistant supports the care role of a registered nurse.

8 What qualifications are needed to train as a registered nurse?

9 Name the four branches of nursing.

10 What kind of skills does a nurse need to work as a ward manager?

11 Name two jobs that involve administrative work.

12 Explain why care organisations need to employ a range of ancillary workers.

13 Explain why a practice manager is an 'indirect' rather than a 'direct' care worker.

Working in social care

Social care involves providing various forms of non-medical help to people who are vulnerable and in need of support. It can include forms of direct care such as counselling or indirect care such as arranging housing or access to other support services. Social care services are provided by care practitioners who have a variety of different jobs titles, including social workers, youth workers and social care support workers.

Social work

A social worker is a person who has gained a professional social work qualification (normally a diploma or degree in social work) and who has experience of working with people experiencing social, financial and emotional problems. Many of the people who require social work assistance are socially excluded or experiencing some form of life crisis. Social workers work with members of all client groups in a variety of community, hospital, residential home, education and day care settings.

Most qualified social workers are employed as field social workers working directly with service users. This means that they have a caseload of people they work with in community and institutional settings. Some social workers specialise in working with members of particular client groups, such as 'at risk' children, vulnerable older people or adults with mental health problems. However, other social workers work as care co-ordinators or care managers and specialise in assessing clients' needs and purchasing care packages for them. Social workers assess the needs of people referred to them. They then have to decide whether the person is eligible for social care services and, if so, what kinds of help and support they can be offered. Packages of support are then organised and managed to meet

Over to you!

Make a list of reasons why social work is sometimes a difficult and stressful job.

the service user's particular needs. It is important that care packages are reviewed regularly to ensure that they are actually meeting the care needs of the person or family they are designed for.

Family support worker

Family support workers are employed by local authorities and voluntary organisations to give emotional and practical support, help and advice to families who are experiencing difficulties. These difficulties may be the result of one or more parent experiencing ill-health, drug or alcohol problems, financial difficulties, disability or mental health problems, for example. The purpose of family support is usually to keep the family together at a time when there is some risk that one or more of the children may be taken into care. Family support workers are often managed by social workers who plan and monitor the kind of support that the family requires. This could involve, for example, demonstrating parenting skills, helping parents to understand and respond to their children's behavioural difficulties or showing them how to promote learning through play. No specific qualifications are needed to become a family support worker. However, maturity and experience of working with children and families in statutory or voluntary services are usually required.

Investigate ...

Find out more about the role of a social worker by looking at the Social Work careers website (www.socialworkcareers.co.uk). This provides information on the role of social workers and training courses. You might also be able to get information by looking at other careers websites, on the Internet, or by obtaining a job description when a vacancy for a social worker is advertised in your local paper.

Case study

Bhupinder Mann is employed as a family support worker by a local authority. She works with one family at a time, often working a shift system that can include days, nights and weekend work. She has taken an NVQ Level 2 course in Children's Care, Learning and Development, and has also completed food hygiene and counselling courses. Bhupinder works with children and families in their own homes. She has recently helped a family where the parents are physically disabled and needed help washing, dressing and feeding their baby. Bhupinder showed both parents how to do this and helped them reorganise their home to make child care easier. Bhupinder enjoys the practical side of her job and feels that it is important to be well organised and understanding to do her job efficiently.

"My job is quite tiring but I think it's important to help people. I enjoy the practical work and think of my clients as friends as well."

Working in early years

There is a wide range of care roles and career opportunities in the child care and early years field. Child care and early years work involves lots of busy, hands-on activities with children. Care workers in this area are responsible for the safety and development of the children they care for and work with. Some early years workers specialise in working with children who have physical or sensory impairments whereas others specialise in working with children who have learning difficulties. Some of the similarities and differences in the roles of different child care and early years workers are described below.

Exploring Health, Social Care and Early Years Provision

Figure 2.25 Work roles in early years services.

Nursery nurses

A qualified nursery nurse has achieved a qualification such as an NNEB, CACHE or BTEC Diploma in Nursery Nursing. Most nursery nurses are employed in private and local authority nurseries, usually providing direct care and education for healthy children under five, though some nursery nurses have specialist roles in hospitals and special education units for sick and disabled children. The main care role of a nursery nurse involves:

- Supporting and encouraging children's physical, intellectual, emotional and social development through play

- Providing basic physical care for children in the form of feeding, washing and cleaning

- Observing children's participation in play, monitoring their progress, identifying any problems and reporting back on this to colleagues and parents

- Managing the health and safety of children in the nursery environment.

Portage workers

Portage workers provide home-based services for pre-school children who have physical or learning disabilities or additional development needs. Portage workers work alongside parents, focusing on ways of encouraging a child's learning and development through play and other day-to-day activities. The day-to-day care role of a portage worker might include:

- Observation of children to identity existing skills.
- Identifying a child's development needs.
- Suggesting and planning activities for a child to develop their skills.
- Providing support and motivation for parents to carry out planned activities.
- Visiting children and parents at home to monitor progress or agree new goals.
- Writing reports about children who have been assessed.

Teacher

Early years or nursery teachers work in pre-school, nursery and reception classes with children between 3 and 5 years of age. Early years teachers promote and develop children's intellectual, social and emotional development. Play and activity-based methods of learning are common ways of doing this. Early years teachers must have a degree in education and experience of working with young children. Good communication skills and the ability to provide and assess learning experiences for children are an essential part of the work role. Early years teachers often have contact with other health and social care practitioners who may also be working with a particular child, especially if they have complex health and development needs.

School reception staff

The people who work in pre-school and early years school receptions have an indirect care role in early years services. Reception staff are the first people that parents and children will meet when they arrive at school. They need to be organised and friendly to welcome people and put them at ease. Reception staff often have to deal with parents and children who become anxious or have worries about where their mum/dad or child is. Reception staff also play a part in managing the health, safety and security of children and teaching staff. Greeting and monitoring visitors and making sure that children don't unexpectedly leave the premises are a part of this. Due to their frequent contact with service users and visitors to their school, reception staff are also an important source of information about children and their families and play a key role in receiving and passing on information about a child's attendance or arrangements to collect them, for example.

Over to you!

Further Education colleges provide a lot of child care and early years courses for full and part-time students. Find out what's available at your local FE college by looking at their website or by obtaining a prospectus of courses.

Knowledge Check

1 What qualifications are needed to train as a social worker?
2 What kinds of care services do domiciliary care workers provide?
3 Name two client groups that domiciliary care workers are most likely to work with.
4 What qualifications do nursery nurses usually have?
5 What skills do you think are needed to work with children under the age of eight?
6 Describe how the work of a nursery nurse is different to that of an early years teacher.

Topic review

The box below provides a summary of the areas covered in Topic 2.4. Tick the areas that you feel you understand and would be confident about when writing your assignment. If there are any areas that you don't understand or are not confident about, you will need to return to them before you begin planning or writing your assignment.

Types of care role
- Health care roles ☐
- Social care roles ☐
- Early years roles ☐
- Direct care roles ☐
- Indirect care roles ☐

Work roles in health care
- Doctor/Medical Practitioner ☐
- Nurse ☐
- Midwife ☐
- Health visitor ☐
- Health care assistant ☐
- Physiotherapist ☐
- Occupational therapist ☐
- Manager / administrator ☐

Work roles in social care
- Social worker ☐
- Social care worker ☐
- Family support worker ☐

Work roles in the early years sector
- Nursery nurse ☐
- Portage worker ☐
- Teacher ☐
- School reception staff ☐

Assessment Guide

Your learning in this unit will be assessed through a controlled assignment. This will be set by Edexcel and marked by your tutor.

The assignment will require you to produce a report based on an investigation of the needs of one service user and how these needs are met by service providers and care practitioners.

You will need to show evidence of:

● The main roles and skills of people providing health, social care and early years services.

The range of direct and indirect work roles in the health, social care and early years sectors have been explained in Topic 2.4.

Your assignment report should demonstrate that you can identify and describe the work roles of the direct and indirect care workers who are providing services for your chosen service user.

Topic 2.5

Care values

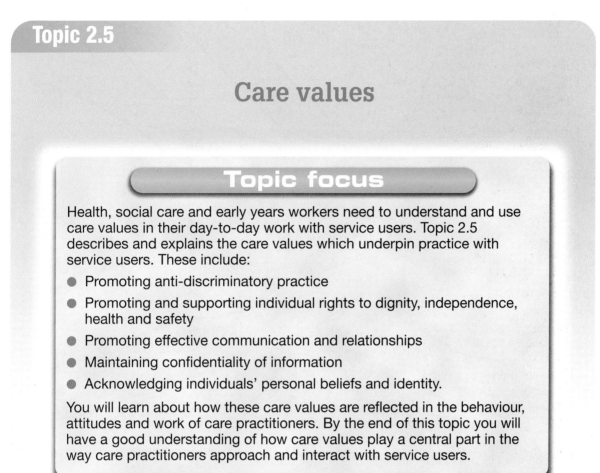

Topic focus

Health, social care and early years workers need to understand and use care values in their day-to-day work with service users. Topic 2.5 describes and explains the care values which underpin practice with service users. These include:

- Promoting anti-discriminatory practice
- Promoting and supporting individual rights to dignity, independence, health and safety
- Promoting effective communication and relationships
- Maintaining confidentiality of information
- Acknowledging individuals' personal beliefs and identity.

You will learn about how these care values are reflected in the behaviour, attitudes and work of care practitioners. By the end of this topic you will have a good understanding of how care values play a central part in the way care practitioners approach and interact with service users.

What are care values?

What are 'care values'? This slightly odd sounding phrase really means something quite simple. If you value something, you feel that it is important or worthwhile. For example, you probably expect your friends to be honest with you and to respect your feelings. Why? Because you probably believe that telling the truth and showing respect is the right way to behave, and that telling lies and being disrespectful is wrong. Care values are beliefs about the right ways to treat care service users.

Care values are now seen as an essential part of the work of all care practitioners. Service users, for example, expected to be treated fairly and not to be discriminated against. You would probably expect your GP (family doctor) to say 'I try to treat all people equally, whoever they are'. Similarly, if somebody asked why you were having counselling, you would probably expect your counsellor to say 'It's important to keep the things my client talks to me about confidential'.

Registered care practitioners (such as nurses, physiotherapists and doctors, for example) have a professional responsibility to understand and use care values in their work. For example, they are expected to follow the codes of practice and guidelines about care values that are issued by their professional bodies.

Over to you!

How do you expect care workers to behave towards you when you use care services? Try to link your own ideas to the list of care values above.

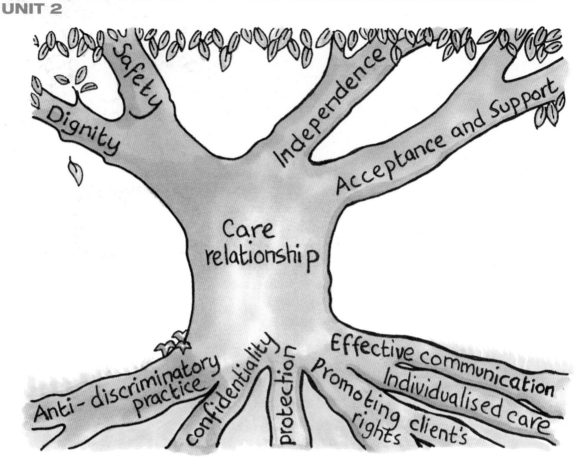

Figure 2.26 Examples of care values.

for more on this). Breaking their profession's code of practice or not following guidelines is likely to result in a care practitioner being 'struck off' the professional register. This will prevent them from working in their care profession.

Promoting anti-discriminatory practice

Unfair discrimination occurs when individuals or groups of people are treated differently, unequally and unfairly in comparison to others. For example, an employer who refused to interview candidates under the age of 25 for a nursery manager post saying 'in my experience, younger people are not good at accepting responsibility', would be treating this group of people unfairly.

The main cause of unfair discrimination is **prejudice**. When an individual is prejudiced in some way, they hold negative feelings and attitudes towards another person or group of people. These feelings, ideas and attitudes will usually be based on untrue, ill-informed or exaggerated ideas or beliefs. In the United Kingdom, some of the social groups that tend to experience unfair discrimination based on prejudice include:

- minority ethnic groups
- minority religious groups
- women
- lesbians and gay men
- older people
- people with learning or physical disabilities
- people with mental health problems.

Over to you!

It's hard to admit to having prejudices. Often people are not aware of their own prejudices until they are put in a position where they feel threatened by or angry about something. Think about your own views on 'race', religion, sexuality and disability. Do you have any prejudices that may lead you to treating some people unfairly?

Members of these groups may experience unfair discrimination because of their race or colour (racism), gender (sexism), age (ageism), disability (disablism), sexuality (homophobia), religious beliefs or health status. Carers should never unfairly discriminate against service users. Wherever they receive care, all patients and clients are entitled to non-discriminatory treatment. However, anti-discriminatory practice does not just mean treating everybody the same. It also means challenging and reducing any form of unfair discrimination that might be experienced by service users. Care workers who take an **anti-discriminatory approach** are:

- aware of the different forms of unfair discrimination that can occur in care settings
- sensitive to the ethnicity, social background and cultural needs of each individual for whom they provide care
- prepared to actively challenge and try to reduce the unfair discrimination experienced by service users.

Promoting and supporting individual's rights to dignity, independence, health and safety

The relationship that a care worker develops with a service user is the cornerstone of all the work that they do as a care provider. A care practitioner who establishes good care relationships will respect a service user's right to have their dignity respected, will support them in making their own decisions, and ensure that the service user's safety and security are protected whilst they are receiving care.

Dignity and privacy

Care settings can be difficult and impersonal places in which to live. However, service users should always have privacy when personal care is being provided. They should not be exposed to the view of others when they are being dressed, undressed, taken to the toilet or being helped to wash. Care practitioners need to take simple practical precautions like closing doors, keeping curtains drawn and not leaving individuals partially undressed in situations where other people may walk in or see them. In addition, care practitioners should be respectful of individuals' rights to privacy in their room. Knocking before entering and checking that it is alright to come in is much more respectful than simply throwing the door open, carrying out tasks without asking or sitting on a person's bed or chair without asking permission. Showing respect for each person's dignity and privacy is a very important way of showing the person that you value them as an individual. It also shows that the care practitioner acknowledges the service user's rights whatever their needs, problems or personal difficulties.

Choice

Individuals receiving care need to be encouraged to make their own choices and should be enabled to make decisions on the basis of their own wishes and preferences. Few care workers would dispute the idea that giving individuals choices is a good thing. However, it can be challenging to find ways of putting this into practice on an everyday basis. Ideally, care workers and

Over to you!

Imagine that you are in hospital, unable to leave your hospital bed because you are recovering from an operation. You are in a mixed sex ward. What would you want the nurses to do to ensure your dignity and privacy were protected?

service users should develop partnerships in which the service user feels equally involved. This kind of relationship is **empowering** because service users are seen as:

- individuals with rights and choices appropriate to their age and needs
- deserving of respect, regardless of their personal or social characteristics.

Care practitioners can also promote and support choice by:

- Finding out what each individual's likes and dislikes are.
- Developing a unique relationship with each of the people they provide care for.
- Adapting their communication style to ensure each individual can communicate as effectively as possible.
- Encouraging and supporting each individual to do what they can for themselves. This is known as providing active support.
- Offering individuals a choice of activities and choices as to whether and how they participate in them.
- Giving people different options on both large and small-scale decisions that affect them.

Some people are unable to make major lifestyle or treatment choices independently. However, every person should be given the opportunity to make the choices and decisions that they are able to make. To support service users in doing this, a care worker needs to be aware of the person's particular wishes and abilities. If a care worker develops an effective relationship with the service users they are caring for, these people will feel more confident about making their wishes and preferences known. If a person is unable to make their needs or preferences known, a care practitioner should always do what is in the service user's best interests, not what is quickest or easiest for the practitioner.

Protection, health and safety

Working in any setting that contains people, equipment, illness, disease and disability and a lot of work pressures can be risky! One of the golden rules of work in a care setting is that the health and safety of individuals, colleagues and anybody else present should be the main concern. People should not be at risk of injury or harm in a care setting. Care practitioners should, at least, do no harm. As a result, awareness of health and safety issues and safeguarding (protection) principles is a basic competence all care practitioners are expected to have.

Many people who use care services are at a vulnerable point in their life and put a lot of trust in care practitioners to provide them with the protection, help and support that they need. Some groups of service users, including children, older people, disabled people and people with mental health problems are vulnerable to exploitation and abuse by others. Other service users may also find it difficult to follow basic health and safety precautions that protect them from the dangers of everyday life as well as abuse or exploitation by others. This can be a result of the problems that they have, such as learning disabilities or memory problems, or because they are easily influenced by unscrupulous people. As a result,

Investigate ...

Find out about the work of the Health and safety Executive by visiting www.hse.gov.uk. Select Health Care in the 'Your Industry' search for information on health and safety in care services.

many people who need or who are receiving care face a greater risk of experiencing harm or a form of abuse (physical, emotional or sexual for example).

Protecting service users from harm or potential abuse is something that all care workers should feel is important. Care workers should assess the relationships that their clients have with other people for any signs of abuse and should always act to prevent this occurring or stop it happening when they become aware of it. A care practitioner should also:

- Ensure that their own health and hygiene does not pose a threat to the health and safety of others and that they manage their personal safety at work.
- Follow the infection control, moving and handling, accident and waste disposal procedures set out in their employer's health and safety policies.
- Make use of any risk assessments that have been carried out to minimise health and safety hazards.
- Respond appropriately to security risks in the workplace.
- Report health and safety and security issues to relevant people.

Promoting effective communication and relationships

For care workers	For service users
Effective communication helps carers to give and receive information that is relevant to an individual's care and wellbeing.	Effective communication enables a service user to feel secure and respected as an individual at a time when they may be physically and emotionally vulnerable.
Effective communication enables care practitioners to express trust, acceptance, understanding and support.	Co-operation, involvement and partnership in a care relationship requires open and supportive communication.
Effective communication allows a care practitioner to identify and meet the individual needs of each service user.	Effective communication empowers service users by allowing them to express their needs, worries and wishes.
Effective communication enables a care practitioner to identify and support service users' abilities and reduces dependency.	Service users need to maintain their sense of identity while receiving care. This can only be achieved if they have opportunities to express themselves and to be understood by their carers.

Table 2.27 The benefits of effective communication

Good care relationships depend on effective communication skills. Being sensitive to what other people are saying, thinking and feeling, showing service users respect, and protecting their dignity and rights, are all features of empowering care practice. To be able to do these things, care practitioners need to be sensitive to the spoken and unspoken communication of service users. They also need to be aware of how they themselves think, feel and behave in their interactions with service users.

Over to you!

Are you an effective communicator? Identify your main communication strengths and the areas where you need to improve your skills further.

People communicate most effectively when they feel relaxed, when they are able to empathise with the other person, and when they experience warmth and genuineness in the relationship:

- **Empathy** involves putting yourself in the place of the other person and trying to appreciate how they 'see' and experience the world. Being empathetic improves a care practitioner's ability to communicate.

- Expressing warmth is important. It makes the person feel accepted, secure and builds trust with them.

- Genuineness involves being yourself and communicating with honesty and integrity. Care practitioners who are genuine will avoid being authoritarian, defensive or emotionally detached. Genuineness also involves making sure that verbal and non-verbal 'messages' match or support each other, being consistent in the way service users are treated and being open and honest with people.

Maintaining confidentiality of information

Care service users must be able to trust the people who provide them with care services. If you cannot trust another person with your thoughts, feelings and dignity you are unlikely to develop a strong or deep relationship with them. The care relationship is based on trust and particularly on the need for care practitioners to maintain **confidentiality** whenever possible.

There are times in care work when it is important to keep confidences and information that you have about service users to yourself. For example, if a child at the nursery where you do your work placement swore at you and misbehaved one afternoon, or an elderly resident at a nursing home refused to bathe after wetting herself, you would be breaching confidentiality to reveal these things to your friends. You should not breach confidentiality in situations where service users have a right to privacy or where their comments or behaviour do not cause harm or break the law. Where care workers gossip or talk publicly about events or issues that happen at work they are betraying the trust that service users and colleagues put in them.

However, there are sometimes situations where it is necessary to disclose information about a service user that has been given in confidence. For example, where a service user requests that what they say is kept a secret, this can be overridden if:

- what they reveal involves them breaking the law or planning to do so

- they say that they intend to harm themselves or another person

- they reveal information that can be used to protect another person from harm.

If a service user commits an offence that could have been prevented by a care practitioner disclosing information given to them in confidence, the care practitioner could be brought to court to face charges. As a result care practitioners should never promise service users that what they say will be absolutely confidential. They should explain that there are times when they may have to share information with their colleagues and other authorities.

Over to you!

What kinds of personal information about yourself do you expect your GP to keep confidential?

Over to you!

Read the following confidentiality situations. For each scenario, explain:

● why confidentiality may be important to the client
● the dilemma facing the care worker
● whether you would break confidentiality and why.

− Darren has an appointment with the school nurse for a BCG booster injection. He's worried about it making him ill. He says that he's just taken some ecstasy and pleads with the nurse not to tell anyone.

− Jennifer goes to her GP for contraceptive pills. She asks her GP not to tell her parents. She is 14 years old.

− Eileen has terminal cancer. She tells her district nurse that she's had enough of living and is going to end her own life tomorrow. She says it's her choice and asks the district nurse not to interfere.

− Yasmin tells her new health visitor that her boyfriend is violent and is beating her. She asks the health visitor not to say anything as she is frightened of what might happen. Yasmin and her boyfriend have a three-month-old baby.

− Lee turns up at a hostel for the homeless. He says that he has run away from home because his father has been beating him. He asks the social worker not to contact his family. He is 16 years old.

− A man with a stab wound arrives at the hospital casualty department. He won't give his name and asks the nurse not to phone the police. He says that he will leave if she does. He is bleeding heavily.

Confidentiality is about sharing, transmitting and storing information about individuals in ways that are appropriate to their care needs. It is definitely not about keeping information 'secret'. This means that 'confidential' information can be shared with other care team members who also need to know about and use it. Beyond this, a care practitioner must consult the service users they work with and respect their wishes about who should be informed or given access to information about them.

Acknowledging individuals' personal beliefs and identity

Care practitioners should be open-minded and adaptable so that they can meet the health, development and welfare needs of all potential service users. This is a challenge because services have to meet the needs of people of different ages, different genders, different sexual orientations, different ethnic and cultural backgrounds, and people with a broad range of abilities, disabilities, illnesses and impairments. In addition, service users hold a wide range of spiritual and religious beliefs and personal values. These may affect the ways that different individuals want care services to be provided for them. For example, people who have an active faith may have particular worship, dietary and personal care needs that they wish to have met.

Care practitioners should try to communicate that they accept and value people for who they are and what they believe in. On a personal level, a care practitioner may not always share the beliefs and lifestyle of the person they care for but should still show that they accept that person's individuality. For example, if a care practitioner worked with a person who had different

Exploring Health, Social Care and Early Years Provision

religious beliefs and practices to their own, the care practitioner should ensure that the service user is given opportunities to practise and celebrate their faith when this is important to them. Ultimately, care practitioners have to be positive about social and cultural diversity in order to provide care in a fair and equal way to service users of all backgrounds. Lack of awareness of social, religious or cultural difference can lead to insensitive care. Deliberately ignoring a person's particular needs because of prejudice or a lack of respect for diversity and difference is unacceptable and discriminatory.

> ### Investigate ...
> How do care service users expect to be treated by care workers? Carry out a brief survey of your friends and family to identify which of the care values we've covered they feel are the most important.

Codes of practice, policies and procedures

To help ensure that care workers respect clients' rights, codes of practice, policies and procedures have been developed by professional organisations and employers. Examples of these are now used in all care settings.

Codes of practice

A **code of practice** is a document that outlines an agreed way of working and dealing with specified situations. Codes of practice aim to reflect and set a standard for good practice in care settings. A number of codes of practice have been developed for care workers such as registered nurses, occupational therapists and physiotherapists, social workers and nursery staff. Codes of practice establish the general principles and standards for care workers and should always refer to equality of opportunity.

Policies and procedures

A **policy** is different to a code of practice in that it tells care workers how they should approach specific issues in a particular care setting. For example, most care homes will have a policy on confidentiality. This will explain in detail how this issue is dealt with in the particular home. Policies should promote equal treatment and equality of opportunity for everyone likely to be affected by them.

A **procedure** describes the way that staff in a particular care setting are expected to deal with an issue or activity that they may be involved in. For example, care homes for older people usually have written procedures that describe how to deal with a situation where a resident goes missing from the home. The procedure will set out in detail all the steps that the staff should take in trying to locate the person and report them missing to the relevant authorities.

Policies and procedures should always incorporate the main values of the care profession. They should ensure that service users' rights are respected and that activities are always carried out in the service users' best interest.

Knowledge Check

1 Identify three important values that are applied by care workers.

2 Explain what a care value is.

3 What is a care value base?

4 Name three groups who often experience unfair discrimination in the UK.

5 What is the main cause of all forms of unfair discrimination?

6 In your own words, explain what care workers do if they take an anti-discriminatory practice approach to their work.

7 What does keeping something confidential mean?

8 Why is confidentiality important in care work?

9 When should a care worker break confidentiality?

10 Do you think that a GP (family doctor) should tell a teenager's parents if she requests to be prescribed the contraceptive pill?

11 Explain why care service users need to be protected from abuse.

12 What is 'individualised' care?

13 What can happen if service users don't receive individualised care?

Topic review

The box below provides a summary of the areas covered in Topic 2.5. Tick the areas that you feel you understand and would be confident about when writing your assignment. If there are any areas that you don't understand or are not confident about, you will need to return to them before you begin planning or writing your assignment.

Care values
- Promoting anti-discriminatory practice ☐
- Promoting and supporting individual rights to dignity, independence, health and safety ☐
- Promoting effective communication and relationships ☐
- Maintaining confidentiality of information ☐
- Acknowledging individual personal beliefs and identity ☐

How care values are used in practice
- Behaviour ☐
- Attitudes ☐
- Interactions ☐
- Codes of practice, policies and procedures ☐

Assessment Guide

Your learning in this unit will be assessed through a controlled assignment. This will be set by Edexcel and marked by your tutor.

The assignment will require you to produce a report based on an investigation of the needs of one service user and how these needs are met by service providers and care practitioners.

You will need to show evidence of:

● The principles of care and values which underpin all care work with service users.

The range of care values that underpin care practice with service users have been outlined and explained in Topic 2.5.

Your assignment report should demonstrate that you can apply your knowledge and understanding of care values to describe and explain the work of the care professionals who are working to meet your chosen individual's needs.

Promoting Health and Wellbeing

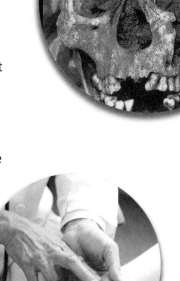

Introduction

This unit is about the different ways that people think about and try to achieve personal health and wellbeing. You will learn about:

- Definitions of health and wellbeing

- Common factors affecting health and wellbeing and the different effects they can have across the human life span

- Methods used to measure an individual's physical health

- Ways of promoting and supporting health improvement for an individual or for a small group.

As a care student, and possibly a future care practitioner, health and wellbeing are concepts that you should understand. It is important that you are able to identify what good physical health involves and that you have an understanding of some of the measures of health used by care practitioners. You should be able to explain the effects of a range of factors on an individual's health and wellbeing. Learning about the positive and negative effects that a range of factors can have on health and wellbeing will be of benefit if you choose to work with people in care situations. Knowledge and understanding of how health and wellbeing can be promoted and improved will also be helpful to you in your personal as well as your professional working life.

Topic 3.1

Understanding health and wellbeing

Topic focus

Health and wellbeing are important concepts that all care practitioners need to understand. This might seem obvious but it is also important to know about and understand the different methods used by care practitioners to define health and wellbeing. These include:

- **Holistic** definitions of health, based on a combination of PIES factors
- Positive definitions of health, based on achieving and maintaining things like physical fitness and mental stability
- Negative definitions of health, based on the absence or lack of physical illness, disease and mental distress

Topic 3.1 will introduce and explain these different types of definitions. It will also cover how ideas about health and wellbeing change over time, differ between cultures and vary according to a person's life stage. By the end of the topic you will understand that the terms health and wellbeing can be defined and used in different ways by care practitioners and service users.

Defining health and wellbeing

What is health? Is it something you're born with, something to do with your body and the way that it works? Or is it more than this? 'Health' is a word that people use all the time but what does it mean?

The ideas you have about health are those that other people in your society and culture use and have probably taught you. We tend to take these ideas for granted and generally assume there is only one way of thinking about 'health'. In fact, there are many different ways of understanding health and wellbeing. Chinese and Indian cultures, for example, adopt very different approaches to the Western **biomedical approach** that is generally used by health care practitioners to understand health and ill-health in the United Kingdom.

The biomedical approach

In Western societies, health professionals use a biomedical approach to define health and wellbeing. This approach includes several different terms that identify when a person's health is lacking or poor. For example, the terms disease, illness and ill-health are commonly used to describe an unhealthy state. Disease is a term used by doctors and other health care workers to refer to a physical change in the body's correct structure or

Over to you!

List as many words as you can which describe being or feeling 'unhealthy'. Identify the main words that you use when talking about health with your friends and family. Are these different to the words you use when talking to your GP or other health care workers?

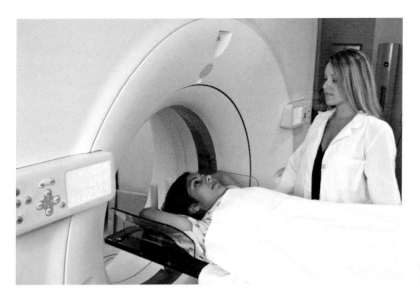

Scanning machines can show disease inside the body.

way of working. Health professionals use the term 'disease' only when they can measure, see or picture (using X-rays or scans perhaps) some type of abnormality. A disease is diagnosed when the health care practitioner can observe signs of abnormal physical change in the individual's body or the way that it is functioning.

The term illness, on the other hand, is generally used to describe a mental or physical state that is causing the person pain, distress or is affecting their ability to function in some way. Health care practitioners use the term 'illness' more broadly to describe ill-health that is identified from the symptoms that the person complains about, such as aches, pains and feeling sick. These symptoms can't always be directly seen or observed by others. This doesn't mean that the person is making up their symptoms or that there is nothing wrong with them! It means that they don't feel in good health and that physically, emotionally or mentally they're not at their best. Illnesses are usually seen as less serious or a more temporary threat to health than diseases. Even so, Western doctors and other health professionals see a lot of people each day who feel ill and want their help to get over their temporary health problems.

It is also important to note that a person can have a disease (a change in their body) without feeling ill or noticing that anything is wrong. This is one of the reasons for having **screening programmes**. Cervical smears, breast screening after the age of 50, childhood blood tests and chest X-rays are all carried out to identify diseases that, in their early stages, often don't cause people to feel ill.

Positive and negative definitions

The Western biomedical approach to defining health and wellbeing is based on the idea that a person is healthy if they don't have any illnesses, injuries or diseases or if they simply feel 'okay'. This is known as a negative view of health because being healthy is defined as not being or feeling unwell! A health care practitioner who uses this approach would assess whether an individual is experiencing any physical illness, disease or mental distress. If they are not, the care practitioner would say the

Over to you!

Can you think of an example of a disease and an illness? Use the explanation above to guide your choices.

person is 'healthy'. This type of definition is widely used by hospital doctors and GPs who look for evidence of illness and disease when they examine patients.

An alternative, positive view of health that is also used in Western societies involves identifying the qualities and abilities that a person ought to have in order to be healthy. For example, being physically fit, the correct weight for their height and feeling happy might be seen as evidence that a person is healthy. A care practitioner who uses this approach would assess whether an individual is physically fit and mentally stable. If the person met these criteria, they would be seen as 'healthy'.

Holistic definitions

There is a third approach to health that takes a broader view than either the positive or negative approaches described so far. The holistic approach to health suggests we should take all aspects of a person's life into account when we're looking at their health. This approach is concerned with the 'whole person' and includes an individual's:

- physical (bodily) health and wellbeing
- intellectual (thinking and learning) wellbeing
- social (relationship) wellbeing
- emotional (feelings) wellbeing.

The term 'wellbeing' is linked to, but also different from, health. **Wellbeing** is used in Western societies to refer to the way people feel about themselves. If people feel 'good' (positive) about themselves and are happy with life they will have a high level of wellbeing, and vice versa. As individuals, we are the best judges of our personal sense of wellbeing.

The World Health Organisation takes a positive and a holistic view when it defines health as:

'a state of complete physical, mental and social wellbeing, not merely the absence of disease or infirmity'

(WHO, 1946).

Life stage differences

The way in which we think about and judge whether or not a person is 'healthy' is affected by the person's life stage. Being able to walk ten miles may be a sign of good physical health (or fitness at least) in an 18-year-old, but it isn't something you would expect a 90-year-old person to do even if they were very healthy for their age. That last bit, 'for their age', is the important point. The way we think about health should take into account a person's age-related needs and abilities. So, we could say that a physically active 90-year-old man might be just as physically healthy, considering his age, as his 18-year-old great grandson.

The social construction of health and wellbeing

Health and wellbeing can be seen as **socially constructed** ideas. This means that the ways in which people think about health and wellbeing are not fixed but change over time and make sense within a particular society at a certain period in its history. People have defined health and wellbeing differently in the past and members of other, non-Western cultures also have alternative ways of thinking about health and wellbeing to those we have discussed so far.

Health in the past

People have thought about health and wellbeing in a variety of different ways for thousands of years. Many of these ideas seem unusual to us by present day standards. Ideas about health have changed over time, but many present-day thoughts and theories about what it means to be healthy have also been developed from these earlier ideas.

Whatever historical period they've lived in, people have always needed to know how to avoid disease and illness, how to deal with sickness and how to remain 'healthy'. It is hard to get evidence from prehistoric times (around 17,000 years ago). However, a possible source of evidence about health ideas is found in the skulls discovered by archaeologists that belong to this period. Some of these skulls had holes drilled in them. One theory is that prehistoric people did this to release the 'spirit' of a person who had died. However, many of the skulls show evidence that the person survived this operation and was therefore alive when it happened! Was this procedure, known as **trepanning**, part of the health beliefs and treatment approach of prehistoric people?

More recent evidence from nomadic and non-industrialised societies shows that in the not too distant past some more modern cultures also based their beliefs about health and the causes of illness on the existence and work of spirits and gods. In some of these cultures, good and bad spirits were seen to affect everyday life and to cause a person to suffer from illness, or even die, by entering their body. The cure for this was to rid the body of the evil spirit. A religious leader or traditional healer would be called on to banish the spirit from the person and return them to health. These ideas are very different from those of present-day Western societies.

It's important to remain open minded about the various ways of thinking about health and the causes and best ways of treating ill-health. Even though they don't fit in with present day medical views, many of the apparently old and unusual ideas about health from earlier times and different cultures continue to be used in the UK and throughout the world. This is often because they work by helping people to get over health problems and by making them feel better. Ongoing research into traditional cures and treatments also shows that the ideas of the past were sometimes based on good sense and played an important part in improving people's lives at the time. For example, modern scientists are now finding that the plants and herbs that were used by ancient civilizations as painkillers and sedatives provide very effective forms of 'natural' treatment. In fact, many modern day medicines are produced from plants and herbs - aspirin, for example, comes from willow bark.

Ideas about health and ill-health in the United Kingdom changed with the development of scientific thinking in the eighteenth century. People began to move away from the belief that magic,

A trepanned skull.

Health ideas from the past

- Ancient Egyptians used a sand-paste to clean their teeth.
- Aboriginal peoples used a casing of mud and clay to set broken limbs, and cleared their camps of human waste and debris to stop their enemies stealing their spirits
- Aztec Indians used human hair to stitch (suture) body wounds.

evil spirits or a disapproving God controlled health and illness. The development of microscopes, knowledge about human anatomy and growing understanding of body chemistry resulted in medical and scientific approaches to health and new ways of dealing with ill-health. Based on theories and observations of how the human body works, these ideas about health and ill-health are those that we currently recognise and use as 'true'. Instead of having religious leaders and traditional healers to banish evil spirits, we now have doctors and other health professionals to put these biomedical ideas about health into practice.

Health in other cultures

Western ideas about health and wellbeing are different from those of some other cultures. For example, Chinese herbal medicine is based on ideas about health that are 2000 years old. **Chinese herbal medicine** deals with both physical and mental health problems. It also provides ways of strengthening a person's recovery power, their immunity and capacity for wellbeing. Chinese herbal medicine is growing in popularity and is being used by an increasing number of people in western countries.

Chinese herbal medicine practitioners try to diagnosis the 'patterns of disharmony' affecting the individuals who come to see them. They try to work out whether the individual has a blocked, deficient or disturbed 'energy' (ch'i). Once they discover how the individual's 'energy' is blocked, the Chinese herbalist will prescribe a range of herbal medicines and give advice on how they can restore their normal energy balance.

If you visited a Chinese herbalist they would ask you what kind of 'complaint' you are suffering from. You would need to tell them where it is located, whether it comes and goes, how intense it is, what makes it better or worse (e.g. food, activity, time of day) and what you have done about it. This information tells the herbalist about your 'patterns of dysfunction'. The herbalist would also feel your pulse and look closely at your tongue for signs of 'imbalance'. According to the Chinese system, healthy people need to achieve a mind-spirit balance, an energy balance, a blood balance and a body fluids balance. The herbal medicines that are often prescribed are said to strengthen the individual's organs or to 'clear' from their body the unhealthy factors that are preventing balance and blocking energy flows.

Over to you!

Are you superstitious about anything? Think about your superstitions and how they affect the ways that you act or behave. Are any of your superstitious beliefs linked to ideas about health or ill-health?

Over to you!

The six people described opposite have different lifestyles, attitudes, values and needs. In some ways they may be 'healthy', in other ways they may not be. Read through each case study and answer the questions at the end.

Lois, age 30, has a job as a stockbroker. She buys and sells shares and must reach certain targets each week. She works out in the company gym each morning and then works very hard from 7.30 a.m. to 7.30 p.m. five days a week. She admits to feeling stressed most of the time. Before going home, she usually goes for a few drinks with her colleagues to wind down. She has made a lot of money but says that she has little time for other things.

Richie is a 27-year-old packer in a factory. He says his job is very boring. His life really revolves around sport and fitness training. He goes to a gym five nights a week to do weight training. Before work each day, he jogs or swims. He cycles everywhere he goes. Richie is very concerned about his diet and his physical appearance. He thinks about exercise even when he isn't doing it. He always wants to do more to improve his body. He has recently started taking anabolic steroids to help him build up his physique.

Amira describes herself as 'just a housewife'. She is 23 and has two children under five. She lives on income support, but occasionally gets help from her mother who lives a few miles away. She says that the children take up most of her time so she doesn't go out very often. Her favourite pastime is television. After the children are in bed she likes to watch soap operas and quiz shows. She always has a box of chocolates, some crisps and a few cans of lemonade while she watches TV.

Linda is a 19-year-old student of geology. In her first year at university, she joined a rock climbing group and went on most of their climbing trips. She recently went on a trip to Snowdonia. This time, she says, she 'just lost her nerve'. She got stuck on a cliff face and had to be taken off by rescue helicopter. She's been feeling 'on edge' ever since and has fallen behind in her studies this term.

Alex, age 47, gave up his job as a business studies lecturer two years ago to live in France and write books. He used to spend a great deal of time out of doors, cycling around the countryside. Last year he damaged his ankle in a fall and can no longer ride very far. Although he's made a few friends, he rarely has enough money to go out. Last winter he felt lonely. He caught pneumonia because he couldn't afford to heat his house. He's now working as a tourist guide to make money until he gets a book published.

 Gary is a 55-year-old nurse working on a hospital medical ward. He works seven days a week, sometimes doing two seven-hour shifts (one in the morning the other in the afternoon) and finishing at 9.30 p.m. He's very concerned about hygiene and always uses disposable gloves at work. Gary washes his hands several times during the day. He carries an extra suit of clothing to change into between shifts. He's worried he might contract a serious disease and insists that his house is cleaned every day, with a fresh set of bed linen put on every other day. His spare time is spent sleeping.

- In what way is each person healthy or unhealthy? Make notes of your ideas. You might want to give each person a score (10 = extremely healthy, 1 = extremely unhealthy) for physical, emotional, social and intellectual health.

- Compare and discuss your ideas and scores with other people in the class.

- What sort of approach to health are you using in making your decision about each person? (Hint: is your approach to health positive, negative, holistic or based on another type of definition?)

Knowledge Check

1 Name three ways of defining 'health'.

2 How would a care practitioner using a negative definition go about assessing an individual's health?

3 Which approach to health and wellbeing focuses on the 'whole person'?

4 What does the term 'wellbeing' mean?

5 Explain why a person who is physically fit and the correct weight for their height might not be healthy.

6 When is a person 'healthy'? Write an answer to this in your own words.

7 Explain why most people living in modern Western societies no longer believe that health and illness result from the action of 'evil spirits'.

8 Name two physical features that a Chinese medical herbalist would look at closely when assessing a person's health problems.

9 What, according to Chinese herbal medicine, happens to cause a person to be unwell?

10 Describe the purpose of the herbal medicines that are prescribed by Chinese herbal practitioners.

11 Explain, using examples, how ideas about 'health' can vary over time and between different cultures.

Investigate ...

Produce a range of questions that explore ideas about health and wellbeing. Use your questions to carry out a survey of friends, relatives or school colleagues to find out how they think about health and wellbeing. Summarise your results by comparing what different people say about the various approaches to 'health' we have looked at.

Topic review

The box below provides a summary of the areas covered in Topic 3.1. Tick the areas that you feel you understand and would be confident about when writing your assignment. If there are any areas that you don't understand or are not confident about, you will need to return to them before you begin planning or writing your assignment.

Definitions of health and wellbeing
Disease and illness ☐
Positive definitions ☐
Negative definitions ☐
Holistic definitions ☐

The social construction of health and wellbeing
Changing definitions over time ☐
Cultural differences in definitions ☐
Life stage differences ☐

Assessment Guide

Your learning in this unit will be assessed through a controlled assignment. This will be set by Edexcel and marked by your tutor.

The assignment will require you to plan and carry out investigations and produce a health improvement plan in response to case study material provided by Edexcel about the health and wellbeing of an individual.

You will need to show evidence of:

● Definitions of health and welbeing.

Topic 3.2

Factors affecting health and wellbeing

Topic focus

Would you like to be healthy? Most people would answer 'yes' to this question. Research has shown that people say being healthy is just as likely to make them feel happy as winning lots of money. Winning lots of money relies on luck. However, being healthy is a bit easier to achieve if you understand how different factors affect health and wellbeing. These factors include:

- Physical factors such as genetic inheritance, illness, disease, diet, exercise, alcohol and smoking
- Social, cultural and emotional factors such as family, friends, educational experiences, employment and unemployment, community involvement, religion, gender, ethnicity, sexual orientation, culture and relationship formation
- Economic factors such as income, wealth, employment status, occupation, social class, poverty and material possessions
- Physical environment factors such as pollution, noise, housing conditions and rural/urban lifestyles
- Psychological factors such as stress, relationships within the family, friends and partners
- **Health monitoring** and illness prevention services (such as screening and vaccination).

Topic 3.2 will help you to gain an understanding of how each of these factors can affect health and wellbeing in either a positive or a negative way.

Physical factors

The physical factors that affect health and wellbeing are those things that have a direct influence on a person's physical health experience. They include:

- The *genes* we inherit from our biological parents
- The *illnesses* and *diseases* that we experience
- The *diet* we eat
- The amount of *exercise* we take
- How much *alcohol* we consume
- Whether we *smoke* cigarettes.

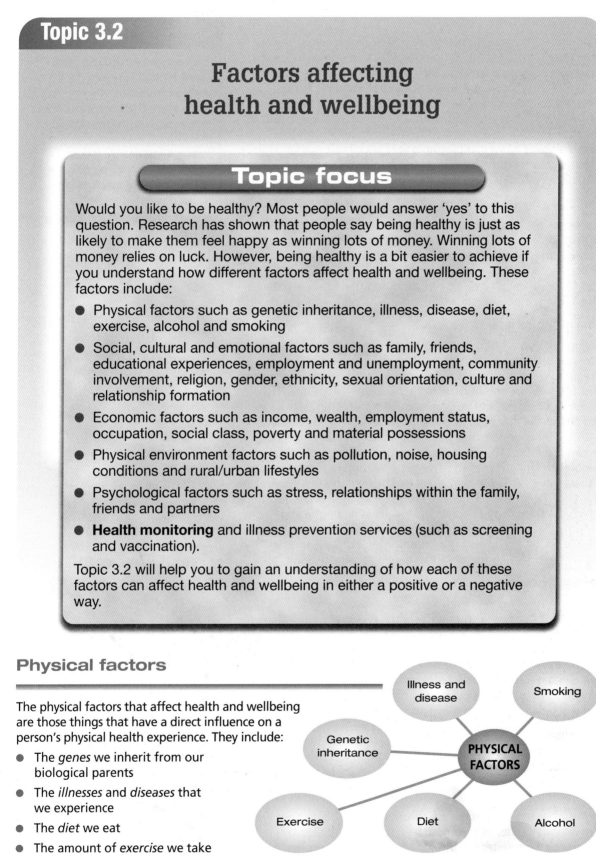

Figure 3.1 Physical factors affecting health and wellbeing.

Genetic inheritance

Biologically, you are unique. Your biological uniqueness results from the particular combination of genes that you've inherited from your biological parents. Each human body cell contains two sets of 23 chromosomes – one set from each parent. These chromosomes contain up to 4,000 different **genes**. The physical characteristics that you share with your parents are one result of genes being inherited or passed from one generation to the next. However, as well as playing a very important role in your physical growth and appearance, the genes you've inherited may also make you vulnerable to certain diseases and health problems.

Inheriting health problems

The genes we inherit from our parents are the biological 'instructions' or codes that tell our body's cells how to grow. Some people inherit one or more genes that are defective or faulty. These faulty genes can, but won't always, result in a person experiencing a disease or condition that has a negative effect on their health and wellbeing.

Dominant gene defects

We inherit one set of genes from each of our biological parents. Some of these genes are identical, whilst others differ. For example, we may inherit a blue-eye-colour gene from one parent and a brown-eye-colour gene from the other. Where this happens, one gene will be dominant over the other. In this case, the brown-eye-colour gene wins! However, if the dominant gene is also a faulty or defective gene, the child will inherit the disease or condition for which it provides instruction. For example, people who inherit the defective gene leading to Huntington's disease have a fifty per cent chance of developing the disorder. Huntington's disease is a slowly progressing, fatal brain disorder which develops in middle age and results in dementia and uncontrollable movements. There is now a diagnostic test for people with a family history of Huntington's disease to assess the risk of them passing the defective gene to their offspring.

Recessive gene defects

A gene that isn't dominant is known as a recessive gene. Normally the genetic information in the recessive gene will be overruled by that in the dominant gene. This happens in the case of eye colour: the blue eye-colour gene is recessive. However, if a person inherits two faulty or defective copies of a recessive gene this will have an effect on their health and wellbeing. A person who inherits just one copy will not have the disease or condition but will be a 'carrier' and may pass it on to their children. Cystic fibrosis is a disease inherited as a result of recessive gene defects. Even though about one in every 25 people is a carrier of the faulty recessive gene, only one in every 2,000 children is born with cystic fibrosis.

Chromosomal defects

Some inherited conditions result from a person being born with the wrong number of chromosomes. These include Down's syndrome, Klinefelter's syndrome and Turner's syndrome. All these conditions affect the growth and development of the people who inherit them.

> **Investigate …**
>
> Tuberous sclerosis, achondroplasia (dwarfism), Marfan's syndrome and neurofibromatosis are all conditions that can be inherited as a result of dominant gene defects. Use medical dictionaries, encyclopedias and the Internet to investigate one or more of these conditions. Identify the possible effects that each condition may have on a person's health and wellbeing.

> **Investigate …**
>
> Cystic Fibrosis, Friedrich's ataxia and sickle cell anemia are all conditions that can be inherited as a result of recessive gene defects. Use medical dictionaries, encyclopedias and the Internet to investigate these conditions. Identify the possible effects that each can have on a person's health and wellbeing.

Case study

Ajay Khan is 20 years of age. He is an active, sporty person who tries to keep his weight within acceptable limits and who manages his diet carefully. Ajay avoids eating fatty food wherever he can, has never smoked and doesn't drink. Ajay is very health-conscious because he is aware of his family history of high blood pressure and heart disease. Ajay's father and grandfather both had high blood pressure and both died of heart conditions in their mid-fifties. Ajay's GP has told him he needs to be aware that there is a genetic component to these health problems and that he may be susceptible to them unless he manages his lifestyle carefully.

- What does Ajay's GP mean when he says that there is a 'genetic component' to high blood pressure and heart disease?
- Identify two lifestyle factors that can contribute to heart disease.
- What is Ajay doing that might help to reduce his genetic risk of heart disease and high blood pressure?

The conditions and disorders that result from dominant and recessive gene defects and chromosomal defects are relatively rare. Other more commonly experienced health problems that also have a significant genetic component to them include:

- Eye disorders, such as glaucoma
- High blood pressure
- Heart conditions
- High cholesterol
- Haemophilia.

Even though a person may be genetically vulnerable to a particular disorder, lifestyle and other biological factors can limit or even prevent some genetically inherited conditions from occurring.

Illness and disease

The illnesses and diseases that an individual experiences throughout their life may have a significant impact on their health and wellbeing. This can happen where the illness or disease affects the person's ability to function normally, where it affects their quality of life, or where it presents a threat to their life or is life-limiting.

Many of the diseases and illnesses that we experience are short-lived and can be treated and cured by taking medication or through other treatments. Illnesses and diseases that used to account for a large number of deaths in childhood, such as polio, diphtheria and whooping cough, are now prevented through vaccinations given in early childhood. Similarly, tuberculosis and influenza (flu) are less of a threat to the health and wellbeing of the UK population than they used to be but can still be very damaging to health when they occur. Infectious diseases and degenerative conditions (see figure 3.2) are two types of disorder that can affect an individual's health and development at different points of the life course. Many of the diseases can become chronic conditions that can only be managed rather than cured. HIV infection, for example, may affect a person's health for the rest of their life and is likely to reduce both the quality and the length of the person's life.

Infectious diseases	Degenerative disorders
Polio	Alzheimer's disease
Tuberculosis	Multiple sclerosis
Rubella	Motor Neurone disease
Diptheria	Huntington's disease
HIV	Parkinson's disease
Influenza	Cancers

Figure 3.2 Types of illnesses and diseases.

UNIT 3

Diet

Food plays a very important role in health. The food we eat should be nutritious if it is going to be beneficial to our physical health. This means it should contain a variety of **nutrients**. Nutrients are naturally-occurring chemical substances found in the food we eat. The five basic nutrients help the body in different ways:

- Carbohydrates and fats provide the body with energy
- Proteins provide the chemical substances needed to build and repair body cells and tissues
- Vitamins help to regulate the chemical reactions that continuously take place in our bodies
- Minerals are needed for control of body function and to build and repair certain tissues.

As well as eating food that contains a balance of these five nutrients, we also need to consume fibre and water. Although these are not counted as nutrients they are vital for physical health.

A healthy intake of food, also known as a **balanced diet**, contains suitable amounts of each of the five basic nutrients. The amount and types of foods that are healthy for a person to eat, varies for each individual. The following factors will affect how much and what types of food we need to consume:

- age
- gender
- body size
- height
- weight
- the environment (for example, whether you live in a cold or a warm country)
- the amount of physical activity you do in your daily life.

Nutrition is very important in the early years of life. Babies and infants need the right types of food to help them grow and develop normally, and to prevent them from developing certain illnesses. Children and adolescents also need the right types of food to promote their physical growth and to provide 'fuel' or energy for their high level of physical activity.

People who have special diets, for example vegetarians and vegans, leave out or include specific food groups to meet their personal values or special physical needs. Vegetarians don't eat meat or fish but they can still get all the nutrients they need. They can get proteins from cereals, beans, eggs and cheese. Vegans, who eat no animal products at all, can still get all their essential nutrients provided their food intake is varied. For example, they can get protein from nuts and pulses.

Exercise

Do you like doing exercise? Some people really enjoy playing sports, going to the gym or taking exercise classes. You might be one of them. Or you might be one of the large number of people who don't do enough exercise. Unfortunately exercise isn't as

Over to you!

Family member	Day	Breakfast	Lunch	Snacks	Dinner
Tom age 40	Saturday	Boiled egg, toast, coffee	Ham roll, crisps,	Doughnut, coffee	Pizza, salad, baked beans, baked potatoes, beer, chocolate cake
	Sunday	Fried egg, bacon, toast, coffee	Roast chicken, roast potatoes, peas, carrots, tinned fruit, ice cream, white wine	Chocolate bar, coffee	Cheese and pickle sandwich, fruit cake, tea
Laura age 30	Saturday	Boiled egg, toast, tea	Crispbread, cottage cheese, herb tea,	Apple, diet coke	Pizza, salad, diet coke, orange, coffee
	Sunday	Toast, marmalade, orange juice, tea	Roast chicken, peas, carrots, ice cream, wine, coffee	Banana, diet coke	Fruit cake, tea
Rachel age 8	Saturday	Cornflakes, orange juice	Ham roll, crisps, blackcurrant squash	Chocolate bar, cola drink	Pizza, salad, baked potato, blackcurrant squash, chocolate cake
	Sunday	Fried egg, toast, orange juice	Roast chicken, roast potatoes, carrots, ice cream, wafers, grape juice	Cheese sandwich,	Chocolate milkshake; sponge cake
Danny age 3	Saturday	Ready breakfast cereal, milk	Tuna sandwich, apple, orange juice	Chocolate bar, milk	Pizza, salad, blackcurrant squash, chocolate cake
	Sunday	Toast, savoury spread, milk	Roast chicken, roast potato, peas, ice cream, wafers, grape juice	Chocolate milkshake	Fruit yoghurt, sponge cake, blackcurrant squash
Audrey age 73	Saturday	Grapefruit, crispbread, marmalade, tea	Roll, cottage cheese, tomato, herb tea	Apple	Pizza, salad, chocolate cake, tea
	Sunday	Boiled egg, toast, tea	Roast chicken, roast potato, peas, carrots, tinned fruit, ice cream, wine, coffee	Nothing	Tuna sandwich, fruit cake, tea

This is a diet record sheet showing the weekend food consumption for members of the James family. Use the diet sheet to answer these questions.

1 Which nutrients can be found in the foods eaten by the family?

2 What effect does each nutrient have on the body?

3 How nutritional is this family's diet?

4 Do you think that individual family members are getting a balanced diet?

5 Are there any deficiencies or excesses in their nutritional intakes?

Using examples from the record sheet, write a paragraph explaining your views on the last three questions. What advice would you give to the parents of Danny and Rachel about the type of diet needed to promote healthy growth and development in children?

Investigate ...

Monitor your diet over a 3-day period by keeping a food diary. List all of the food you eat (including meals and snacks). Identify the range of nutrients that you consume in each meal or snack. Does your diet over the three days suggest that you are or are not eating a balanced diet?

popular as eating food and is one of the things in lists of top health tips that many people struggle with. But it's still important, and is very good for your physical health.

Exercise has a positive effect on both physical and mental health. But it's important not to do too much exercise. People are advised to find a balance between physical activity and rest in order to maintain good physical health and a sense of wellbeing. Too much exercise can lead to excessive weight loss and may result in physical damage or chronic injuries, to joints or ligaments for example.

So, what kinds of exercise should you do? The type and level of exercise that an individual can do safely will depend on their age, gender and health status. For example, moderate exercise can be safely undertaken by older and less physically mobile people, including women in the later stages of pregnancy and people with physical disabilities. Younger people who are physically fit can safely undertake more vigorous exercise.

Lack of physical exercise can lead to ill-health and disease. For example, lack of exercise is linked to an increased risk of diseases such as coronary heart disease, stroke, obesity (being excessively overweight or very fat) and osteoporosis (brittle bones). Obesity is now a major health problem in the UK and is closely linked to people overeating and not exercising. There are many reasons why people don't take more exercise. These include not having enough time, not liking sport and being frightened of injuries.

Alcohol

Alcohol is a very popular, widely available and accepted part of social life in the United Kingdom. Many people enjoy a drink and there is usually nothing wrong with that. In small, controlled quantities alcoholic drinks can be part of a pleasurable social occasion. In fact, some types of alcoholic drink, such as red wine, have been shown to be good for health.

The health benefits of alcohol

Studies have shown that people who regularly drink small amounts of alcohol tend to live longer than people who don't drink at all. This is because alcohol protects against the development of coronary heart disease. It also has an effect on the amount of **cholesterol**, or fat, carried in the bloodstream,

Benefits of exercise

Exercise…

…keeps the heart healthy

…improves circulation

…helps muscles, joints and bones to remain strong

…improves stamina

…reduces blood pressure

…increases self-esteem and self-confidence

…helps to control and maintain weight

…makes you feel more energetic

…is a good way of socialising

…helps the body to stay supple and mobile.

Case study

Jack is 14 years old. He lives on a small estate on the edge of town with his parents. Jack plays a lot of computer games on his console. He's also a keen keyboard player, practising for a couple of hours each day. Jack is popular at school, partly because he is very funny. He uses his humour to defend himself when people laugh at his size. Jack is about 3 stone overweight. His parents are concerned about this although his mum insists he does not overeat. She believes that lack of exercise has led to his weight problem.

- What factors might be contributing to Jack being overweight?

- Why is Jack's weight likely to lead to health problems if he doesn't do something about it?

- Suggest three ways Jack could increase the amount of exercise he takes each day.

making it less likely that the clots which cause heart disease will form. Maximum health advantage can be achieved from drinking between one and two units of alcohol a day. There is no additional overall health benefit to be gained from drinking more than two units of alcohol a day. However, there are possible negative effects from doing so.

When consumed, alcohol is rapidly absorbed into the bloodstream. The amount of alcohol concentrated in the body at any one time depends on how much a person drinks, whether the stomach is empty or full and the height, weight, age and sex of the drinker.

The risks associated with alcohol

Nearly all the alcohol a person drinks has to be burnt up by the liver. The rest is disposed of either in sweat or urine. The human body can get rid of one unit of alcohol in one hour. Smaller than average people, younger or older people and people who are not used to drinking are more easily affected by alcohol and take longer to get it out of their bodies.

Alcohol is a depressant. This means that it reduces certain brain functions and affects judgement, self-control and coordination. This is why alcohol causes fights, domestic violence and accident-related injuries. It has been estimated that up to 40,000 deaths per year could be alcohol-related.

The health risks associated with alcohol result from consuming it in large quantities, either regularly or in binges. People who frequently drink excess amounts of alcohol have an increased risk of:

- high blood pressure
- coronary heart disease
- liver damage and cirrhosis of the liver
- cancer of the mouth and throat
- psychological and emotional problems, including depression
- obesity.

Health professionals recommend safe limits of alcohol consumption. The recommended limits for women are two to three units a day, or less. It is recommended that men limit their consumption to between three and four units a day or less. One unit of alcohol is the same as one small glass of wine,

Drinking alcohol can have positive and negative effects on health.

think about drink

There's more to a drink than you think

Alcohol is a positive part of life for most people. By following the guidelines in this leaflet you can make sure that you can drink alcohol without putting yourself or others at risk.

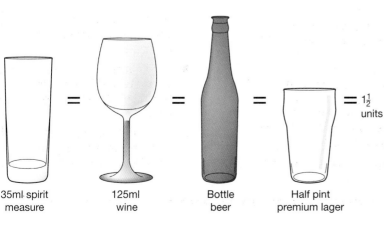

| 35ml spirit measure | 125ml wine | Bottle beer | Half pint premium lager | $1\frac{1}{2}$ units |

Figure 3.3 Each of these contains $1\frac{1}{2}$ units of alcohol.

UNIT 3

Case study

Jodie started drinking when she was 14 years of age. She used to drink in her local park with some older teenagers and a couple of her friends. At weekends Jodie drank a couple of bottles of cider and any vodka that was available. Jodie thought that drinking was fun and that it made her happy. She realised when she was 19 years of age that the opposite was true. Jodie found herself thinking about alcohol during work and would go to the pub for a few drinks at lunchtime. Jodie was eventually sacked from her job as a trainee hairdresser for coming to work smelling of alcohol. After making a promise to her mum and dad Jodie hasn't drunk any alcohol for three months. They told her about the physical effects that binge drinking and long-term alcohol abuse could have on her health.

- Suggest some reasons why young teenagers like Jodie start drinking alcohol.

- Identify four effects of binge drinking or long-term alcohol abuse on physical health.

- What are the recommended limits (in units) for alcohol consumption that Jodie should stick to if she does start drinking alcohol again?

half a pint of ordinary strength lager, beer or cider, or a 25ml pub measure of spirits. If men and women follow this guide there should be no significant risks to their health from alcohol. However, if women regularly drink three or more units and men drink four or more units a day, the risk to health is increased.

You should be aware that these recommended limits are based on 'pub measures'. People who drink at home, or buy alcohol from an off-licence or supermarket to consume elsewhere, usually pour themselves larger measures of wines and spirits or consume stronger beer than that sold in licensed premises.

Smoking

Do you smoke cigarettes? If not, you probably know people who do. Smoking cigarettes is a prominent part of some people's social life. However, despite it being legal for people age 18 or over to buy and smoke tobacco, cigarettes have got a very bad reputation with health professionals.

Cigarettes, and tobacco smoking of any kind, have no health benefits at all. Instead, smoking cigarettes directly damages your physical health. This is one of the most important pieces of information that health professionals regularly give out to people. Their advice is always to stop smoking. You should be told this if you smoke cigarettes. People who fail to take note of this warning run a considerable risk of causing themselves long-term health damage and dying, as a direct result of their smoking habit. The health problems associated with smoking tobacco include:

- coronary heart disease
- stroke
- high blood pressure
- bronchitis
- lung cancer
- other cancers, such as cancer of the larynx, kidney and bladder.

Investigate ...

Using the Internet, investigate the health impact of drinking excessive amounts of alcohol. Produce a poster designed to inform 14–16 year old adolescents about the links between alcohol consumption and health problems.

Smoking cigarettes is harmful to health because the smoke inhaled and substances circulated deep into the body are harmful. These substances include nicotine, carbon monoxide and tar.

Nicotine is a powerful, fast-acting and addictive drug. Smokers absorb it into their bloodstream and feel an effect in their brains seven to eight minutes later. Some smokers say this is 'calming'. However, the physical effects of smoking also include an increase in heart rate and blood pressure and changes in appetite. Cigarette smoke contains a high concentration of carbon monoxide, a poisonous gas. Because carbon monoxide combines more easily with haemoglobin (the substance in blood that carries oxygen), the amount of oxygen carried to a smoker's lungs and tissues is reduced. This reduction in oxygen supply to the body then affects the growth and repair of tissues, and the exchange of essential nutrients.

The carbon monoxide inhaled by a smoker can also affect their heart. The changes in the blood associated with smoking can cause fat deposits to form on the walls of the arteries. This leads to hardening of the arteries and to circulatory problems, causing smokers to develop **coronary heart disease**.

Cigarette tar contains many substances known to cause cancer. It damages the cilia, small hairs lining the lungs that help to protect them from dirt and infection. Because these lung protectors get damaged, smokers are more likely than non-smokers to get throat and chest infections. About 70 per cent of the tar in a cigarette is deposited in the lungs when cigarette smoke is inhaled.

The use of tobacco is now less widespread and less socially acceptable than it was twenty years ago. However, in 1996–7, just under 30 per cent of adults were still smokers and there were over 120,000 smoking-related deaths. Teenage girls are one of the few social groups who are now more likely to smoke than in the past. Tobacco use is therefore still a major cause of preventable disease and early death in the UK.

Over to you!

What does the graph reveal about trends in cigarette smoking? What percentage of females smoked in 2003?

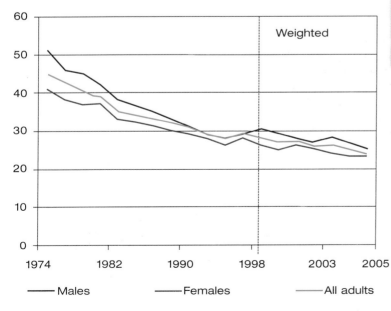

Figure 3.4 Percentage of adults who smoke cigarettes by sex. Great Britain 1974–2005.

Smoking during pregnancy

When women smoke during pregnancy, the ability of the blood to carry oxygen to all parts of the body is reduced. This affects the flow of blood to the **placenta**, which feeds the foetus. Mothers who smoke during pregnancy have a greater risk of suffering a miscarriage. Women who smoke tend to give birth to premature or underweight babies who are more prone to upper respiratory tract infections and breathing problems. The risk of cot death among these babies is also increased.

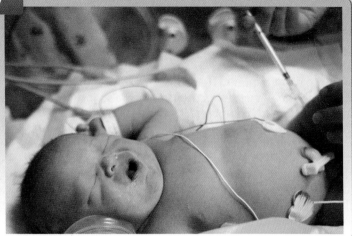

✔ Knowledge Check

1 Identify four different physical factors that affect health and wellbeing

2 Name one inherited disorder that results from a recessive gene defect.

3 Explain how a person inherits a disorder as a result of recessive gene defects of their parents.

4 Describe the effects that Huntington's disease can have on a person's health, wellbeing or development.

5 Name the five basic nutrients that are part of a balanced diet.

6 Identify at least two sources of each nutrient in the food you eat regularly.

7 Describe the factors that affect how much food a person should eat.

8 Explain why a varied and balanced diet is especially important for babies and children.

9 What are the health benefits of taking regular exercise?

10 Identify two health problems that can result from not taking enough regular exercise.

11 Name three negative long-term effects that drinking too much alcohol can have on a person's health and wellbeing

12 What factors should a person take into account when assessing how much it is safe for them to drink?

13 Name three diseases associated with cigarette smoking.

14 Describe the physical effects on the body of inhaling cigarette smoke.

15 Explain what statistics on smoking reveal about the trends of cigarette smoking in the UK.

Social, cultural and emotional factors

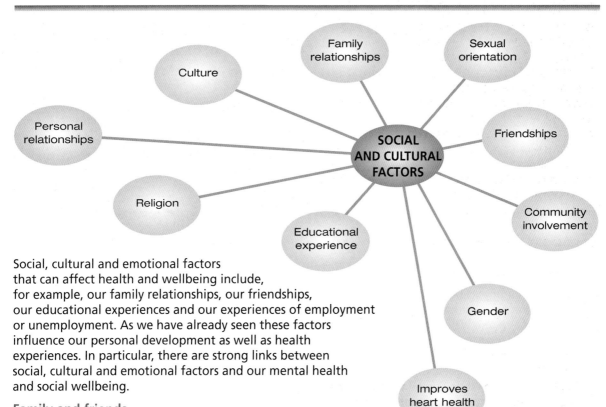

Social, cultural and emotional factors that can affect health and wellbeing include, for example, our family relationships, our friendships, our educational experiences and our experiences of employment or unemployment. As we have already seen these factors influence our personal development as well as health experiences. In particular, there are strong links between social, cultural and emotional factors and our mental health and social wellbeing.

Family and friends

Do you have good friends and relatives who you care about? Hopefully you will be able to think of a variety of people who are emotionally close to you. These people are good for your health and wellbeing. You may have disagreements and fall out with family members and close friends from time to time, but you shouldn't underestimate the important effect they have on your emotional wellbeing and mental health.

Relationships with family members and friends are supportive, and have a positive effect on mental health when the people involved feel emotionally close, cared for and able to trust each other. We need supportive relationships in each life stage to experience wellbeing, and to support our social and emotional development. Babies need to form a close attachment to an adult carer (usually a parent) so that they can experience an emotionally secure relationship. Children also need supportive relationships with their parents (or carers) and with friends to develop their self-concept and self-esteem. Not having friends can lead to a child feeling 'left out' and having low self-esteem. During adolescence close, supportive relationships with friends and parents provide people with a 'safe place' when they feel stress and pressure. These supportive relationships help to boost self-esteem, a sense of belonging and of feeling valued by others. People who experience supportive relationships with family members and friends are more likely to experience a positive sense of social and emotional wellbeing and better mental health than people who lack support and are more socially isolated. Researchers have shown that people who lack close, supportive relationships are much more likely to experience depression.

Figure 3.5 Social, cultural and emotional factors affecting health and wellbeing.

Case study

Robbie is one year old. Monica, his mum, is 22 years old and a lone parent. She has recently found out that she has to go into hospital for an eye operation. Monica is upset and feels frightened about how this might turn out. Her worst fear is that something might go wrong and she won't be able to care for Robbie afterwards. She is also upset about the prospect of being separated from Robbie for a week while she is in hospital.

- How might Robbie react if he feels insecure and unsupported when Monica is in hospital?

- Who would you seek support from if you were in Monica's situation?

- What kinds of support do you think Monica needs at the moment?

- What do you think other members of Monica's family could do to be supportive whilst she is in hospital?

Educational experiences

Personal, social and health education programmes are now a part of every school's curriculum. Children and young people now learn about physical, mental, emotional and sexual health as well as how the use of alcohol, tobacco and illegal drugs can affect their health and wellbeing. Increasingly schools and colleges are also focusing on healthy eating and educating pupils and students about the need to consume a balanced diet. These kinds of educational experiences often shape the attitudes of children and young people and help to make them more informed and more able to make healthy choices about their diet, taking regular exercise, sex and relationships, and the risks associated with tobacco, illegal drugs and alcohol. More informal educational approaches are also used to target adults and older people with forms of health education - through leaflets, booklets, articles and programmes in the media, for example – in order to provide information and shape attitudes towards living a healthier lifestyle.

Employment and unemployment

Work and health experiences are closely linked. For example, a person's health affects their ability to get work and to keep it. People who experience poor health, especially chronic disorders or disabling conditions, often find they are unable to work. In many ways, work has a positive effect on health and wellbeing. Work is good for mental health and social wellbeing because it provides people with:

- A sense of purpose and identity ('what do you do?')
- Self-reliance
- Self-esteem and a sense of self-worth
- Social relationships.

Employment obviously provides the income people need for their financial wellbeing but it also provides people with social contacts and support and a sense of achievement. When people become unemployed they tend to lose their social networks and their relationships with others, and their social skills and motivation may decrease over time. Employment can make a positive contribution to a person's physical health as well as their

Over to you!

What types of jobs do you think would be mentally demanding and good for a person's sense of wellbeing? List five jobs that would stimulate a person intellectually.

intellectual, emotional and social wellbeing if it involves safe, stimulating and satisfying work. However, some types of work can be a risk to health and wellbeing because of the dangerous nature of the work, the long hours that some people work or the high stress levels that can result from demanding workloads, workplace bullying and poor working conditions.

Figure 3.6 Accident statistics for employed people 1999–2000

Severity of injury	Number of injuries	Injury rate*
Fatal	162	0.7
Non-fatal major	28,652	116.6
Over 3-day (minor)	135,381	550.6
All injuries	164,195	668.2

* per 100,000 employed
Source: *HSE: Health and social care statistics* 2000–01

Unemployment is something that most people of working age worry about and hope they can avoid. A person is unemployed when they don't have work. Losing a job or not being able to obtain work affects people in a variety of ways. Few of them are positive. Many older workers dread the prospect of losing their jobs when they reach their forties and fifties. This is because it can be hard for older workers to get work. Older workers often complain that they suffer from age discrimination in the job market, although the Employment Equality (Age) Regulations 2006 have made age discrimination unlawful.

Figure 3.7 Unemployment statistics.

People unemployed* for two years or more: by gender

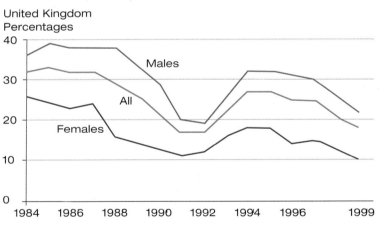

United Kingdom
Percentages

*At spring each year. Percentage of ILO unemployed who have been unemployed for two years or more.
Source: *Labour Force Survey*, Office for National Statistics

Over to you!

How would you feel if an employer told you that, despite all your efforts and your good, conscientious service to them, they were very sorry but your services were no longer needed? Write down a few words that you feel would describe your emotions. Think about how you would feel about yourself as well as how you would feel about the way that you'd been treated by the employer.

Over to you!

In general, has the trend in long-term unemployment gone up or down since 1984? What percentage of females were long-term unemployed in 1999?

But why is unemployment such a bad thing? Wouldn't you like lots of free time and not to have to get up in the morning to go to work? These things might be good in the short term and you might feel a little like you do when you're on holiday. However, unemployed people generally don't feel like they're on holiday. Work is an important source of self-esteem and it plays an important role in our emotional and mental health. Work also provides money that pays the bills. Unemployed people complain that they feel they don't 'fit in', find themselves outside of their normal social groups and they feel a sense of failure and rejection as a result of not having work. Financial problems occur very quickly when people have no income. All of these consequences can be very damaging if a person experiences long-term unemployment. For example, people can feel hopeless, lose motivation and self-confidence and use harmful substances such as tobacco or alcohol to cope with the negative feelings they experience. Unemployment often leads to emotional strain, anxiety and depression and a reduced sense of wellbeing and purpose.

Unemployment can also have an effect on a person's physical health. Long-term unemployed people are more likely to suffer from respiratory problems, alcohol-related disease, arthritis and mental illness. The connection between these illnesses and unemployment are not clear. Do people become ill because they are unemployed? Or do their illnesses cause them to remain unemployed? Perhaps the lifestyle adopted by unemployed people is less healthy than that of people in work. One of the more common explanations is that unemployment is highly stressful. A high level of personal stress has a negative effect on a person's physical and mental health, their sense of emotional wellbeing and their relationships with others. Without adequate support and strategies to use their time constructively and without the hope of finding work or other fulfilling activity, unemployment will damage a person's health and wellbeing.

Community involvement

Involvement in the life and activities of a local community is likely to have a positive effect on an individual's emotional and social wellbeing. Community involvement enables a person to develop a sense of belonging and identity and also provides them with a social network in which friendships can develop and support can be found. A person who is involved with their local community will experience the mental health benefits of social inclusion.

Over to you!

Unemployment usually means a person has a lower income than if they were in work. Explain how this direct effect of unemployment might have an indirect or knock-on effect on an individual's health and wellbeing. Think about the things that people need money for and what might have to be sacrificed if income is reduced.

Case study

George (42), Helena (39) and their daughter Ruby (3) moved to live in a small village in mid-Wales two years ago. George had always wanted to move to the countryside so that he could grow vegetables, keep chickens and enjoy the fresh air and wide open spaces that London lacks. Helena had never been to Wales before they moved. Since arriving she has found it very hard to make friends and still feels unsettled. George, on the other hand, is now a member of the Parish council, goes to the local pub quiz every week and is the main spokesperson for a group campaigning against a dual carriageway being built next to the village. George is well known and popular in the village. He is very happy living there and believes moving from London was a really good thing to do. He is aware that Helena disagrees and would like to 'go home' as she puts it.

- How has moving from London affected George and Helena's emotional wellbeing?
- What effect might a lack of community involvement be having on Helena?
- Suggest some ways in which Helena and Ruby might become more involved in the life of the local community.

An individual who is not involved and lacks connections and support in their local community may become socially isolated and suffer poor emotional and social wellbeing as a result. Social isolation and exclusion are strongly associated with mental distress.

Ethnicity

Research studies and statistics show that different ethnic groups in the UK have differing experiences of health and illness. In particular:

- Members of minority ethnic groups have a shorter life expectancy than the majority white population.

- Members of the white British population experience higher rates of cancer and lung disease than members of minority ethnic groups.

- People belonging to groups from the Indian subcontinent are more likely to die from coronary heart disease than members of other ethnic groups.

- Members of African-Caribbean groups experience higher death rates from stroke but low rates of cancer.

- African people have higher rates of high blood pressure and are more likely to die as a result of accidents, violence and tuberculosis than members of other ethnic groups.

- Infant death rates are higher for most migrant groups but are highest for the infants of Pakistan-born mothers.

- Members of minority ethnic groups rate their personal health in poorer terms than members of the white population.

- Certain diseases that are very uncommon in the general population do affect members of some minority ethnic groups much more often. Sickle cell disorders are an example of this.

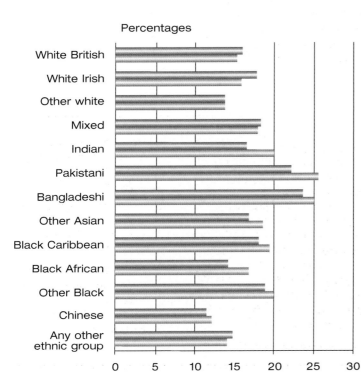

Percentages

Males

Females

Figure 3.8 Limiting long-term illness, by ethnic group and sex, April 2001, England and Wales.

Over to you!

Which ethnic group has the highest rate of limiting long-term illness? Which has the lowest?

The precise reasons for these ethnic differences in the health and illness experience have not been fully explained. Scientists have claimed that genetic, lifestyle and broader social factors all account for some of these differences in health experience. It is the case that members of minority ethnic groups are more likely than members of the white majority population to experience social deprivation (poor housing, low incomes, hazardous jobs) and poverty. These are likely to lead to ill-health and poor social and emotional wellbeing.

Culture

A person's culture has a wide-ranging influence on their way of life and the lifestyle decisions that they make. A person's diet, relationships, attitudes to alcohol, drugs, exercise and education are all influenced by the cultural beliefs and practices that they have been exposed to whilst growing up. As the United Kingdom is a multicultural society in which many different ethnic groups co-exist, it is important to learn about and understand different cultures in order to appreciate the varying lifestyles of people who use health and social care services.

Religion

Religious beliefs can influence an individual's lifestyle in a number of ways. Diet, use of alcohol and the approach a person takes to medical care, for example, may all be influenced by their religious beliefs. Whilst the Christian faith does not forbid the consumption of any type of food, other faiths do. For example, most Hindus are vegetarian and Muslims do not eat pork or other meat that has not been killed using halal techniques. People who follow a strict version of Islam would also avoid alcohol and would prefer to be seen and examined by a health practitioner of the same gender in order to avoid physical contact with a member of the opposite sex.

Gender

Research studies of the health experiences of men and women show a number of gender differences. These are summed up in the phrase 'women are sicker but men die quicker'. Briefly:

- Women are more likely to see a doctor and report higher rates of illness than men

- Women are more likely to experience depression, especially if they are lone parents or look after children at home

- Women live longer lives than men and are less likely to die prematurely as a result of accidents or other risk-related behaviours

- Men are more likely to die from circulatory diseases whilst the main cause of death for women is now cancer

- The high-risk period for men is between 15 and 22 years, with higher death rates resulting mainly from motor vehicle accidents. Boys are also far more likely to die from accidents in childhood than girls.

Gender differences in health experiences between men and women can be explained in a number of ways. It is likely that the reasons for these differences are a combination of genetic, lifestyle and social factors. Women are more likely to experience

Investigate ...

Investigate the cultural beliefs, practices and lifestyle of an ethnic group other than your own. Use your findings to create a poster or leaflet about cultural influences on health and wellbeing.

Investigate ...

Investigate a religion that you are not currently familiar with and look at how the beliefs and ways of life of members of this religion affect their diet and lifestyle. Identify any other areas that may influence their health and wellbeing.

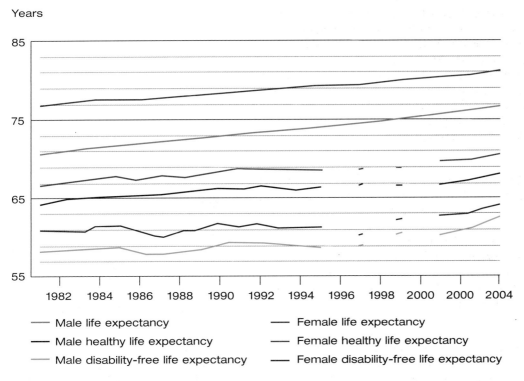

Years

Legend:
- Male life expectancy
- Male healthy life expectancy
- Male disability-free life expectancy
- Female life expectancy
- Female healthy life expectancy
- Female disability-free life expectancy

Figure 3.9 Health expectancy by sex, 1981–2004.

poverty and social deprivation than men, men don't generally consult their doctors often or quickly enough and younger men do seem to take more risks in the way they live their lives than young women, for example.

Sexual orientation

An individual who is comfortable with and able to express their sexual orientation freely, as heterosexual, lesbian, gay or bisexual for example, will tend to have a better sense of self-worth, more personal confidence and higher self-esteem than a person who is ashamed of, confused or anxious about this aspect of their identity. People who do have concerns and worries about their sexual orientation may be more at risk of experiencing anxiety and depression and may lack the confidence required to form and maintain supportive and fulfilling personal relationships.

Relationship formation (including marriage and divorce)

Being in a relationship is generally good for a person's health and wellbeing. Being single is associated with many more health risks than being married. Researchers have found that people who are single tend to live less healthy lives than people who are married. Single people drink more because they tend to socialise more with friends, skip meals, work longer hours and don't have the same level of emotional support as people who are married. Married couples tend to have better diets, more comfortable homes and more stable lifestyles, especially if they also have children. The break-up of a relationship, such as a divorce, tends to have a negative effect on a person's health and wellbeing. Relationship breakdown is generally stressful and reduces a person's sense of emotional and social wellbeing and self-esteem. This is particularly the case where there is continuing conflict with a former partner or where one partner experiences distress because they can no longer be with their children.

Knowledge Check

1 Identify four different social, cultural or emotional factors that affect an individual's health and wellbeing.

2 How can relationships with family and friends contributes to health and wellbeing?

3 Describe how health education can affect an individual's health behaviour and lifestyle.

4 Name one positive effect that work can have on a person's health or wellbeing.

5 Describe the ways unemployment can have an impact on a person's health and wellbeing.

6 Which aspects of health and wellbeing are most likely to be affected by community involvement?

7 Give two examples that suggest different ethnic groups have differing experience of health and illness.

8 How, if at all, is a person's gender linked to their experience of health and illness?

9 How can a person's sexual orientation have an impact on their social and emotional wellbeing?

10 What effect can forming a relationship, such as marriage, have on a person's health and wellbeing?

Economic factors

Money is an economic factor linked to health and wellbeing in various ways. A person's health and wellbeing won't be good simply because they have a lot or even sufficient money to live on. The economic links between money and health are indirect – it is what money can buy and how people use their money that is important. It is also important to recognize that people who don't have enough money to meet their daily living needs are more likely to experience ill-health and poor wellbeing.

Income and wealth

The amount of money that people earn affects their lifestyle and their opportunities. People need enough money (adequate finance) to afford the basic necessities of life, such as food, housing and clothing, which directly affect physical health. People with more money generally have better housing and may eat better quality food. In this way money does affect basic physical health.

People who have a good income are also less likely to worry about being able to cope with everyday life. They don't

Over to you!

When we say that people need 'enough money', what do we mean? 'Enough' for what? For the basic necessities of life usually.

- Identify what you think are the basic necessities of life by completing this checklist.

- How much money would a person need (each week, month or year) to afford your list of basic necessities?

heating ❑	toys for children ❑
an indoor toilet ❑	a warm waterproof coat ❑
satellite TV ❑	a refrigerator ❑
a damp-free home ❑	access to a personal computer ❑
a washing machine ❑	carpets ❑
a bath or shower ❑	three meals a day ❑
a foreign holiday ❑	a bedroom for each child ❑
beds for everyone ❑	two pairs of all-weather shoes ❑
a mobile 'phone ❑	party celebrations ❑
money for public transport ❑	a roast dinner once a week ❑

Case study

Desmond is 35 and has been unemployed for the last six months. He currently lives on his own in a council-owned maisonette. He finds the days very long, boring and stressful. When he does get an interview for a job, he says that he finds the situation very difficult. In particular, he has a lack of self-confidence when talking about his skills and personal qualities. Desmond has had a variety of different jobs in both the building and catering industries in recent years. Currently all the jobs that he sees seem to require computer skills and experience. Desmond doesn't have access to the Internet at home and is cautious about using computers. He says that he feels that he's been 'left behind' and thinks he might be unemployable now. Desmond has no real plans for the future at the moment. He says that he's getting depressed and becoming demotivated in his search for work.

- How is unemployment affecting Desmond's emotional health and wellbeing?
- How might long-term unemployment affect Desmond's physical health?
- What advice or information would you give to Desmond to help him to improve his health and wellbeing?

experience the same stresses as people who are worried about paying their rent or feeding their children, for example. Having a good income allows people to buy luxuries such as holidays, cars, electrical goods and other desirable things. It also has a positive effect on self-esteem as money is highly valued in Western societies. People with lots of money are often seen in a positive way. Being rich and successful is seen as desirable.

Employment status and occupation

Some people live for their work and can't think of a better way to spend their time than by having a busy work life. What do these people get out of work? For many people, work is an important source of self-esteem and status. Work provides these people with a strong sense of emotional wellbeing. It gives them a feeling of being successful, of having a purpose and of being useful. Health workers who choose to be doctors or nurses often do so because they want to be useful and make a difference to peoples' lives. So, having a job that you enjoy, and which you feel is useful and important, can be good for your sense of emotional wellbeing.

Work also provides an opportunity to socialise and build relationships with others. Work is important for social wellbeing because it provides social stimulation as well as a routine and pattern to a person's day. Work gives people social status, confidence and self-respect.

Social class

A **social class** is a group of people who are similar in terms of their wealth, income and occupation. There are a number of different ways of identifying social classes in British society. These include:

- The 3-class scale – consisting of upper, middle and working-class groups. This is a popular but largely inaccurate and out-of-date way of defining a person's social class. It is not used in official statistics or by health and social care professionals to define a person's social class.

- The Registrar-General's scale – this was the official method of identifying social classes until 2001. A person's social class was defined by the occupation of the male head of their household. The scale consisted of six social classes that were organised into a hierarchy that linked occupations to social status.

Figure 3.10 The Registrar-General's Social Class Scale.

Social class	Types of occupation
Class 1 - Professional occupations	Lawyers, doctors
Class 2 - Intermediate occupations	Social workers, managers, shopkeepers
Class 3N – Skilled, non-manual occupations	Clerks, policemen, nurses
Class 3M – Skilled, manual occupations	Electricians, coal miners
Class 4 - Partly skilled occupations	Nursing assistants, farm workers, bus drivers
Class 5 – Unskilled	Porters, cleaners

- This NS-SEC (National Statistics – Socioeconomic Classification) scale is now the official way of identifying social class in Britain. This classification system is based around 8 classes that are designed to reflect the growth of middle-class occupations, the changing nature of work as well as the levels of social esteem that these jobs attract.

Figure 3.11 The NS-SEC.

Social class	Types of jobs included
Higher managerial and professional occupations	Doctors, lawyers, dentists, professors, professional engineers
Lower managerial and professional occupations	School teachers, nurses, journalists, actors, police sergeants
Intermediate occupations	Airline cabin crew, secretaries, photographers, firemen, auxiliary nurses
Small employers and own account workers	Self-employed builders, hairdressers, fishermen, car dealers and shop owners
Lower supervisory and technical occupations	Train drivers, employed craftsmen, foremen, supervisors
Semi-routine occupations	Shop assistants, postmen, security guards
Routine occupations	Bus drivers, waitresses, cleaners, car park attendants, refuse collectors
Never worked or long-term unemployed.	Students, people not classifiable, occupations not stated

Sociological research has repeatedly shown that social class has a greater effect on a person's life chances than other important factors such as their gender, ethnicity, age and experience of disability. Researchers using sociological methods have presented a wide range of data to show that significant and enduring patterns of health and illness experience are linked to social class. A persistent finding is that a person's social class is the most important predictor of health experience and mortality. In particular, the lower a person's social class position the more likely they are to:

- die, at any age, than their counterparts in higher social classes
- experience chronic illness than their counterparts in higher social classes.

Figure 3.12 Death rates using NS-SEC; men aged 25–64, England and Wales 2001–03.

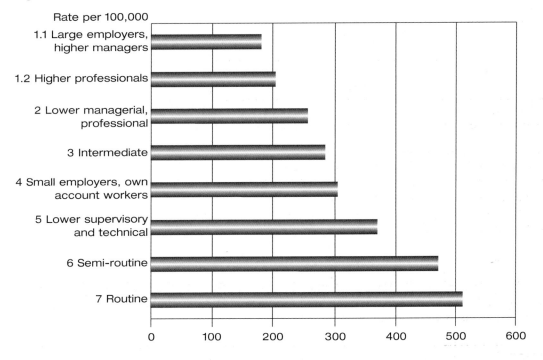

Poverty and material possessions

People who live in absolute poverty have insufficient income to meet their basic needs. People who live in relative poverty have enough money for their basic needs but relatively little money compared to other people. People living in relative poverty can afford the essentials but are unable to enjoy other activities and material possessions that others in their community take for granted. A person is defined as living in poverty in the UK if their income is less than 60% of the average household income.

There are very strong connections between poverty and ill health. The reasons for this are not completely clear-cut. It is possible that people who experience ill health are unable to work as effectively or as frequently as people who are in good health and so earn less money. However, poverty and low income can also be a cause of ill health. Poverty affects an individual's ability to afford a good diet, comfortable housing conditions,

UNIT 3

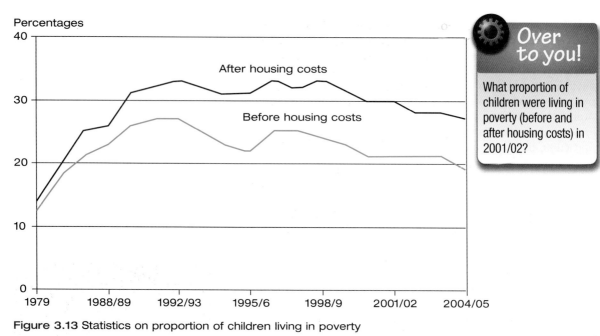

Figure 3.13 Statistics on proportion of children living in poverty

Over to you!

What proportion of children were living in poverty (before and after housing costs) in 2001/02?

stress-relieving holidays and leisure activities, for example. Statistics show that people living in poverty are more likely to experience:

● High infant mortality rates

● Greater risk of low birth weight

● Higher rates of mental health problems

● Higher rates of long-term illnesses.

Economic factors that affect health and wellbeing, income, employment, social class and poverty are all inter-linked. A lack of income, good employment opportunities and social status appear to be predictors of poor health experience.

Environmental factors

Where a person lives can have a direct effect on their health and wellbeing. If the quality of the physical environment is poor because of air and noise pollution or poor housing or the type of area in which the person lives limits their opportunities or causes them to feel stressed, their health and wellbeing may suffer.

Air pollution

Pollution happens when our natural surroundings (including the air, water and landscape) are contaminated with poisonous or harmful substances. Usually, though not always, this involves the release of high concentrations of a substance, such as human sewage or chemicals. Environmental pollution can remain in the environment for a long time, causing health problems for whole populations for many years.

Pollutants can affect the air, sea, waterways and land. Factories and cars that produce carbon-based fumes are common sources of air pollution. Often we only think about the smoke and fumes that we can see in the environment. However, other air

Knowledge Check

1 Identify three different economic factors that can affect health and wellbeing.

2 Describe two ways in which income can have a positive effect on a person's physical health and wellbeing.

3 Identify the social class classification system that is currently used in official statistics about health and illness.

4 How is an individual's social class likely to influence their experience of health and wellbeing?

5 When is a person living in 'poverty'?

6 Describe ways in which poverty can have an impact on physical health and wellbeing.

pollutants are less visible. For example, 'acid rain' is ordinary rainwater that has become acidic because it picks up residues of sulphur and nitrogen oxides that are produced by cars, power stations and other factories, often long distances away from where the rain falls. Acid rain is thought to make respiratory problems, such as asthma, worse because it irritates surface membranes in the lungs.

You may also have heard about 'greenhouse gases' and the 'ozone layer'. Greenhouse gases are chemicals which, when released into the atmosphere, reduce the ozone layer high above the Earth. The ozone is a layer of oxygen high in the atmosphere that acts as a sunscreen. Holes in the ozone layer, caused by the emission of greenhouse gases, result in harmful ultraviolet light beaming down from the sun. This type of pollution increases the risk of skin cancers.

Noise pollution

Noise pollution occurs when human or machine-made sound disrupts the activity or balance of a person's everyday life. Transport systems, particularly cars, airplanes and trains, are the main source of noise pollution. People who live in densely populated residential areas may also experience noise pollution, especially if they live near to industrial buildings.

Noise pollution can lower the quality of life of those people who are exposed to it. Chronic exposure to excessive noise is linked to tinnitus, increased stress levels, disturbed sleep patterns and hearing loss. The World Health Organization (WHO, 2008) has also produced research linking noise pollution to premature death from heart disease that is triggered by exposure to excessive levels of noise. It estimated that 3,030 of the 101,000 deaths from coronary heart disease in the UK in 2006 were caused by chronic noise exposure. The WHO guidelines on noise pollution say that chronic exposure to noise of 50 decibels or more – light traffic noise – may lead to cardiovascular problems. People who are exposed to 42 decibels or more are likely to experience sleep disturbance.

Housing conditions

A person's housing provides them with physical shelter and protection. This is important for physical health. However, the place where you live and spend most of your time is more than just somewhere to stay and keep warm and dry. 'Home' also provides people with a sense of emotional wellbeing and psychological security.

Poor housing can have a direct effect on a person's physical health. For example, lack of adequate heating, dampness and overcrowding can lead to respiratory disorders, stress and mental health problems. Lack of basic amenities (a shower or bath, for example), sharing facilities between too many people (kitchen or bathroom, for example) and cold, damp or unsafe buildings make some homes unfit to live in. Poor conditions like these can lead to health problems. Lack of security, too much noise and lack of privacy can also lead to high stress levels and loss of wellbeing.

Cold and damp housing aggravates many medical conditions, including asthma, bronchitis and other respiratory diseases, and rheumatism and arthritis. These conditions affect people of all

Sources of noise pollution

- Car engines and alarms
- Airplanes
- Trains
- Audio entertainment systems
- Power tools and construction work
- Office machinery
- Factory machinery
- Domestic appliances
- Lighting hum
- Barking dogs
- Noisy people.

Densely populated areas can be noisy and over-crowded.

ages, but are particularly serious for babies, infants and older people. Older people with low incomes sometimes have to choose between buying food and heating their homes. The consequence of not having enough heating can be hypothermia (a fall in body temperature to below 35°C – normal body temperature is 37°C).

Overcrowding encourages the spread of infection and infectious diseases such as tuberculosis and dysentery. Children who live in overcrowded homes are more likely to be victims of accidents. Sleeplessness and stress are also associated with overcrowding.

People living in high-rise tower blocks or bedsits may suffer from poor emotional wellbeing because of social isolation. This in turn can lead to depression and low self-esteem. Many high-rise blocks of flats were built in the UK during the 1950s and 60s (in the post-war years) when there was an acute housing need. The government's long-term plan is now to phase these buildings out and gradually replace them with more appealing housing that is suitable for the wider community. Most housing blocks built in the last few years do not extend beyond four floors.

Over to you!

What is healthy housing? Identify the features you feel are important in making a person's housing 'healthy'. Alternatively, identify the negative features that you would look out for if you were house or flat-hunting. Explain, in terms of their effect on health and wellbeing, why you would try to avoid housing that had these negative features.

Modern housing blocks are now low-rise rather than high-rise.

Case Study

Courtney is three years old. She lives with her mum in a bedsit flat on the edge of a large city. Courtney's mum is very caring and spends all of her time looking after her daughter. The flat where they live is cold and damp. A lot of traffic passes directly in front of the flat and there are few places where Courtney can play outside in the local area. As a result, Courtney doesn't go out very often. She also gets colds and chest infections quite often and is underweight for her age. Courtney's mum has very little money to spend on food, heating or clothes as she is unemployed and claiming benefits. She has recently applied to the council for a change of flat as she believes that her current housing conditions are harming Courtney's health and development.

- Identify two features of the bedsit flat in the case study that may have a negative effect on health

- Describe two modifications to the bedsit flat that would be beneficial for Courtney's health.

Rural/urban lifestyles

Urban lifestyles result from living in cities or large towns where there is a built-up environment, a relatively large and socially diverse population and a lot of hustle and bustle from everyday activities. In some ways this may be good for a person's health or wellbeing. For example, urban areas typically have a range of health and social care services available and provide many work and leisure opportunities for people. However, various physical features of the urban environment are also associated with stress and mental health problems. High population density, general 'hassle', lack of green spaces, noise exposure, litter, vacant housing, crime, drug selling and concerns about physical assault are features of urban living that have all been linked to poor mental health.

Generally there are thought to be a number of advantages to rural lifestyles. These include a closer, more supportive and safer community, an absence of stress, a sense of belonging, and a cleaner, more beautiful environment. For some people, these aspects of rural living are ideal and enhance their quality of life. However, for others there are downsides to rural life that can be harmful to health and wellbeing. A proportion of people living in rural communities may feel isolated and excluded from the local community, and may have problems adjusting to the place where they live. Health and social care services may be more difficult to access and there are likely to be fewer opportunities to meet others and socialise with people from diverse backgrounds.

In the end, urban and rural lifestyles provide both opportunities and challenges for everyone. What suits one person won't suit someone else. However, government statistics do show that where a person lives influences their overall standard of health and life expectancy as well as their general quality of life. Figure xx shows that there are marked variations in patterns of illness and death rates according to where people live.

Psychological factors.

Knowledge Check

1 Identify three examples of environmental factors that can affect an individual's health and wellbeing.

2 Using examples, explain what air pollution is and describe how it can affect health and wellbeing.

3 Identify two examples of noise pollution and describe their effects on health and wellbeing.

4 Which aspect of health and wellbeing is directly affected by inadequate housing?

5 Describe the main features of inadequate housing that are linked to health problems.

6 Explain how a person's housing conditions can affect their emotional wellbeing.

7 Explain how a rural lifestyle can have either a positive or a negative effect on health and wellbeing.

8 Explain how an urban lifestyle can have either a positive or a negative effect on health and wellbeing.

Psychological factors

Psychology is concerned with a person's inner, mental life. A person's thoughts, feelings and relationships are important psychological issues that can have an impact on their health and wellbeing. In particular, psychological factors such as stress levels and relationships with others are directly linked to a person's mental health and emotional wellbeing but also affect their physical health and social wellbeing too.

Stress

People often talk about 'feeling stressed' and stress has a bad reputation with health professionals. So, what is it? Stress is a response to the demands made on a person. Where the demands outweigh a person's ability to cope or adapt, they feel under pressure, threatened, tense or strained. This is 'stress'. It has both psychological and physical symptoms.

Extreme stress, either sudden or more long-term, produces uncomfortable symptoms and can lead to health problems. Stress becomes harmful when it is continuous, disrupts everyday life and relationships and becomes too difficult to cope with. Some people experience temporary health problems from which they recover when they manage to reduce their stress levels. For other people, stress has long-term health effects on both their physical and mental health. Stress can trigger mental health problems such as depression and anxiety-based illnesses.

Many different factors can cause 'stress'. Exams, assignments or being asked questions in class might do it for you. Other common causes of stress in people's lives include relationship problems, money worries, poor living or work conditions, having too much work to do and general lack of satisfaction in life.

Symptoms of stress

- muscle pain
- headaches
- feeling sick
- trembling
- sweating
- dry throat
- disturbed sleep
- changes in appetite
- stomach upset
- fast pulse rate
- feeling faint or dizzy
- irritability
- poor concentration
- feeling panicky.

Health problems associated with stress

- anxiety and depression
- eczema
- asthma
- migraine
- angina (pain around the heart muscle)
- high blood pressure
- heart attack
- stomach ulcers
- accidents.

What can people do to reduce or minimize stress? Exercise, recreation and leisure activity are particularly important for reducing stress levels. Having supportive relationships and satisfying work also helps. Increasingly, people use sports activities to help them to relax and de-stress. Massage, talking to others about problems and feelings, thinking positively and being assertive (saying 'no' to extra work!) are all good ways of reducing stress levels.

Over to you!

Identify three occasions when you've felt very stressed. What were your symptoms? What caused your stress? Make a note of these points or discuss them with a colleague in your class.

Case study

Neville is a 37-year-old plumber. He wants to retire as a rich, happy man when he is 50. Neville runs his own plumbing company, working between 60 and 80 hours every week. He is feeling under a lot of pressure at the moment. Neville has complained to his wife that he has had a headache for a week, feels faint at times and is having trouble sleeping. Neville will not go and see his GP as he says he is too busy. His wife is trying to persuade him to take a holiday but he is reluctant to do so because of the amount of work he has to do.

- What symptoms of stress does Neville have?
- What might be causing Neville's current stress problems?
- Explain what might happen to Neville's health and wellbeing if he continues to experience high stress levels.
- Suggest some changes that Neville could make to his lifestyle to reduce his high stress levels.

Relationships

Relationships within the family, with partners or with friends can contribute positively to an individual's health and wellbeing if they are supportive and meet the individual's social and emotional needs. Supportive relationships are good for a person's self-esteem and self-concept. However, relationships can also be a source of problems and can affect a person's emotional wellbeing and mental health if things go wrong or difficulties occur. People who find themselves in unequal relationships where they are subject to bullying, personal criticism or are not given love, affection and respect by their relatives, partner or friends may develop low self-esteem, a negative self-concept and mental health problems such as anxiety and depression.

> ### Knowledge Check
>
> 1 Briefly, explain what 'stress' is.
> 2 Identify five physical symptoms of stress
> 3 Describe how stress can have a negative effect on an individual's health and wellbeing.
> 4 Using examples, describe the reasons why teenagers sometimes experience levels of stress that can harm their health or wellbeing.
> 5 Describe the positive and negative impact that close relationships can have on an individual's social and emotional wellbeing.

Health monitoring and illness prevention

Health care practitioners provide a range of services that are designed to prevent people from becoming ill and to promote a healthy lifestyle. Services are usually provided for particular client groups, or to deal with particular health problems. For example, illness prevention services include:

- **Vaccinations** against infectious diseases such as polio, diphtheria and measles; against viruses, such as influenza (flu), that affect many older people; and against tropical diseases, such as malaria, that can affect overseas travellers visiting areas where the virus is prevalent.

- Advice and information services to help people change their unhealthy behaviour and live healthier lives. GPs, for example, provide advice about stopping smoking and ways of losing weight.

- Classes where health workers teach people ways of improving their health. For example, relaxation, pilates and yoga for people who are stressed, or opportunities for people to meet and talk about their problems.

The general health of the UK population is much better now than it was at the beginning of the twentieth century. The evidence for this can be seen in the much higher proportion of children who survive early childhood and the fact that both men and women can now expect to live much longer lives. The widespread use of screening and vaccination has been important in this.

Screening

Screening is a health monitoring strategy. It is used to detect disease in individuals who have no obvious signs or symptoms of that disease. The aim of screening is to identify disease early enough to treat people and hopefully prevent them becoming more unwell. Common screening tests for adults include blood pressure measurement, blood cholesterol tests, cervical smears and mammograms for breast cancer. Screening tests can help with early diagnosis of health problems and plays a key part in enabling early treatment. However, screening tests can also lead to misdiagnosis and give some people who were thought to be clear of a particular disease a false sense of security if symptoms do occur at a later stage.

Vaccination

Vaccination is an illness prevention strategy. It involves giving an individual a vaccine (usually but not always by injection) that produces immunity to a disease. Vaccinations are the most clinically effective and cost-effective way of preventing infectious diseases. Babies and young children are given a number of vaccines as part of an immunisation programme (see figure 3.14) to protect them from infectious diseases. Older people (65+ years) and those with chronic heart and respiratory diseases are also encouraged to have an influenza ('flu) vaccination each year.

Figure 3.14 Typical immunisation programme.

Vaccine	When given
Diptheria Tetanus Pertussis (whooping cough) Polio Hib (*Haemophilus Influenzae*) Pneumococcal infection	2 months
Diptheria Tetanus Pertussis (whooping cough) Polio Hib (*Haemophilus Influenzae*) Meningitis	3 months
Diptheria Tetanus Pertussis (whooping cough) Polio Hib (*Haemophilus Influenzae*) Meningitis Pneumococcal infection	4 months
Meningitis C and Hib	Around 12 months
MMR (Measles, mumps, rubella) Pneumococcal infection	Around 13 months
Diptheria Tetanus Pertussis (whooping cough) Polio MMR	3 years
Human papillomavirus (cause of cervical cancer)	Girls 12–13 years
Diptheria Tetanus Polio	13–18 years

Investigate ...

Look at the immunisation programme. Research three of the diseases that are listed in Figure 3.14 on the left. Use the information to make a leaflet or poster that informs parents about the dangers of these diseases.

Health monitoring can also be carried out using simple self-monitoring techniques that can be learnt, such as breast or testicle self-examination. Checking your weight, looking after your skin and hair and having regular dental check ups and eye tests are also ways of monitoring personal health. Using health monitoring and illness prevention services, and assessing your own health regularly, are important to achieve and maintain good physical health and wellbeing.

Testicular cancer

Testicular (or testes) cancer is now the most common form of cancer in men aged 20 to 34. More than 8 out of 10 people who get it are cured.

Men – know your body
1. Anus
2. Scrotum
3. Urethra
4. Penis
5. Foreskin
6. Glans
7. Testicles

Symptoms
An enlargement or 'hardness' of the whole testicle or a lump in part of one testicle. It is usually painless but some men notice an ache or 'heavy' feeling in the affected testicle. Testicular cancer usually affects only one of the testicles.

Cancers found early are those most easily cured. You should regularly carry out a self-examination after a warm shower or bath, when the skin of the scrotum is relaxed.

Who is at risk?
Potentially all men are at risk. However:

• men with an undescended testicle (absent testicle) who did not have the problem surgically corrected in early childhood are 5 times more likely to contract testicular cancer

• men between the ages of 20 and 34 are most at risk

• other risk factors include a close relative who has had testicular cancer (for example, father or son)

Case study

Gemma is 30 years old. She has been trying to get pregnant since marrying Phil 2 years ago. When she made an appointment with her GP, Gemma was hoping that there might be a quick and simple solution to the problem. Dr Foster, her GP, said he would need to take a range of health measures and carry out some checks to assess her current state of physical health. He also talked to Gemma about her lifestyle and health behaviour. At the end of the consultation, Gemma was encouraged to eat a more nutritious, balanced diet, to lose some weight and to enrol in relaxation and Pilates classes. Dr Foster said that Gemma should also monitor her own health for the next three months to see if the changes she made had any effect. He reminded her that being in good physical health would help her to conceive.

● What aspects of Gemma's physical health would you expect Dr Foster to check?

● How could Gemma monitor her own health over the next three months?

● What kind of health monitoring and screening services are available to young women like Gemma in your local area?

Knowledge Check

1 Name two methods used by health care practitioners to prevent ill-health.

2 Describe one way in which a person can monitor their own physical health.

3 Name three health problems or diseases that people can be screened for.

4 Explain what screening involves.

5 Identify four infectious diseases which children under the age of 1 are vaccinated against.

6 Explain what vaccination involves.

Topic review

The box below provides a summary of the areas covered in Topic 3.2. Tick the areas that you feel you understand and would be confident about when writing your assignment. If there are any areas that you don't understand or are not confident about, you will need to return to them before you begin planning or writing your assignment.

Physical factors
Genetic inheritance ☐
Illness and disease ☐
Diet ☐
Exercise ☐
Alcohol ☐
Smoking ☐

Social, cultural and emotional factors
Family ☐
Friends ☐
Educational experiences ☐
Employment / unemployment ☐
Community involvement ☐
Religion, culture and ethnicity ☐
Gender ☐
Sexual orientation ☐
Relationship formation ☐

Economic factors
Income and wealth ☐
Occupation and employment status ☐
Social class ☐
Poverty and material possessions ☐

Physical environment factors
Pollution ☐
Noise ☐
Housing conditions ☐
Rural / urban lifestyles ☐

Psychological factors
Stress ☐
Relationships (family, friends, partners) ☐

Assessment Guide

Your learning in this unit will be assessed through a controlled assignment. This will be set by Edexcel and marked by your tutor.

The assignment will require you to plan and carry out investigations and produce a health improvement plan in response to case study material provided by Edexcel about the health and wellbeing of an individual.

You will need to show evidence of understanding:

● Factors which affect health and wellbeing

● The effects of the factors affecting health and wellbeing

Topic 3.3

Indicators of physical health

Topic focus

The previous topic outlined a variety of factors that can affect a person's health and wellbeing. These include factors that promote good health, such as exercise and a balanced diet, and cigarette smoking which is harmful to health. But how can we know whether a person is healthy or not? One way is to measure specific aspects (indicators) of their physical health. This topic will focus on what these indicators are, how they can be measured and how the results of health assessments can be used to develop realistic health improvement plans. We will look at the following indicators of physical health:

- Blood pressure
- Peak flow
- Body Mass Index
- Hip/waist ratio measures
- Body fat composition
- Cholesterol levels
- Blood glucose tests
- Liver function tests
- Pulse rate.

Topic 3.3 will help you to understand how and why physical health is measured. It won't teach you how to make these measures yourself but will help you to understand how they are used by health care practitioners to develop realistic health improvement plans for service users.

Ways of measuring physical health

You've probably had aspects of your physical health measured many times. This will have happened when you visited your GP (family doctor) or if you've ever been to hospital for assessment or treatment. You've probably also watched television programmes set in hospitals where people seem to spend a lot of time checking the state of their patients' health.

So, how can health care practitioners tell if a person is physically healthy or not? There are, in fact, many different ways of measuring physical health. They are all based on the same basic idea – the health care practitioner measures and records something and then compares the individual's 'score' against a standard scale. You are probably familiar with the way that blood

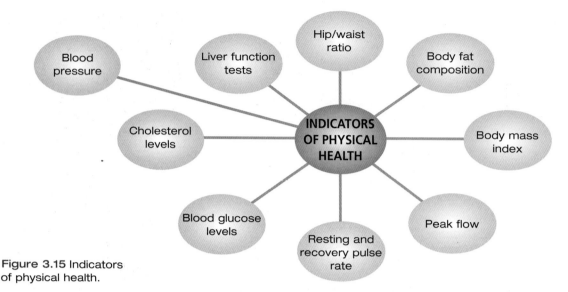

Figure 3.15 Indicators of physical health.

pressure and pulse are measured. However, there are a range of other techniques that provide useful information about physical health too.

Blood pressure

Health care professionals routinely measure their patient's blood pressure as well as their pulse rate. Blood pressure measurement is a direct way of checking heart functioning, and indirectly physical fitness.

When a person's blood pressure is checked, two measurements are taken. The force, or pressure, which the blood puts on the walls of the artery when the heart beats is one of these measurements. This is known as the **systolic blood pressure**. The continuous pressure that the person's blood puts on the arteries between heart beats is the second measurement of blood pressure. This is known as the **diastolic blood pressure**. A person's blood pressure reading is recorded and written as two numbers. The systolic measure comes first, followed by the diastolic measure. On average, a healthy young adult will have a blood pressure reading of 120/80 mm Hg (millimetres of mercury).

Blood pressure is measured with an instrument called a sphygmomanometer or 'sphyg' for short. Some health care professionals use electronic sphygs which measure automatically and display the results on a screen. The other way of measuring blood pressure is to use a manual sphyg.

A person's blood pressure fluctuates throughout the day and night. It increases when the person is active and decreases when they are inactive, resting or sleeping. A person's blood pressure will usually be taken when they are resting. A younger adult should have lower blood pressure than an older adult. If a person's blood pressure is higher or lower than average for a person of their age, it will need to be checked on several more occasions to establish whether this is caused by a health problem. Consistently high blood pressure (hypertension) is linked to a higher risk of heart attacks and strokes. Low blood pressure (hypotension) may be an indicator of heart failure, dehydration or other underlying health problems.

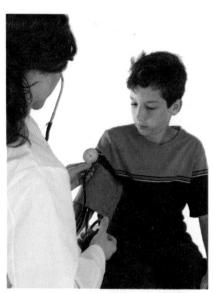

Using a manual 'sphyg'.

Over to you!

Find out what effect each of the following can have on a person's blood pressure:

- a diet high in fat and salt
- regular exercise
- stress
- cigarette smoking.

Peak flow

A person's respiratory health (breathing) can be assessed by recording simple physical measurements. One way of doing this is to use a peak flow meter. You may have seen or used a peak flow meter, especially if you have asthma or have had other respiratory health checks. A person is asked to take a deep breath and then breathe out as hard as they can into the peak flow meter.

A peak flow meter measures the maximum rate at which air is expelled (pushed out) from the lungs when a person breathes out as hard as they can. This is an example of a pulmonary function test. A healthy adult should record a peak flow result of 400–600 litres of air per minute. Peak flow tests are used to monitor several aspects of respiratory function. For example, the peak flow meter can be used to diagnose whether a person has a problem with the use of their lungs, because there is a standard scale of expected scores against which the results can be compared. People with chronic (long-term) asthma usually record a measurement that is lower than 350 on the peak flow scale when they breathe out as hard as they can.

Using a peak flow meter.

Body Mass Index

The relationship between height and weight can be an indicator of good or ill-health in adults. Health professionals recommend that a person's weight should be in proportion to their height. A person is considered obese when their weight is more than 20 per cent above the average weight for people of the same height. People who are obese or whose weight is much greater than recommended run the risk of developing a range of health problems.

Health professionals use the Body Mass Index (BMI) to assess whether a person is overweight. Unlike blood pressure measurement, you don't need to undertake any training to measure a person's BMI. Body Mass Index is calculated by dividing a person's weight in kilograms by their height in metres squared. This produces a number which is then checked against the categories in the table below.

Health problems associated with obesity

- arthritis
- high blood pressure
- increased risk of stroke
- diabetes
- gallstones
- heart disease.

Figure 3.16 - BMI.

Female BMI	Indicates	Male BMI	Indicates
Under 18	Underweight	Under 18	Underweight
18–20	Lean	18–20	Lean
21–22	Normal	21–23	Normal
23–28	Overweight	24–32	Overweight
29–36	Obese	32–40	Obese

In most cases a person's BMI result will provide some useful information about their physical health. Being over or underweight can have significant negative effects on physical health, for example. However, one of the limitations of BMI scores is that they don't take a person's body shape and composition into account. A very fit and muscular person, such as a rugby player or weightlifter, may have a lot of heavy muscle and little fat. Their BMI score may still suggest they are overweight or even obese when this isn't the case.

Hip/waist ratio measurements

Measurement of a person's hip/waist ratio provides a way of assessing the proportion of body fat that is stored around their waist and hips. People tend to store fat either around their middle (giving them an apple shape) or around their hips (giving them a pear shape). People who carry extra fat around their waist have an increased risk of developing health problems compared to people who carry extra weight around their hips or thighs.

The hip/waist ratio is calculated by measuring the circumference of the waist (located just above the hip bone) and dividing it by the circumference of the hips at their widest point. A hip/waist ratio of about 0.7 for women and 0.9 for men is associated with good general health and fertility. Research has shown that women within the 0.7 range are also less likely to develop diabetes, cardiovascular disorders or ovarian cancers. Men within the 0.9 range are also healthier, more fertile and less likely to develop prostate or testicular cancers.

Body fat composition

Measuring a person's body fat composition is a way assessing how much fat they are carrying in comparison to muscle. A person's body shape and health will both be affected by their body fat composition. The exact percentage of body fat a person has generally cannot be determined, but there are several techniques which can be used to accurately estimate it:

- Skinfold tests involve a pinch of skin being measured precisely by calipers at several points on the body. This allows an estimate to be made of the thickness of the person's subcutaneous fat layer. This way of measuring body fat is imprecise but does provide a method of charting changes in body fat composition over a period of time if the skinfold test is repeated.
- Bioelectrical impedence machines can be used to send an electrical impulse through the body. The signal travels quickly through lean tissue and more slowly through fat. The machine can use the information provided by the signal to work out a person's body fat composition.

Cholesterol levels

Cholesterol is a lipid, or fat substance, that is needed to allow the human body to function normally. However, there are two main types of cholesterol – 'good' cholesterol (HDL) and 'bad' cholesterol (LDL). **LDL cholesterol** is carried through the blood to the body's cells. The cells take the cholesterol they need, leaving any excess in the blood. High levels of LDL cholesterol in the blood are associated with a narrowing of the arteries, heart attacks and strokes. **HDL cholesterol**, by contrast, is extra cholesterol produced by the body's tissues that gets transported to the liver where the body eliminates it. This kind of cholesterol is thought to protect against heart disease.

Over to you!

1 Is your BMI measure within or outside of the normal range? If outside, how can you adjust your health-related behaviour to bring it within the normal, healthy range?

2 You can find more information on weight, BMI and weight measurement on several websites. Try those listed below or carry out a search of your own:
- www.teenagehealthfreak.com
- www.surgerydoor.co.uk
- www.weightlossresources.co.uk

Some websites will calculate your BMI for you if you know your height and weight figures.

Cholesterol levels are measured through a blood test. The test results will usually show overall cholesterol levels and the figures for LDL and HDL cholesterol. The overall amount of cholesterol in the blood can range from 3.6–7.8 mmol/litre. Levels of cholesterol above 6 mmol/litre are seen as high and are associated with a narrowing of the arteries. Healthy levels of cholesterol are:

- Total cholesterol – less than 5 mmol/L
- LDL cholesterol – less than 3 mmol/L
- HDL cholesterol – more than 1 mmol/L.

Blood glucose levels

Blood glucose levels are also measured through blood tests. Blood is made up of a number of different kinds of cells and other compounds. One of these is glucose (a sugar). Blood glucose levels refer to the amount of glucose present in a person's blood. Glucose is a main source of energy for human body cells, particularly those in the brain and nervous system. The concentration of blood glucose is normally closely controlled by the human body. It stays within quite narrow limits (4–8 mmol/litre) throughout the day. Blood glucose levels are higher after meals and lowest in the morning before breakfast has been eaten.

If a person's blood glucose levels drop too low they develop a condition called hypoglycaemia. The symptoms of this are lethargy, reduced mental functioning, irritability and loss of consciousness. Brain damage and death can result from severe hypoglycaemia. If a person's blood glucose is too high they develop a condition called hyperglycaemia. Diabetes is the most common long-term health problem resulting from a failure of the body to control blood glucose levels. Abnormally high or low blood glucose levels can also indicate that a person has other underlying health problems that are affecting their blood glucose levels.

A number of different methods can be used to measure a person's blood glucose levels. These include:

- Random glucose tests. This is carried out on two separate occasions. The person's finger is pricked to draw blood, this is then wiped onto a special strip and inserted in a machine that identifies the blood glucose level. A reading above 11.1 mmol/l usually indicates diabetes.

- Fasting glucose tests. This test is carried out in the same way as the random glucose test, again on two separate occasions. However, the person is tested after fasting overnight. A reading above 7.0mmol/l usually indicates diabetes.

- The glucose tolerance test. The individual being tested has to fast, usually overnight, for between 8 and 14 hours. The person's blood glucose levels are then measured. They are then given a special drink that contains glucose. The person's blood glucose levels are repeatedly measured after 30, 60, 90 and 120 minutes. A reading above 11.1 mmol/l after two hours is an indication of diabetes. A reading below 7.8mmol/l is normal.

Liver function tests

A liver function test is a blood test that is carried out by a qualified health care practitioner who sends a sample of blood to

Promoting Health and Wellbeing

a specialist medical laboratory for analysis. Liver function tests provide information about the state of a person's liver. They are a way of detecting and diagnosing liver diseases that may be causing symptoms such as jaundice, loss of appetite and bloody or black bowel movements. Liver function tests report on the presence and levels of enzymes and proteins in the blood that are produced by the liver.

Resting pulse and recovery pulse after exercise

The pulse rate, both before and after exercise, is often used to determine a person's general health or physical fitness. The pulse rate indicates how fast the heart is beating. For adults, the average (or normal) resting rate is usually between 70 and 80 beats per minute. Babies and young children normally have a faster pulse rate than adults.

The pulse can be felt at any artery. In conscious people, it is usual to use the **radial artery**, which can be felt at the wrist. In unconscious people, the **carotid artery**, which can be felt at the neck, may be used (Most conscious people would find it uncomfortable if you pressed on their carotid artery!). A person's pulse rate increases when they exercise, when they are emotionally upset, or if they develop a form of heart or respiratory disease. Unfit people, smokers and overweight people have a faster resting pulse rate than normal.

Taking a radial pulse.

Knowledge Check

1 Identify five different indicators of physical health that health care practitioners can measure and monitor.

2 Identify and describe two methods of measuring a person's cardiac (heart) health.

3 Using your own words, explain what the systolic and diastolic numbers in a blood pressure reading are measuring.

4 Explain what a high diastolic measurement would tell you about a person's blood pressure.

5 Explain the purpose and use of a peak flow meter.

6 Identify the two measures needed to calculate a person's Body Mass Index (BMI).

7 What effects can obesity have on an individual's health and wellbeing?

8 Describe two ways of measuring a person's body fat.

9 Describe how a cholesterol test is carried out.

10 Explain why high cholesterol levels are likely to lead to health problems.

11 What do blood glucose tests measure?

12 What health problems might high and low levels of blood glucose be an indicator of?

Over to you!

How might each of the following factors have an impact on an individual's pulse rate?
- Stress
- Blood loss
- Drugs
- Strenuous exercise
- Age
- Infection
- Sleep.

Investigate ...

Measure your own, or another person's, pulse rate (using the radial pulse!) for one minute. Compare the resting pulse rate with the pulse rate taken after some brief exercise.

Topic Review

The box below provides a summary of the areas covered in Topic 3.3. Tick the areas that you feel you understand and would be confident about when writing your assignment. If there are any areas that you don't understand or are not confident about, you will need to return to them before you begin planning or writing your assignment.

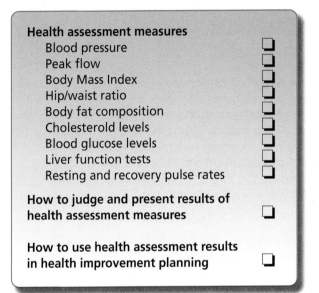

Health assessment measures
Blood pressure ❑
Peak flow ❑
Body Mass Index ❑
Hip/waist ratio ❑
Body fat composition ❑
Cholesterold levels ❑
Blood glucose levels ❑
Liver function tests ❑
Resting and recovery pulse rates ❑

How to judge and present results of health assessment measures ❑

How to use health assessment results in health improvement planning ❑

Assessment Guide

Your learning in this unit will be assessed through a controlled assignment. This will be set by Edexcel and marked by your tutor.

The assignment will require you to plan and carry out investigations and produce a health improvement plan in response to case study material provided by Edexcel about the health and wellbeing of an individual.

You will need to show evidence of understanding:

● Methods used to measure individual physical health.

UNIT 3

Topic 3.4

Promoting and supporting health improvement

Topic focus

Have you ever set yourself a goal of 'being healthier' or 'getting fit'? A common time to do this is just after Christmas, when people often feel they've had too much to eat or drink, or a few months before going on holiday. We've probably all wanted to improve our health and wellbeing at one time or another. However, health improvement needs to be based on more than good intentions. Topic 3.4 will help you to apply the knowledge and understanding you have about factors that affect health and wellbeing and about measures of health to health improvement situations. It will show you how to design a health and wellbeing improvement plan for an individual or group of individuals. Your plan will need to include:

- An assessment of the present health status of the individual or group.
- Appropriate health promotion materials to motivate and support the person or people involved.
- A clear health and wellbeing improvement plan that includes both short- and long-term targets.
- An assessment of the difficulties the person may experience in implementing the health and wellbeing improvement plan.
- An outline of support needed to implement the plan.

Designing a health improvement plan (HIP)

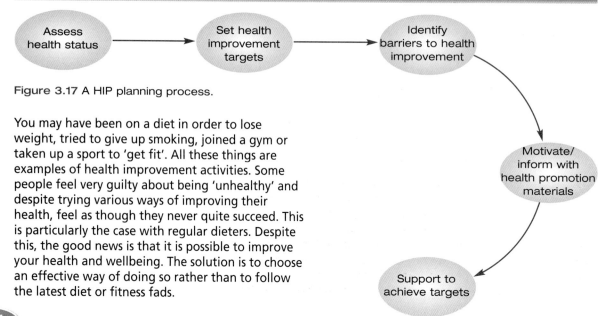

Figure 3.17 A HIP planning process.

You may have been on a diet in order to lose weight, tried to give up smoking, joined a gym or taken up a sport to 'get fit'. All these things are examples of health improvement activities. Some people feel very guilty about being 'unhealthy' and despite trying various ways of improving their health, feel as though they never quite succeed. This is particularly the case with regular dieters. Despite this, the good news is that it is possible to improve your health and wellbeing. The solution is to choose an effective way of doing so rather than to follow the latest diet or fitness fads.

Assessing health status

Health improvement planning should begin with thorough and honest health assessment. This involves collecting basic health-related information and also measuring physical health indicators. Figure 3.18 identifies the lifestyle issues that a health care professional might ask about and the range of physical measures they may take as part of an individual's health assessment.

Figure 3.18 Health assessment information

Lifestyle information	Physical measures
Dietary intake	Height
Amount of sleep	Weight
Units of alcohol consumed	Pulse (before and after exercise)
Exercise pattern	Blood pressure
Use of cigarettes or drugs	Cholesterol levels
	Blood glucose levels
	Body Mass Index (BMI)
	Hip/waist ratio

The information that the health practitioner collects is used to provide a baseline, or starting point, from which to work. The service user who is motivated to improve their health may be asked to complete a questionnaire or might be interviewed about their health and wellbeing by the health care practitioner to obtain this information. In some cases service users are asked to keep a health and lifestyle diary for a couple of weeks. The aim is to record what they eat and drink, their sleep and exercise pattern, and their cigarette and alcohol consumption, for example. The health diary, combined with physical measures, enables the practitioner to identify some of the factors (such as lack of exercise, poor diet) that may be contributing to a health problem (such as obesity). It also provides a basis on which to set realistic improvement targets.

Before any health improvement targets are identified, it is important to compare the service user's physical health measures to those recommended or expected for someone of their age and physical characteristics. This allows the care practitioner to identify whether, and if so how far, any of the person's physical health indicators (blood pressure, for example) are outside the expected range and a cause for concern. The health care practitioner will then know which areas they need to concentrate on to improve the service user's physical health and wellbeing.

Setting health improvement targets

The next stage is to set targets for improvement. Health care practitioners must ensure that the health improvement targets they set for service users are safe, realistic and achievable. For example, it is important not to plan for unrealistically rapid weight loss that can only be achieved through 'crash dieting' or exercise binges. People regain weight lost in this way very quickly and can damage their physical health in the process. Instead, there should be a clear, logical plan for setting particular health

Investigate ...

Talk to somebody who helps others to 'get fit' – such as a PE teacher, a personal fitness trainer or an aerobics instructor. Find out how they assess fitness, how they set targets and what methods they use to motivate people to improve their fitness.

Case study

Philip (17), Lara (19), Erica (44) and Pauline (62) all work in a nursing home for older people. They have recently volunteered to take part in a health improvement programme being run by the local primary care trust. Each member of the group has agreed to have their physical health measured and to provide some basic lifestyle information. This will help the primary care staff to assess their current state of health and develop a health improvement plan for each individual. The health measurements that have been recorded are provided below.

Measure	Philip	Lara	Erica	Pauline
Height	6′1″	5′8″	5′4″	5′2″
Weight	13.5 stone	7 stone	14 stone	8.5 stone
Resting pulse	80 per minute	65 per minute	125 per minute	87 per minute
Blood pressure	120/80	90/65	200/135	135/85
Cigarettes per week	None	Smokes 10 cigarettes a day	Smokes 10 cigarettes a day	None
Units of alcohol per week	Drinks beer. 6 units per week	Drinks vodka. 30 units per week	Drinks lager. 40 units per week	Drinks wine. 10 units per week
Hours of exercise	Football 3 hours. Gym 3 hours	Gym 7 hours	None	Yoga. 2 hours. Walking 2 hours
Diet	Eats a regular balanced diet	Eats snacks and salads. Avoids fatty food	Eats a lot of burgers, chips and kebabs	Eats a regular balanced diet

- Who do you think is the most healthy and least healthy person out of the four people in this group? Give clear reasons for your choices.

- Describe the ways in which the remaining two members of the group appear to be healthy or unhealthy.

- Identify three lifestyle factors that should be taken into account when interpreting the various health measurements.

improvement targets that can be achieved in a reasonable timescale. Many health care practitioners set short, medium and long-term targets, and build in regular reviews, so that service users can see their progress and address any difficulties they are having in reaching the targets.

The methods that are used to work towards, and achieve, health improvement targets should be safe and, ideally, should fit in with the service user's current lifestyle. For example, improving physical fitness can be achieved in many different ways. Walking more, cycling to school or work or going to an exercise class once a week are all relatively straightforward and won't disrupt a person's lifestyle too much. Running a marathon or swimming the English Channel may enable the person to achieve the same weight loss or fitness targets but probably aren't realistic or safe methods of doing so! An individual is not likely to achieve or benefit from such ambitious targets.

It is important to view health improvement as a gradual process that needs to be worked at. Sudden changes in weight, fitness or behaviour are unlikely to be maintained. If you need to develop a health improvement plan for another person, remember to take their age and physical characteristics into account when conducting the health assessment. You will also need to ensure that the person agrees with the health improvement targets and is personally motivated to achieve them. If not, they'll never reach them.

Using health promotion materials

There are a range of different types of health promotion material available on a wide variety of health-related subjects. Health care practitioners use health promotion materials to raise awareness of health issues, to motivate people to change their health behaviours and to support people who set themselves health improvement targets. The particular type of health promotion material that a health care practitioner chooses will generally be selected because of its particular advantages and because it is appropriate in the circumstances. Figure 3.19 below identifies a number of different types of health promotion material and outlines some of their strengths and limitations.

Figure 3.19 Strengths and limitations of health promotion materials.

Over to you!

Develop a simple but realistic plan for improving your personal health and wellbeing.

- Collect information about the health-related aspects of your lifestyle and record as many of your basic physical indicators of health as you can. You may want to produce a diary for the first part of this task and get some help in doing the second part.
- Compare your personal results to those recommended for someone of your age and physical characteristics.
- Identify those aspects of your health you need to improve and set yourself a couple of short, medium and long-term targets.
- Identify ways of working towards and reaching your targets.

Health promotion material	Strengths	Limitations
Leaflets	- Can be read in own time - Easy and cheap to make - Can summarise a lot of information	- Information can be too general - Requires good reading skills - Easy to ignore or lose
Videos	- Can show real-life situations - Easy to use and engage with - Can be seen by a lot of people	- Requires specialist equipment - Can become out dated quickly - Viewers may not think about what they watch
Posters	- Easy way to raise awareness of a topic or issue - Can give basic information to a lot of people - Easy and cheap to produce	- Can deteriorate quickly - People learn to ignore them/don't read
Websites	- Can provide a lot of information to a lot of people - Can be easily updated - Can be viewed/used in own time - Can be eye-catching and interactive	- Requires computer and internet access - Not suitable for all age groups - Need to know website exists and be able to find it on Internet

Investigate ...

Visit places in your local area where you would expect to find health promotion information. These might include your GP surgery, local library, a sports centre or a youth club. Identify examples of health promotion material on display. Write a brief report describing the information that was available, explaining who it was aimed at and what the health messages were. You could also say whether you think the material and the way it was presented was effective and what other information could be displayed or provided to promote health improvement.

UNIT 3

Identifying barriers to health improvement

A number of factors are likely to influence the effectiveness and ultimately the success of a health improvement plan. These are summarised in the table below:

Figure 3.20 Factors affecting health improvement plans.

Factor	Positive effect	Negative effect
Motivation	The person has enough willpower and the desire to succeed	The person lacks commitment and loses heart easily
Involvement	The person identifies their own targets	The person doesn't understand or agree with the targets
Values	The person sees health and fitness as important	The person doesn't see the need to change their health behaviour
Stress levels	The person is not too stressed by work and personal life	The person is already very stressed and can't cope with more changes
Peer and social pressure	The person responds positively to encouragement of others to change health behaviour	The person feels embarrassed by or rejects encouragement of others to change health behaviour
Self-concept	The person is able to adjust their self-concept to see themselves as fit and 'healthy'	The person is reluctant to change self-concept or doesn't accept they can be fit and 'healthy'.

Case study

Men don't often talk to each other about their personal health and wellbeing. They are also less likely than women to visit their GP if they do have health concerns. This means that some men don't get the appropriate treatment for health problems that could be prevented or cured. Avoiding contact with health care services and being unaware of disease symptoms may result in some men developing serious health conditions, such as testicular or prostate cancers, that become untreatable.

- Suggest some aims for a health promotion campaign targeted at men.
- What methods could be used to promote both health awareness and a preventive approach to health with men as the target group? Explain why you would use these methods.
- What barriers would your health promotion campaign have to overcome before it made a difference to men's health?

Over to you!

Teenagers are very sensitive about being 'told what to do' even if this is intended as health promotion advice. Imagine that you are a health promotion officer. You've been asked to:

- Identify three key health topics affecting teenagers.
- Suggest a health message for each topic about which teenagers ought to be aware.
- Propose a way of getting each health message across to the teenage target group.

Think about this health promotion challenge and write down your suggestions.

Supporting implementation of the HIP

An individual who has begun their health improvement plan and is working to achieve their targets is likely to need help and support to keep going and reach their goals. Health care practitioners use a range of strategies to support the implementation of health improvement plans that they develop with service users. These include:

- Using diaries and record-keeping forms to help the person monitor their own progress and their feelings about the plan or the targets they have to achieve.

- Encouraging people to attend support groups, or contribute to online forums with other individuals who are also seeking to improve their health. Some health care practitioners help service users to establish supportive 'buddy relationships' with others in a similar position so that they can talk to and support each other.

- Using substitutes, such as nicotine patches, or recommending lower fat or lower calorie alternatives to foods that a person has difficulty giving up.

- Reward systems, such as scoring or grading improvements, identifying a slimmer of the week or month, for example, or encouraging the person to treat themselves as a personal reward for making progress towards their targets.

- Review meetings that acknowledge difficulties and give positive feedback to the person for their efforts and the progress they have made. Review meetings also allow the health care practitioner and the service user to adjust targets if they reach them early or if they appear to be unrealistic.

Case study

Elsie Stevens is a 60-year-old woman. Since recently retiring from her job as a secretary, Elsie has decided that she needs to get fit to make the most of her retirement. Elsie currently does no exercise at all. She is two stone overweight. In her youth, Elsie was a keen swimmer and also enjoyed walking.

- Suggest three types of exercise Elsie could take as a way of reducing her weight and getting fitter. Explain how these particular choices would benefit Elsie and also fit into her lifestyle.

- Plan a three-month exercise/activity programme for Elsie based on the range of opportunities and facilities available in your local area. Set out your programme in a table format.

Knowledge Check

1 Identify three factors that must be assessed before a health improvement plan can be written.

2 Describe how health behaviour and lifestyle can be assessed as part of a health improvement programme.

3 Explain why individual health assessment and target setting are essential before an effective health improvement plan can be constructed.

4 Explain why it might be damaging to an individual's health to set unrealistic health improvement targets.

5 Identify a range of factors that are likely to affect the success of a health improvement plan.

6 Describe four different forms of health promotion material that can be used to deliver health improvement messages to the general population.

7 How can an individual be motivated and supported to improve their health?

Topic review

The box below provides a summary of the areas covered in Topic 3.4. Tick the areas that you feel you understand and would be confident about when writing your assignment. If there are any areas that you don't understand or are not confident about, you will need to return to them before you begin planning or writing your assignment.

Health improvement planning

Assessment of health status ☐

Identifying health improvement targets ☐

Designing health improvement plan ☐

Using health promotion materials ☐

Assessment of barriers to health improvement ☐

Ways of supporting health improvement efforts ☐

Assessment Guide

Your learning in this unit will be assessed through a controlled assignment. This will be set by Edexcel and marked by your tutor.

The assignment will require you to plan and carry out investigations and produce a health improvement plan in response to case study material provided by Edexcel about the health and wellbeing of an individual.

You will need to show evidence of understanding:

- Ways of promoting and supporting health improvement

Health, Social Care and Early Years in Practice

Introduction

Practitioners in health, social care and early years need a comprehensive knowledge and understanding of the core principles which underpin their work. Unit 4 aims to develop your knowledge and understanding of these core principles. Unit 4 draws on and reinforces key aspects of what you have learnt through studying Units 1, 2 and 3. In particular you will learn about:

- The range of care needs of major client groups
- Care values commonly used in practitioner work
- The development of self-concept and personal relationships
- Promoting and supporting health improvement.

Unit 4 is assessed through a written examination that is set and marked by Edexcel examiners. The examination will assess your ability to apply knowledge and understanding of core principles of health, social care and early years work to case studies and short scenarios involving service users in a variety of care settings. You will be required to analyse and evaluate the information and problems presented in case studies and short scenarios and to present conclusions based on reasoned judgements that are informed by your understanding of these core principles.

Topic 4.1

The range of care needs of major client groups

Topic focus

The range of care needs of major client groups is covered in detail in Topic 2.1 of Unit 2. Topic 2.1 outlines the physical, intellectual, emotional and social needs of infants, children, adolescents, adults and older people and explains how these affect an individual's health, development and wellbeing. Topic 4.1 will reinforce your earlier learning by:

- Outlining the basic physical, intellectual, emotional and social needs of service users
- Summarising the care needs of the major client groups
- Identifying how expected and unexpected life course events and lifestyle choices affect human growth and development.

Case studies and short scenarios with questions for you to answer are a key learning feature of this topic. You should work through as many of the case studies and scenarios as possible. Applying knowledge and understanding of the range of care needs of major client groups will be a feature of the external examination for this unit.

Basic needs of service users

Health, social care and early years services are designed to meet the physical, intellectual, emotional and social needs of different client groups. A client group is a group of service users who, because they are in the same life stage, have a similar range of basic needs. PIES identifies the physical, intellectual, emotional and social needs that all human beings must meet to:

- be physically healthy (physical needs)
- develop their knowledge, skills and abilities (intellectual needs)
- develop communication skills and personal relationships (social needs)
- feel secure and have good mental health (emotional needs).

A person's physical, intellectual, emotional and social (PIES) needs are affected by their:

- stage of development (life stage)
- health status
- how well they are able to meet their needs independently.

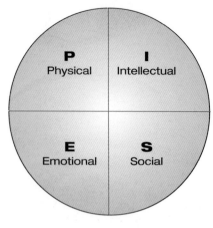

Figure 4.1 PIES.

Type of needs	Examples of needs
Physical needs	• A balanced diet and sufficient fluids • Warmth • Shelter • Exercise • Sleep and rest • Good hygiene • Protection from harm, illness and injury
Intellectual needs	• Interesting and purposeful activities • Learning opportunities • Mental challenges and new experiences
Emotional needs	• Love, support and care • A sense of safety and security • Self-confidence and self-esteem • Opportunities to express feelings
Social needs	• Attachment to a trusted carer • Relationships with other people, including friendships, work relationships and intimate and sexual relationships • A sense of identity and belonging within a community

Figure 4.2 Examples of PIES needs.

For example, a healthy infant is almost completely dependent on others (their parents or carers usually) to meet all of their PIES needs. By contrast, a physically and mentally healthy adult is generally able to meet their needs without much assistance from others. If a person experiences ill health or development problems, they will have specific care needs.

Over to you!

Think about the last time that you were physically unwell and unable to attend school or college. Which aspects of your PIES needs did you require assistance with? Did you have any specific care needs as a result of your ill-health?

Infants' care needs

An infant has a range of care needs. These range from the need for assistance with feeding to the need for play and communication opportunities that stimulate their thinking,

Figure 4.3 The care needs of infants.

Care needs	Purpose of care	Ways of meeting care needs
Physical care	Provision of basic physical care and protection	• Assistance with feeding • Being washed/cleaned regularly • Having nappies changed • Being dressed • Receiving vaccinations to prevent infections • Having physical health monitored • Having personal safety monitored and safeguarded
Intellectual stimulation	Development of basic thinking and language skills	• Stimulating toys and books to play with • Being read stories or rhymes and sung to • Encouragement to babble and make sounds
Emotional support	Establishing basic attachment relationship	• Consistent, emotionally responsive relationship with a parent or carer • Reassuring, soothing and comforting response when upset
Social support	Development of relationship and interaction skills	• Attachment relationship with a parent or carer • Regular contact with parents or other carers • Opportunities and encouragement to play

UNIT 4

language development and social skills. Infants have a wide range of care needs because they are vulnerable and dependent on others for their survival and development. A summary of the care needs of infants who are healthy and developing normally is presented in figure 4.3 above.

An infant who has physical health or developmental problems is likely to require specialist assistance from health and early years practitioners to meet their specific care needs. Examples of these are outlined in figure 4.4.

Infants need a lot of basic care.

Figure 4.4 Examples of services for infants.

Childrens' care needs

Children are more physically robust, and have a range of physical skills that enable them to be more independent, than infants. For example, most three-year-old children can safely walk up and down stairs without assistance, can use a spoon to feed themselves and can occupy themselves with toys and other play activities. As a result of their physical, intellectual, emotional and social development, an individual's care needs change throughout childhood. The care needs of a five-year-old child are likely to be very different to those of a nine-year-old child because of this ongoing development. Care in childhood focuses on encouraging development and increasing an individual's capabilities.

Social needs become important during childhood.

The range of care needs of major client groups

Figure 4.5 The care needs of children.

Care needs	Purpose of care	Ways of meeting care needs
Physical care	Provision of physical care and protection to enable further development to occur	• Encouragement to eat a balanced diet • Provision of warmth and shelter • Help and encouragement to wash and dress • Opportunities and encouragement to exercise and develop physical skills • Regular rest and sleep • Protection from harm
Intellectual stimulation	Stimulation and support of intellectual abilities to develop knowledge, understanding and skills	• Play opportunities • Educational support and encouragement to learn basic reading, writing and numeracy skills • Books to read, television to watch, music to listen to • Friends and adults to learn from and talk to
Emotional support	Building self-confidence, emotional security and self-esteem	• Supportive parents or carers to provide love and affection • Respect and feeling of being valued by parents, friends and other adults • Opportunities to have fun, feel happy and express own feelings • Encouragement and positive feedback from parents, teachers and others which boosts self-esteem
Social support	Supporting development of social skills and relationships	• Help and support to develop friendships with other children and safe relationships with adults outside of the family • Opportunities to play and learn alongside other children • Opportunities to experience a range of social activities and events • Development of basic organisational skills to deal with everyday activities

A child may have additional or specific care needs because they experience:

• problems with their physical or mental health

• difficulties with learning, behaviour or relationships with others

• social or financial problems affecting their family.

A range of health, educational and social care services are provided to meet the specific or additional care needs of children. Examples of these are outlined in figure 4.6.

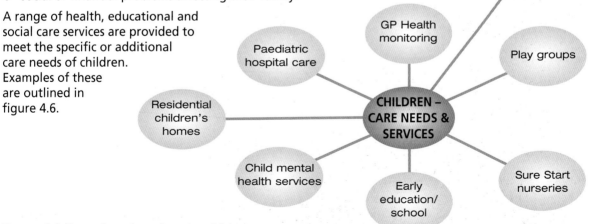

Figure 4.6 Examples of services for children.

Adolescents' care needs

Adolescents' care needs are an extension of those of children. Adolescents are moving towards independent adulthood but still require help, support and guidance from adults around them to feel safe, secure and cared for. As an adolescent moves towards adulthood, their sense of personal identity and need for independence becomes more of a personal concern. As a result, many adolescents benefit from the emotional support that their parents and other relatives provide as a kind of 'safety net' whilst they seek out and experiment with new friendships and more personal and intimate relationships with partners. Care in adolescence focuses less on directly meeting basic needs and more on providing opportunities, encouragement and support so that the individual can gradually take on the responsibility of meeting their needs independently.

Over to you!

How do you think the parents of an older adolescent (16–17 years) could encourage and enable them to be more independent whilst also providing an appropriate level of support and assistance?

Figure 4.7 The care needs of adolescents.

Care needs	Purpose of care	Ways of meeting care needs
Physical care	Maintenance of good physical health and wellbeing to support growth and development through puberty	• Encouragement to eat a balanced diet • Shelter, physical security and warmth • Encouragement and facilities to ensure good personal hygiene • Opportunities and encouragement to be physically active and to exercise
Intellectual stimulation	Stimulation and extension of intellectual skills and abilities	• Education and learning opportunities • Opportunities to work and train in areas of interest • Stimulating books, music, television • Opportunities to talk and explore ideas and beliefs with others
Emotional support	Provision of supportive relationships to enable development of personal identity, self-confidence and self-esteem.	• Supportive relationships with parents or carers to provide love and affection • Friendships that are supportive and stimulating • Respect and feeling of being valued as a capable person by parents, friends and other adults • Opportunities to have fun, feel happy and express own feelings • Encouragement and positive feedback from parents, teachers and others which boosts self-esteem
Social support	Promoting a sense of belonging and social inclusion	• Active and supportive circle of friends • Opportunities to socialise with others • Opportunities to take part in leisure activities and meet new people

As in childhood, an adolescent may develop additional or specific care needs because they experience:

- problems with their physical or mental health
- difficulties with their learning, behaviour or relationships with others
- social or financial problems affecting their family.

A range of health, educational and social care services are provided to meet the specific or additional care needs of adolescents. Examples of these are outlined in figure 4.8.

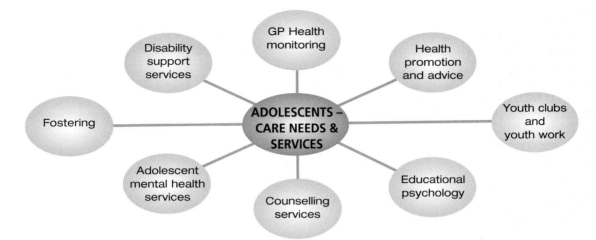

Figure 4.8 Examples of services for adolescents.

Adults' care needs

Adulthood is often seen as the life stage in which individuals are independent and able to meet their own needs. To some extent this is true but nobody is truly independent – we all need other people and tend to live in ways in which we both support others and are supported by them in adulthood. Because adults have largely completed their physical growth and have developed many of the skills, abilities and attributes that they will make use of throughout the rest of their life, an adult's care needs tend to focus on maintaining and refining the different aspects of their health and wellbeing.

Care needs	Purpose of care	Ways of meeting care needs
Physical care	To maintain physical health and wellbeing and minimise effects of ill-health	• A balanced diet and adequate fluids • A warm, safe place to live • Good hygiene • Opportunities to exercise • Sleep and rest • Access to health facilities
Intellectual stimulation	To provide a focus for using and developing intellectual abilities	• Stimulating work or other occupation • Stimulating relationships with others • Access to books, television, music etc • Learning opportunities and educational guidance and support
Emotional support	To achieve and maintain fulfilling and stable personal relationships, positive self-esteem and personal identity	• Love and support from close relationships (partner, family, children) • Respect from and feeling valued by others • A sense of personal identity • Independence and opportunities to make own decisions • Stable and fulfilling personal relationships
Social acceptance and involvement	To establish and maintain a social network and an active social life	• An active and supportive circle of friends • Opportunities to take part in social activities • Opportunities to enjoy leisure activities

UNIT 4

An adult may develop additional or specific care needs because they experience:

- problems with their physical or mental health
- difficulties in their personal or work relationships
- social or financial problems.

A range of health, welfare and social care services are provided to meet the specific or additional care needs of adults. Examples of these are outlined in figure 4.9.

Over to you!

How might financial problems affect an adult's ability to meet their basic physical care needs?

Figure 4.9 Examples of services for adults.

Older peoples' care needs

Later adulthood is the final stage in an individual's life. It is also a stage in which an individual's care needs are likely to increase. Many older people are very healthy and live active, enjoyable

Figure 4.10 The care needs of older people.

Care needs	Purpose of care	Ways of meeting care needs
Physical care	To maximise physical health and wellbeing and minimise ill-health and disabling effects of ageing	• Housing that provides warmth, shelter and safety • A balanced diet and adequate fluids • Provision of mobility support and assistance • Glasses / hearing aids / other prostheses • Opportunities to be physically active and to exercise • Access to health facilities
Intellectual stimulation	To maintain and use intellectual capabilities in ways that are stimulating and interesting	• Learning opportunities • Stimulating activities and hobbies • New experiences • Opportunities for reminiscence • Books, TV, magazines and newspapers • Conversation
Emotional support	To maintain supportive relationships, self-esteem and strong personal identity	• Supportive and loving relationships with partners, friends and family members • Being treated with respect and dignity by others • Being given opportunities to make choices and to be as independent as they would wish • Stable relationships
Social support	To maintain social network and active social life	• Contact with friends and relatives • Opportunities to socialise • Participation in leisure activities

lives. However, the loss of physical and sensory abilities in particular is a common feature of ageing as is the reduction in a person's social network as they retire from work and see less of old friends. As a result, the care needs of older people tend to focus on using support, services and adaptations to maximise independence, maintain an active lifestyle and minimise the effects of illness and ageing.

Figure 4.11 Examples of services for older people.

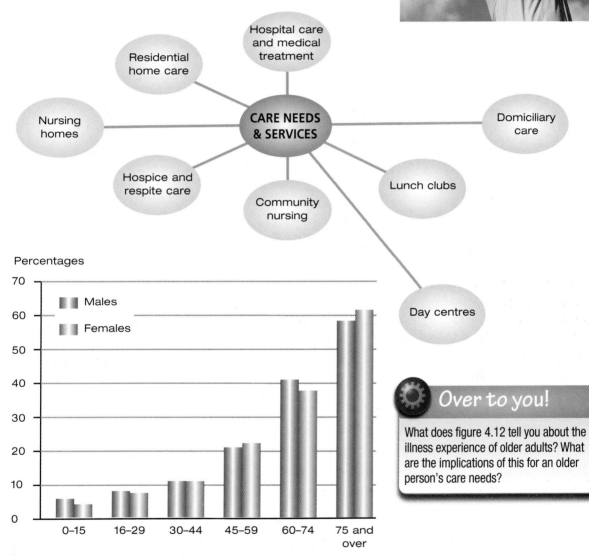

Percentages

Figure 4.12 Prevalence of limiting long-term illness: by age and sex, UK 2001 (ONS)

Over to you!

What does figure 4.12 tell you about the illness experience of older adults? What are the implications of this for an older person's care needs?

Individuals with specific care needs

An individual can have specific care needs because they experience:

● Learning difficulties

● Physical disabilities

● Sensory impairments (hearing, visual)

● Mental health problems.

UNIT 4

Examples of the different kinds of care services provided for people with specific care needs are outlined in figure 4.13 below. Because people experience these problems in different ways, their care needs will also vary to some extent.

Figure 4.13 Services for individuals with specific care needs.

Knowledge Check

1 Identify three examples of basic physical needs that all service users have.

2 What type of need do relationships with others meet?

3 Describe two ways of meeting the physical care needs of an infant.

4 Describe two ways of meeting the intellectual needs of a child.

5 Explain how an adolescent's emotional care needs are different to those of a child.

6 What type of need does stimulating work and access to leisure opportunities meet for an adult?

7 Describe two ways of meeting the emotional care needs of an older person.

8 Identify three reasons why individuals may have specific care needs in addition to their basic care needs.

Factors affecting human growth and development

A number of factors can affect human growth and development in both positive and negative ways. This part of Topic 4.2 is designed to remind you of some of these factors and to provide you with an opportunity to apply your understanding of them to a number of case studies and short scenarios.

Lifestyle choices

Human growth and development is partly influenced by the way in which an individual chooses to live their life. As we've seen, people have a variety of different health and development needs that they have to meet in each life stage. The choices a person makes about their diet, exercise and social, or recreational (leisure) activities have definite consequences for their growth, development, health and wellbeing.

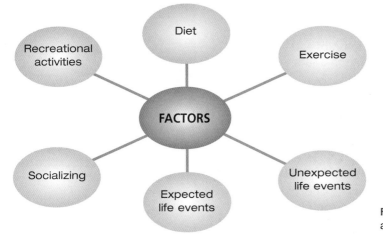

Figure 4.14 Lifestyle factors affecting health and wellbeing.

Diet

- A balanced diet is the basis of good physical health in all life stages.
- The amount and type of food that a person requires depends on their age, physical build, gender and activity levels.
- People who have physically demanding jobs or physically active lives will need to consume more calories than people with sedentary jobs and less physically active lives in order to meet their higher energy needs.
- An individual's dietary needs may change as a result of illness, pregnancy or changes in their level of physical activity.
- Diets that are high in sugar or fat or which lack certain food groups, such as vitamins and minerals from vegetables, are not nutritious and can be harmful to a person's physical health, growth and development.
- Being significantly over- or under-weight can lead to physical and mental health problems.

Not all food is healthy and nutritious!

Exercise

Exercise is important for physical growth and development in every life stage. Infants and children need to be physically active in order to develop and strengthen their muscles, ligaments and bones. Adolescents, adults and older people also need to exercise to keep their bodies in good physical condition. Lack of exercise or physical activity, can lead to obesity, lack of physical fitness and a range of health problems, including:

- heart disease
- high blood pressure
- **osteoporosis**
- constipation
- strokes.

Over to you!

Identify two forms of physical exercise that you most enjoy taking part in (or would like to try). What are the possible benefits for your personal development, health or wellbeing of participating in these activities?

Being physically active promotes physical health and can also help people to meet their emotional and social needs. Taking part in sport or exercise classes helps to reduce stress and is a good way of socialising and forming friendships. Exercise can boost self-esteem and have a positive effect on a person's mood too.

Socialising with others

Human beings need each other – we are social animals. Spending time and mixing with others has a positive effect on an individual's social and emotional wellbeing. Social relationships with friends and family provide:

- Opportunities to develop close relationships and express a range of positive and negative feelings in a safe, supported way
- Opportunities to give and receive emotional support and feel valued by others
- An important boost to self-esteem and contribute to our sense of personal identity
- Protection against feeling isolated, lonely and depressed.

Having good friends, an active social life and opportunities to form new friendships all contribute to a person's emotional wellbeing and social development. An individual needs to socialise with others in each life stage in order to experience emotional wellbeing and to maintain their social skills and relationships.

Recreational activities

If you want to live a healthy life, it is important to have a balance between work and non-work activity. Leisure time, including having hobbies, enjoying a social life and simply relaxing, is part of a healthy life. The recreational activities that people take part in during their leisure time contribute to health and wellbeing because they:

- Help people to form social relationships with each other
- Provide opportunities to communicate with and feel valued by others
- Enable people to develop social skills
- Provide opportunities to develop and use physical and intellectual abilities and skills, depending on the recreational activity
- Provide people with an important sense of belonging to a group or team.

The impact that lifestyle choices such as diet, exercise, socialising with others and recreational activity have on human growth and development have been covered in detail on pp. 37 – pp. 41 of Unit 1. You may want to refresh your memory of the main issues by reading these pages again as part of your preparation for the external assessment.

Expected life events

Life events are transitions or turning points in a person's life that affect their personal development. Some life events, such as starting school, getting a job, getting married or living with a

Over to you!

What impact might not having friends or being excluded from a friendship group have on an adolescent's personal development?

Over to you!

What kind of recreational activities do you regularly take part in? What impact does your choice of recreational activity have on your health and wellbeing?

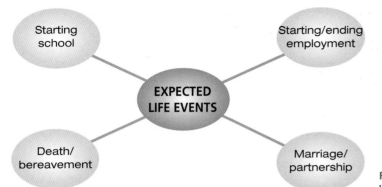

Figure 4.15 Examples of expected life events.

partner, can be predicted and are expected life events. Each person's development is shaped by the impact of the particular life events they experience. The impact of expected life events can be:

- Positive – such as when a person gets married, starts school or succeeds in getting the job that they want. In this situation, a person's self-esteem may be boosted, they will experience emotional wellbeing and their self-concept may change in a positive way

- Negative – such as when a partner, relative or close friend dies. In this situation, a person's emotional wellbeing may decline due to the sadness and grief that they feel as a result of their loss. The person's self-concept may also change in order to adjust to the absence of this person in their life.

Starting school

Starting school is one of the first expected life events that an individual experiences and is very significant for personal development. Beginning primary school:

- involves spending time away from parents or carers
- widens the circle of people a child has contact with
- leads to considerable intellectual development
- provides opportunities for social and emotional development through friendships and regular contact with other children and adults
- leads to changes in self-concept as children compare and contrast themselves with others.

Some children may see starting school as a negative life event if they are very anxious about leaving the security of their parents. However, most children do adjust to starting school and come to see it as a positive experience. At 11 years of age children in the United Kingdom move from primary to secondary school. This change is also a major life event as it requires a range of adjustments to be made to self-concept, relationships and everyday routines.

Going to school contributes to all aspects of a child's personal development. It provides opportunities for a lot of new learning, much of which helps the child to understand themselves and other people more. A child's self-concept, self-esteem, relationships, communication skills and knowledge and understanding of the world around them will all change as a result of starting school.

Over to you!

Can you remember what your first day at primary school was like? If not, ask one of your parents how you reacted to going to school and how you changed as a person during your first year at school.

Health, Social Care and Early Years in Practice

UNIT 4

Marriage/partnership formation

Marriage, or partnership formation, is a life event that generally occurs in early adulthood. When they first get married or begin cohabiting, the couples involved – as well as their friends and relatives – are usually very positive about their future together. However, the couple have to adapt to their new relationship and marital roles and may find that their relationships with friends and family members change as a result too. Marriage and partnership formation:

● Leads to changes in self-concept

● Can have a positive effect on emotional development where the participants establish a deep commitment to each other

● Can boost self-esteem and change a person's self-image.

However, not everyone adjusts to married life or close personal relationships so well. Some people experience a loss of freedom and see marriage as restricting their friendships and work opportunities. As a result, marriage or partnership formation can have both a positive and negative effect on social and emotional development.

Over to you!

What does figure 4.16 reveal about the trend in marriages? What does the graph reveal about the trend in divorces?

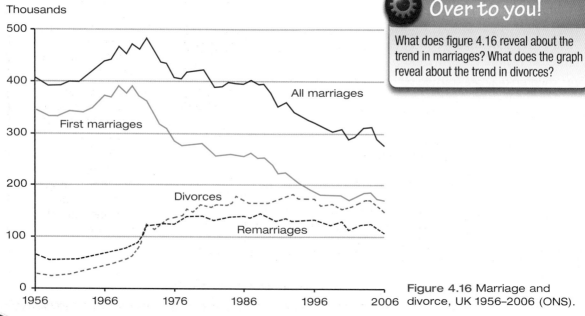

Figure 4.16 Marriage and divorce, UK 1956–2006 (ONS).

Employment

Everybody finishes studying at school, college or university at some point in their life. A large proportion of people then enter employment. Starting work affects personal development because it:

- places a different set of responsibilities and expectations on people
- requires people to behave more independently without the support of parents or teachers
- provides opportunities for intellectual development through training and acquiring new knowledge and skills
- provides opportunities to develop new social relationships and social skills through time spent with work colleagues
- leads to changes in self-concept as individuals gain experience, progress and higher status in a particular field of work.

An individual's self-concept is likely to change significantly when they enter employment if their work identity becomes a part of 'who' they are.

Death / bereavement

A person's death may be anticipated and prepared for because of their old age or because they have a terminal illness, for example. Though the loss of a loved one can be anticipated in this way, it may still be difficult to accept. The often overwhelming feelings of grief (bereavement) that can occur may be hard to cope with. Bereavement may be even more traumatic and psychologically difficult when a person's death is unexpected because of an accident, serious injury or suicide, for example. Bereavement can result in:

- short and long-term change to self-concept as the person adjusts to the loss of a partner, friend or relative
- acute emotional distress

Case study

Laura and Ian decided to go on holiday to Costa Rica as a way of celebrating their first wedding anniversary. They were really enjoying their first week away, taking part in snorkelling and diving trips and just enjoying themselves on the beach. At the beginning of their second week, Ian and Laura went out for a meal to a beachside restaurant. Both had some wine to drink and agreed that this was their best holiday together. On the walk back to their hotel, Ian persuaded Laura that they should go for a quick swim in the sea. Neither of them knew the beach or were aware that there were dangerous tides in the area. Ian quickly got into trouble. Laura lost sight of him in the waves but managed to get herself back to the beach despite the strong tide pulling her out to sea. Ian's body was washed up on another beach the next morning. Laura says that she still thinks about the incident every day and is still grieving for Ian. She hasn't returned to work since the incident six months ago, takes anti-depressant tablets to help with her mood and is beginning to lose touch with friends who have tried hard to support her.

- Describe the impact of Ian's death on Laura's emotional wellbeing.
- How might the unexpected loss of her husband affect Laura's self-concept?
- Which care practitioners might be able to provide help and support for Laura?

- the loss of friendships and other social relationships if the person who died – such as a husband or wife - played a significant part in the individual's social life, for example.

The death of someone close can have a profound effect on an individual's life. Some people are able to adjust to their loss once they have grieved and find ways of continuing with or changing their own life in the person's absence. However, bereavement can also have long-term effects that are damaging to a person's emotional wellbeing and mental health if they are unable to adapt to life without their loved one.

Unexpected life events

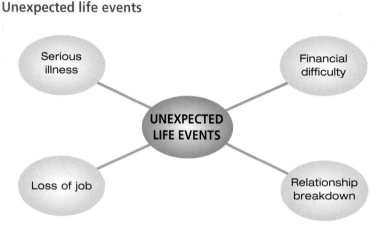

Figure 4.17 Examples of unexpected life events.

Some of the major events that shape and change a person's life occur unexpectedly. Life events such as serious illness, relationship breakdown, financial difficulties or the loss of a job can happen unexpectedly and can affect anyone. These life events may occur on their own or may become linked as part of a more involved and problematic series of personal difficulties. In either case, unexpected life events can have a major effect on a person's life resulting in significant change because of the need to overcome them and adapt to new life circumstances. Unexpected life events are usually thought of as having a negative effect on a person's development and wellbeing but they can sometimes lead to positive change in a person's life because they provide opportunities for new learning and a new direction in life.

Serious illness

An unexpected, serious illness can have a dramatic effect on a person's health, development and lifestyle. Serious illness can affect:

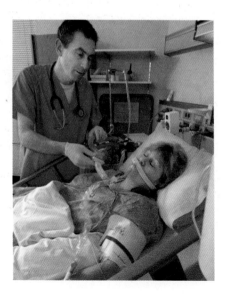

- *Physical* development and wellbeing, particularly where an illness or condition, such as a heart attack, stroke, or a degenerative condition such as multiple sclerosis, Parkinson's disease or cancer, affects a person's ability to look after themselves or live independently.

- *Intellectual* development where the illness or condition, such as a brain injury or sensory impairment, affects a person's ability to learn or use their existing skills.

- *Emotional* development if the person is traumatized by the illness or experiences depression or other psychological difficulties in adapting to the effects the illness or condition has on their life.

- *Social* development if the individual finds that their relationships with others change because they need practical help or care because of their illness.

Serious illnesses are often life-changing events because people who survive them learn a lot about themselves and change their values and priorities to get as much out of their life as possible. An individual's self-concept is likely to change significantly too.

Relationship breakdown

Relationship breakdown tends to be unwanted, unexpected and emotionally distressing when it occurs. For example, most people who marry don't expect their relationship to end in divorce but divorce is quite common in the United Kingdom. One in three marriages is likely to end in divorce. The ending of close friendships or family rifts are other examples of relationship breakdown that can have a significant impact on a person's development and wellbeing. In all of these situations an individual may experience:

- Physical health problems as a result of poor sleep, loss of appetite, weight gain

- Emotional distress due to the loss of a close bond

- A reduction in self-esteem if they see the relationship breakdown as a personal rejection

- Disruption to their social relationships if other friends and relatives 'take sides'.

Though relationship breakdowns can have a negative effect on the lives of those involved, the ending of a relationship that is causing problems for one or other of the people involved may still be preferable to continuing with an unsatisfactory relationship.

Investigate ...

Use the Internet or library resources to investigate the impact that either stroke (cerebro-vascular accident) or Parkinson's disease can have on an individual's health and wellbeing. Use your findings to produce a short leaflet or poster that describes the physical, intellectual, emotional and social effects that these serious health problems can have.

Case study

Jenny hasn't spoken to or seen her mother for the last eight years. Jenny is now thirty years old. She started having disagreements and arguments with her mother shortly after Stacy, her first child, was born. Jenny's mother was often quite critical of the way she looked after Stacy, particularly how she fed and clothed her. This annoyed Jenny but she coped with it by ignoring her mother's comments and having a bit less contact with her. When Shaun, Jenny's second child, was born eight years ago Jenny's mother made a comment about 'getting it right this time'. This led to a big argument and Jenny cut off all contact with her mother. Jenny's mother has sent cards and presents to her grandchildren over the last eight years but hasn't spoken with Jenny or made any attempt to apologise. When Jenny thinks about her mother she feels stressed and agitated. She is still very angry about her mother's criticisms but also wishes that the problems could be solved so that her children could experience what she calls 'a proper family life'.

- Describe the emotional impact on Jenny of the rift with her mother.

- How might the relationship breakdown have affected Jenny's self-esteem?

- What effect might resolving their relationship problems have on the self-concepts of both Jenny and her mother?

UNIT 4

Financial difficulty

Money is an economic factor linked to health and wellbeing because it affects an individual's quality of life, their lifestyle choices and the opportunities open to them. People can experience financial difficulties because they are:

- unable to work because of illness or disability
- made redundant
- unable to find work
- employed in low-paid work
- struggling to afford debts or high living costs.

A person facing financial difficulties may not be able to afford the basic necessities of life (food, shelter, clothing) and may have to make difficult decisions about how to spend the little money they do have. This might lead to them eating a poor diet, living in poor housing conditions and experiencing high stress levels. As a result a person facing financial difficulties is likely to experience a decline in their physical health, emotional and psychological problems, or low self-esteem. A person's financial difficulties may be short-term and might be resolved when they do find work or are able to change their living circumstances. In these situations, people often learn things about themselves and how they should live their life that are helpful to them. However, where a person is unable to change their circumstances, the financial difficulties that they face may result in them making fundamental decisions – about moving house, relocating to another area or changing career – that have a lasting impact on their personal development.

Loss of job

A person may lose their job because they are made redundant or because they are dismissed. In either situation, the loss of a job is a life event that may lead to:

- Loss of confidence and self-esteem
- Loss of identity and self-respect
- Loss of status
- Increased stress levels

Case study

Adam Akehurst is 35 years of age. He has worked as an accountant in a large, prestigious city firm for the last ten years. Adam's firm is currently facing a lot of financial problems. The board of directors have recently said that they will have to make almost half of the employees redundant. Adam is now very worried that he will lose his job. He has spent most of last weekend worrying about the possible consequences of this. He hardly slept and is not eating well. Adam has started thinking that he will 'lose everything' if he is made redundant.

- What impact is the threat of redundancy having on Adam's wellbeing?
- How might redundancy affect Adam's self-esteem and social relationships?
- How might Adam's self-concept change if he is made redundant?

- Problems with sleeping, eating and mood
- Loss of social relationships with work colleagues
- Increased strain in personal and family relationships.

People who lose their jobs often feel rejected and devalued. This can make them feel angry and self-critical at the same time. Losing a valued job can destabilize a person's life, taking away their usual routine and the structure of their day and leave them wondering about their own worth and abilities. However, even though the loss of a job may be unexpected, some people find that it is a positive turning point in their life where they are able to identify a new direction and pursue new opportunities.

In general, expected and unexpected life events have a powerful effect on social and emotional wellbeing and shape an individual's self-concept. Individuals often learn new things about themselves, others and life in general as a result of the life events that they experience. This typically leads to a new phase or direction in the person's life.

Knowledge Check

1 Identify three lifestyle choices that influence an individual's physical health and development.

2 Explain how diet has an impact on health and development.

3 Suggest three reasons why socialising with others can have a positive impact on personal development.

4 How can taking part in recreational activities contribute to an individual's health and wellbeing?

5 Identify three examples of expected life events that can affect human development.

6 What impact might marriage or partnership formation have on an adult's social and emotional development?

7 Identify three examples of unexpected life events that can affect human growth or development.

8 Explain how losing a job might affect an individual's social development and emotional wellbeing.

Topic review

The box below provides a summary of the areas covered in Topic 4.1. Tick the areas that you feel you understand and would be confident answering exam questions about. If there are any areas that you don't understand or are not confident about, you will need to return to them before you begin your exam revision.

Basic needs of service users
- Physical needs ☐
- Intellectual needs ☐
- Emotional needs ☐
- Social needs ☐

Factors affecting growth and development
- Life style choices
  - diet ☐
  - exercise ☐
  - socialising ☐
  - recreational activities ☐
- Expected life events
  - starting school ☐
  - marriage/partnership formation ☐
  - employment ☐
  - death/bereavement ☐
- Unexpected life events
  - serious illness ☐
  - relationship breakdown ☐
  - financial difficulty ☐
  - loss of job ☐

Assessment Guide

Your learning in this unit will be assessed through a one hour and fifteen minute examination.

The examination will consist of a series of structured questions based on case studies and short scenarios.

You will need to show that you understand:

- The range of care needs of major client groups

Topic 4.2

Care values
commonly used in practitioner work

Topic focus

You may remember reading about the way care values are commonly used in practitioner work in Unit 2. Topic 2.5 describes and explains a range of care values that play an important part in guiding the way care practitioner's work with service users. Topic 4.2 will reinforce your earlier learning by:

● Reminding you about the care values practitioners use in their interactions with service users.

● Describing how health, social care and early years practitioners promote and use care values in their work with service users.

● Explaining the effects and consequences of not implementing care values in work with service users, including the possibility of discrimination, social exclusion, or a service user's self-concept and self-esteem being damaged.

Case studies and short scenarios with questions for you to answer are a key learning feature of this topic. You should work through as many of the case studies and scenarios as possible. Applying knowledge and understanding of care values commonly used in practitioner work will be a feature of the external examination for this unit.

Using care values in practice

Care values are important and widely used in health, social care and early years work. They help care practitioners to:

● recognise and respond to each service user's particular care needs

● respect individual differences

● ensure each individual is treated equally and fairly

● protect individuals from poor-quality care, neglect, discrimination and mistreatment.

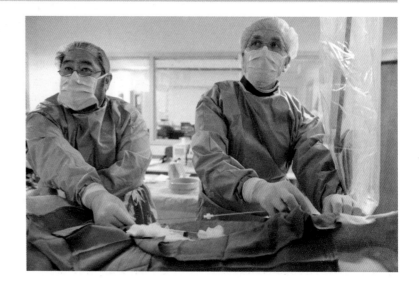

Case study

Delia and Bob Evans recently inherited a very large sum of money. They decided to invest this money in a residential home for young disabled adults. Neither Delia or Bob have any care training or any experience of caring for vulnerable people. Delia says that 'doing the right thing for people, being kind and making sure everyone is fed and happy is probably the best we can offer them really'. Delia and Bob intend to continue employing the staff currently working at the home. Delia has recently been told by a friend who is also an experienced care home manager that she must ensure that all of her staff understand and implement care values in their practice.

● Explain to Delia what 'care values' are.

● Why is it important for care practitioners to understand and use care values in their work?

● What might be the consequences of not implementing care values in this care setting?

Care practitioners put care values into practice through the use of effective communication and the supportive care relationships that they develop with individuals.

Reviewing care values

The care values that you have studied so far include:

● Promoting anti-discriminatory practice

● Promoting and supporting individual rights to dignity, independence, health and safety

● Promoting effective communication and relationships

● Maintaining confidentiality of information

● Acknowledging individual's personal beliefs and identity.

Care practitioners should implement a range of care values in their work with service users. This often happens when care practitioners interact and communicate with the people they provide care for. The way in which care practitioners approach their work and the quality of the relationships they develop with service users are central to this. Positive, respectful care practice is based on and always occurs through effective relationships with service users. To some extent care relationships rely on care professionals having appropriate personal qualities. For example, being kind, understanding, sensitive and compassionate towards others plays a part in this. However, by themselves these personal qualities are not enough. Care professionals must also find ways of putting care values into practice through the way they work with service users.

Promoting anti-discriminatory practice

According to the equality laws of the United Kingdom, all service users should be treated fairly and equally. These laws do deter some people from acting on their prejudices and also provide a way of punishing others who discriminate unfairly. The basic principles of anti-discriminatory practice are that:

● All service users are entitled to non-discriminatory treatment.

● Care practitioners should never unfairly discriminate against service users.

Figure 4.18 Ways of implementing care values.

- Care practitioners should challenge and try to remove any form of unfair discrimination against a service user that they become aware of.

A care practitioner who takes an anti-discriminatory approach in the way they work will be aware of:

- different forms of prejudice and unfair discrimination (sexism, racism, ageism, homophobia, for example)
- the needs, beliefs and traditions of people from diverse ethnic, social and cultural backgrounds
- the legal rights of service users to fair and equal treatment
- the need to challenge any incidents of prejudice or unfair discrimination against service users.

Anti-discriminatory practice is a way of applying equal opportunities ideas to everyday work situations. Care practitioners who use an anti-discriminatory approach to practice:

- Use non-discriminatory language (non-sexist, non-racist, non-disablist words and phrases)
- Become self-aware, tolerant of difference and are prepared to change their ideas and views about people
- View people as diverse and different but of equal value regardless of their physical, mental or cultural characteristics
- Accept people's physical, social and cultural differences as a positive and interesting feature of care work rather than as a problem.

Promoting and supporting individual rights to dignity, independence, health and safety

A person who requires care is likely to be at a vulnerable point in their life because of the onset or progression of illness, disease, impairment or other social or emotional problems. Receiving personal care, emotional support or assistance from care professionals can be difficult and even feel humiliating unless the care professionals involved are respectful of the individual's right to dignity, independence, health and safety. For example, dignity and independence become important issues when an individual needs assistance with personal tasks such as washing, dressing,

Over to you!

How would you go about challenging someone whom you heard being racist, sexist or homophobic to a service user? Identify strategies you could use.

Case study

Ingrid Henry is a 76-year-old woman who has a recent diagnosis of dementia. Ingrid's social worker has found a nursing home for her that is close to where her only son now lives. She feels that the nursing home has the right kind of facilities and the right kind of specialist staff that Ingrid requires. Two members of the nursing home staff recently assessed Ingrid in hospital. They have just written to her social worker saying that the nursing home is 'not suitable' for Ingrid and that she would 'struggle to fit in' with the other residents.

- Do you think that the nursing home staff are discriminating unfairly against Ingrid?
- What form of unfair discrimination might be occurring in this situation?
- What should the social worker do if she is using an anti-discriminatory approach in her practice?

Figure 4.19 Ways of promoting dignity.

eating and using the toilet. Being unable to carry out these personal tasks independently may be damaging to a person's self-esteem as they may feel they are a burden on others, helpless or somehow incapable. To promote and support the individual's right to dignity and independence care professionals should:

- try to understand each individual's feelings
- provide the emotional and practical support each individual needs
- respond to each individual's wishes and preferences as much as possible.

It would be disrespectful and abusive for a care practitioner to draw attention to a service user's problems or to criticise or complain about any difficulties they may be having in meeting the individual's particular needs. It is also unethical and in breach of health and safety laws to provide any form of care that may be unsafe or to work with equipment or in care environments where health and safety risks have not been assessed and minimised.

Promoting effective communication and relationships

Care practitioners have an important role to play in helping individuals and their relatives to talk about personal matters and issues that concern them. Effective communication begins when

Over to you!

Make a list of the things that you would expect a care practitioner to do in order to protect your dignity if you required their assistance to use the toilet, wash and dress.

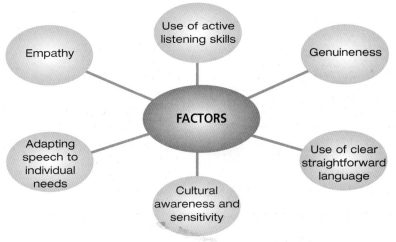

Figure 4.20 Factors affecting quality of communication.

Health, Social Care and Early Years in Practice

a rapport or basic 'communication connection' is established with the service user. A good rapport provides a basic platform on which to build a care relationship and is the first step in getting to know the service user better. Effective communication also requires two-way interaction between care professionals and service users. This is why speaking *and* listening are both equally important skills for care professionals to develop. Care professionals encourage effective communication by:

● Not interrupting an individual when they are speaking

● Listening carefully to what the other person says

● Using straightforward words that are easy to understand

● Speaking clearly and at an appropriate pace.

Care professionals who are effective communicators try to actively involve service users in discussions and decisions that affect them. This allows the service user to contribute and have a chance to communicate their needs and preferences.

Maintaining confidentiality of information

Confidentiality is not about keeping information 'secret'. It is about sharing, transmitting and storing information about service users in ways that are appropriate to their care needs. This means that 'confidential' information can be shared with care team members who also need to know about and use it. However, it is not acceptable for a care practitioner to reveal an individual's personal details or to comment on their care or treatment to relatives or other people outside of the care team without first gaining the approval of the individual.

There is a limited range of circumstances in which a care practitioner cannot agree to keep information confidential. These include situations where breaking confidentiality is necessary:

● to protect an individual's health

● to protect the health and safety of others

● to prevent a crime happening

● to assist an investigation into suspected child abuse

● if a court or tribunal orders disclosure.

As a result, a care practitioner can never promise a service user 'absolute confidentiality'. However, it is important to only use personal or private information about the individual in ways that are legally and ethically acceptable.

> **Over to you!**
>
> Identify health or social care workers whom you have given confidential information about yourself to. What do you expect them to do to maintain this confidentiality?

Case study

Jane is a nursery assistant at the Tumbledown Day Nursery. She recently overheard one of her nursery nurse colleagues giving confidential information about the recent ill-health of three-year-old Joel to the mother of another child whom Joel is friendly with. Jane has told her supervisor that she feels this wasn't right or in Joel's best interests, but that she is not sure what she should do about it.

● Has there been a breach of confidentiality in this situation?

● Why is it important that confidential information relating to Joel's health status should be protected?

● If you were Jane's supervisor, how would you deal with this situation?

Acknowledging an individual's personal beliefs and identity

Dress and behaviour often express identify and beliefs.

Acknowledging people's personal beliefs and identity means that care practitioners should try to communicate that they accept people for who they are and what they believe. Care practitioners may not always share the beliefs and lifestyle of the people they care for, but should still show that they accept a service user's individuality. For example, when a care practitioner cares for people who have different religious beliefs and practices to their own, they should give them the opportunity to practise their faith and celebrate their religious festivals at a time when this is important to them. In order to acknowledge an individual's personal beliefs and identity a care practitioner should:

- Ask about service users' beliefs, identity and lifestyle, and listen carefully to them
- Observe a service user's behaviour and treat them as an individual
- Find out about different cultures, religious beliefs and lifestyle practices
- Be open to and tolerant about difference and accepting of cultural diversity.

Case study

Erica Fleming is an evangelical Christian. She has a very strong religious faith, reads the Bible for a couple of hours every day and always attends a church service on a Sunday. Erica believes that her life has been touched by God and that praying is helping her to recover from a depressive illness. Some of the staff at Erica's residential home help Erica to practise her faith by booking a taxi to transport her to church on a Sunday. John, one of the newer support workers, recently suggested to Erica that she was wasting her time and money going to church 'because God doesn't exist anyway'. This upset Erica a great deal although John was unapologetic and has since refused to book a taxi to take her to church.

- Is John entitled to express his views about religion or is he making a mistake here?

- What should a care worker whose views were different to Erica's do in this situation?

- Is John failing to implement any care values by refusing to arrange a taxi to take Erica to church?

Promoting care values through practice

Care values are now seen as an essential part of the work of all care practitioners. Care professionals are required to put care values into practice during their interactions with service users and in the way that they approach their work, or care practice. To help ensure that care professionals have adequate guidance and advice on how to do this professional organisations and employers have developed codes of practice and policies and procedures. Examples of these are now used in all care settings.

Codes of practice

A **code of practice** (also known as a code of conduct) is a document that outlines an agreed way of working and dealing with specified situations. Codes of practice aim to reflect and set a standard for good practice in care settings. A number of codes of practice have been developed for care workers such as registered nurses, occupational therapists and physiotherapists, social workers and nursery staff. Codes of practice establish the general principles and standards for care workers and should always incorporate the range of care values described earlier. Breaking or failing to follow a code of practice may result in a registered care practitioner being 'struck off' the professional register. This will prevent them from working in their care profession.

Policies and procedures

A **policy** is different to a code of practice in that it tells care practitioners how they should approach specific issues in a particular care setting. For example, most care homes will have a policy on confidentiality. This will explain in detail how this issue is dealt with in the particular home. Policies should promote equal treatment and equality of opportunity for everyone likely to be affected by them.

A **procedure** describes the way that staff in a particular care setting are expected to deal with an issue or activity that they may be involved in. For example, care homes for older people usually have written procedures that describe how to deal with a situation where a resident goes missing from the home. The

Investigate . . .

Use the Internet to find information on the codes of conduct of nurses and midwives (www.nmc-uk.org) or the code of practice of social workers (www.gscc.org.uk). Try to identify the main care values that are covered by the codes that you look at.

Knowledge Check

1 Identify three care values that are commonly used to guide the work of care practitioners.

2 Describe the basic principles of anti-discriminatory practice and explain why many care practitioners adopt this approach in their work with service users.

3 Give two examples that demonstrate an anti-discriminatory approach to care practice.

4 Explain why it is important for a care practitioner to promote and support an individual's rights to dignity and independence.

5 Give an example of one thing a care practitioner could do to promote a service user's independence.

6 Identify three things a care practitioner could do to encourage effective communication with a service user.

7 Explain what confidentiality involves.

8 Explain why a care practitioner should normally maintain confidentiality in their relationships with service users.

9 What can a care practitioner do to acknowledge the personal beliefs and identity of a service user?

10 What is a code of practice and how is it related to care values?

procedure will set out in detail all the steps that the staff should take in trying to locate the person and report them missing to the relevant authorities.

Policies and procedures should always incorporate the main values of the care profession. They should ensure that every service user's rights are respected and that activities are always carried out in service users' best interests.

When care goes wrong

People who train for and work as care practitioners are usually very motivated to help others and are very committed to providing high quality care for the vulnerable people they work with. However, despite the best intentions of many care practitioners, for various reasons care situations and relationships with service users do sometimes go wrong.

Treated like a dog, used as a punchbag

(Daily Mail)

A short life of misery and pain   *(BBC News)*

Baby P – Hidden Horror Revealed

(News of the World)

In some cases it is the care practitioners themselves who are responsible for care going wrong. This can happen where a service user's partner, relative or the care professional themselves become the perpetrator of neglect or abuse. Whoever the perpetrator is, the neglect or abuse of a service user is never acceptable and cannot be justified. Some of the risk factors that make neglect and abuse more likely include care-givers:

● being very stressed because they feel powerless and isolated

● feeling resentful and hostile towards the individual/service user

● having deeply held prejudices towards members of particular social groups

● becoming financially dependent on the individual

● having unrestricted and unmonitored access to the individual's finances

● lacking care training and having poor practical care skills

● not being monitored or supervised effectively.

People who need care and support are not always grateful or pleasant to be with. Experiencing complaints, unpleasantness or hostility from service users or their relatives can be difficult for care practitioners. In these situations care practitioners sometimes feel angry and retaliate. This is not an acceptable or appropriate way of responding and can lead to the service user experiencing neglect ('I'm not helping you anymore then') or some form of abuse.

Over to you!

Why do you think that care practitioners and others who care for vulnerable people sometimes hurt or neglect the people they are supposed to be providing care for?

Over to you!

How might a team approach help care practitioners to avoid becoming involved in neglect or abuse situations?

Forms of neglect and poor practice

Neglect of a service user can occur if a care practitioner or a team of care workers ignore or fail to give an individual the help or assistance that they are known to require. There can be a range of reasons for this, including:

- Prejudice against a particular group of people (sexism, racism, homophobia, for example)
- Personal dislike, hostility or disagreement ('personality clash') between the care practitioner and service user
- Incompetence by the care practitioner due to lack of knowledge and skills
- Poor standards of practice by the care practitioner
- Failure of the care practitioner to follow policies and procedures .

It is sometimes difficult to identify that an individual is experiencing neglect. Neglect may be easier to identify in an individual's own home, but can, and does, happen in in-patient and residential care settings. Some of the indicators of neglect include:

- Incontinence because the individual cannot access toilet facilities
- Poor physical condition due to unwashed, dirty skin, uncombed, matted and dirty hair, excessively long fingernails and toenails
- Lack of stimulation and isolation of an individual in their room
- The individual is relieved or overly pleased to see visitors and seems to feel safer while they are there
- Noticeable loss of weight, possibly because of food and drink being withheld
- Excessive drowsiness or confusion due to being sedated or over-medicated

Investigate ...

Use the Internet or library resources to review national newspapers for stories about poor care practice or the neglect of service users. Summarise a case that has come to public attention and provide a brief account of the reasons why care seems to have gone wrong in this situation.

Case study

Heinz Brandt, aged 83, is a resident at Riverview Residential and Nursing Home. Heinz is confused at times and has short-term memory loss. However, Heinz's long-term memory is still very good. He has particularly strong memories of being a prisoner of war during the Second World War. Recalling this period of his life causes Heinz some distress. Eddie, one of the night care assistants, was spotted whispering something to Heinz that caused him to become distressed and to start calling out. Eddie then left Heinz sitting on the toilet unattended for ten minutes and turned out the light in his room. Eddie was discovered sitting on the end of Heinz's bed in the dark by Denise, the nurse in charge of the night shift. When she had finally calmed Heinz down and got him back to sleep, she questioned Eddie about the incident. Eventually Eddie said that he'd whispered 'Achtung, zer Germans, zer Germans are here' and also claimed 'it was just a joke, that's all'. He couldn't explain why he had left Heinz sitting on the toilet, why he had turned the light off, or why he was sitting on Heinz's bed instead of helping him.

- Is Eddie guilty of neglecting Heinz in this situation?
- Why do you think Eddie might be treating Heinz in this way?
- Is there any evidence that Eddie may also be guilty of abusing Heinz in some way?

- Return of illness or disease symptoms due to not being given prescribed medication
- Obvious evidence of self-harm (cutting, refusing food, pulling own hair out, self-neglect) that has not been noted or responded to by carers.

In practice care professionals should be alert to any changes in mood, behaviour or appearance that are out of the ordinary for the people they provide care for. However, it is also important to remember that there are circumstances where unexpected marks, unusual behaviour or unexplained changes in an individual's circumstances or appearance have a very different and straightforward explanation.

Types of abuse

Many care service users are at a point in their life where they are vulnerable, relatively powerless and dependent on others to provide them with help, support and assistance. As a result they put a lot of trust in care practitioners and informal carers to help them to meet their needs. This also makes them vulnerable to abuse and exploitation.

There are a number of different types of abuse:

- Physical abuse, including hitting, kicking, pushing or treating a person very roughly
- Sexual abuse, including inappropriate touching or forcing a person to take part in sexual activity
- Verbal abuse, including shouting at, insulting or threatening a person
- Emotional abuse, including teasing, undermining, mocking or deliberately distressing a person
- Financial exploitation, including stealing from or manipulating a person to spend their money
- Unfair discrimination.

Protecting service users from potential abuse is something that all care practitioners should feel is important. Care practitioners should ensure that their own relationships with service users are positive and supportive. They should also be alert to any indications that the people they provide care for are being neglected or abused by others. If this is the case a care practitioner should follow the policies and procedures of their employer in order to prevent or stop neglect or abuse happening when they become aware of it.

Team work reduces the chance of abuse occurring.

Identifying abuse

The signs and symptoms of physical abuse can include:

○ *Unexplained bruising*, especially bruising on areas of the body that are unlikely to bruise through naturally occurring accidents

○ Any sign of *burns or scalding*

○ *Unexplained cuts and grazes* to the skin or conflicting explanations about how the injuries occurred

○ *Guarding reactions*, such as when an individual unconsciously holds up their hands to protect themselves when approached or touched

○ *Unexplained and unconscious signs of fear*, when a particular person is near, or when a particular procedure (washing or dressing for example) is being carried out.

The signs and symptoms of emotional abuse can include:

○ *Self-imposed isolation*, especially where the person is normally outgoing and sociable

○ *Emotional withdrawal*, especially where the person seems emotionally hurt, fearful or watchful

○ *Lowering of mood*, especially where the person is normally more cheerful and outgoing

○ *Changes in sleeping patterns*, such as nightmares, difficulty going off to sleep or broken sleep

○ *Decline in self-esteem*, especially where the person is not normally self-critical

○ *Loss of confidence* and an increase in anxiety

○ *Self-harming behaviour* or *self-neglect*.

The signs and symptoms of sexual abuse can include:

○ *Fear of physical contact*, such as when accessing toilet or bathing facilities

○ *Unexplained crying* and withdrawal from social contact

○ *Physical trauma* such as scratches, bite marks, bruising or bleeding in the perineal area

○ *Sexualised language* used unexpectedly and inappropriately

○ *Vaginal infections* or *anal bruising* or *bleeding*

○ *Torn clothing*, especially underwear and night clothes.

Unfair discrimination

Care practitioners should never discriminate unfairly against any service user. Similarly, care organisations should encourage equality of access for and fair and equal treatment of all service users. Care practitioners who understand and use care values in their work are unlikely to discriminate unfairly because they will:

● Promote anti-discriminatory practice

● Promote and support individual rights

● Promote effective communication and relationships

● Acknowledge an individual's personal beliefs and identity

Despite the fact that care practitioners are trained to treat service users fairly and equally, and care organisations have policies and procedures that are designed to ensure this happens, members of some social and cultural groups regularly complain that they are treated less fairly or they are unfairly discriminated

Care values commonly used in practitioner work

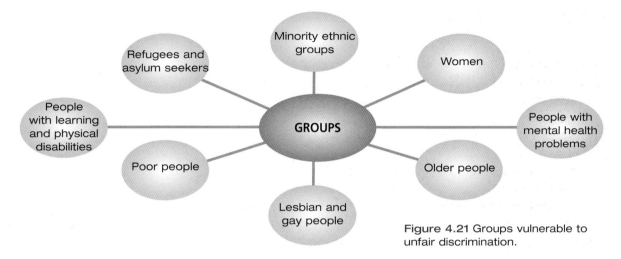

Figure 4.21 Groups vulnerable to unfair discrimination.

against. The danger of not implementing care values effectively is that members of these groups may experience:

- *Direct discrimination* when they are deliberately and unfairly treated in a less favourable way compared to other people. The motive or intention behind such treatment is irrelevant though it is likely to be related to prejudice.

- *Indirect discrimination* where they are inadvertently treated less fairly, perhaps because their particular needs, beliefs or identities are not recognised or taken into account by care practitioners.

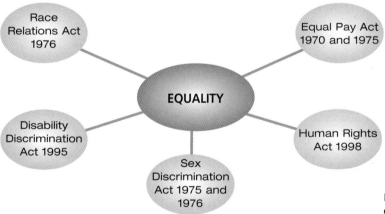

Figure 4.22 Equality and anti-discrimination laws.

Failing to use care values in practice can have real, practical consequences for some service users if this results in them being denied care and being given inappropriate or sub-standard care. Care practitioners who do discriminate unfairly against service users are likely to be disciplined by their employer and **regulatory body** and may lose their job as a result.

The impact of poor care practice

Individuals who receive poor standards of care can be profoundly affected by this. Poor care practice can have a number of consequences, including:

- Increasing the risk of further health problems or injury to the individual (such as from infection)

Investigate ...

Use textbooks, other library resources and the Internet to investigate two of the equality and anti-discrimination laws identified in figure 4.22. Summarise the main provisions and legal protections of your two chosen laws and present them as a handout or poster.

Health, Social Care and Early Years in Practice

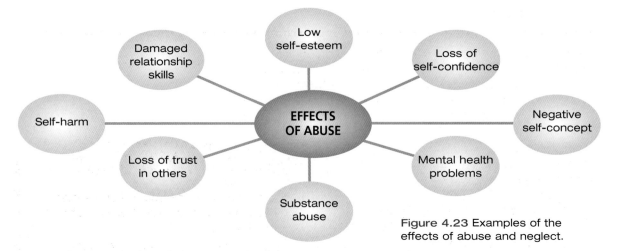

Figure 4.23 Examples of the effects of abuse and neglect.

- Reducing the individual's chances of recovering from health problems or overcoming social or developmental problems
- Damaging the individual's self-esteem by making them feel devalued and unimportant. This can undermine their sense of self-worth
- Having a negative effect on the individual's self-concept by making them feel disempowered and dependent on care professionals who, in the end, don't really care about them as a person.

Care values play an important part in protecting the interests of service users. Care practitioners who fail to incorporate and use care values in their practice, run the real risk of discriminating against some of the individuals they come into contact with. This can have a negative effect on the physical and psychological health and emotional wellbeing of people who are already in a vulnerable state.

Knowledge Check

1 Identify four reasons why care can sometimes go wrong and lead to the neglect or abuse of a vulnerable individual.

2 Explain why care practitioners sometimes neglect care service users.

3 Identify four indicators of physical or emotional neglect.

4 List four different types of abuse that vulnerable people may be subjected to.

5 Give an example of a type of verbal abuse that is unacceptable in a care relationship.

6 Describe the signs and symptoms of emotional abuse that a care practitioner should be alert to.

7 Explain how the use of care values can ensure that a care practitioner does not discriminate unfairly against a service user.

8 What impact might poor care practice have on the personal development and emotional wellbeing of an individual who experiences it?

Topic review

The box below provides a summary of the areas covered in Topic 4.2. Tick the areas that you feel you understand and would be confident answering exam questions about. If there are any areas that you don't understand or are not confident about, you will need to return to them before you begin your exam revision.

Care values used in practitioner work
Promoting anti-discriminatory practice ❏
Promoting and supporting dignity, independence, health and safety ❏
Maintaining confidentiality of information ❏
Acknowledging personal beliefs and identity ❏

The use of care values ❏

When care goes wrong
Neglect and abuse ❏
Unfair discrimination ❏
Effects on self-concept and self-esteem ❏

Assessment Guide

Your learning in this unit will be assessed through a one hour and fifteen minute examination.

The examination will consist of a series of structured questions based on case studies and short scenarios.

You will need to show that you understand:

● Care values commonly used in practitioner work.

Topic 4.3

The development of self-concept and personal relationships

Topic focus

The development of self-concept and personal relationships is covered in detail in Topic 1.1 and Topic 1.2 of Unit 1. Topic 1.1 describes and explains how self-concept develops across the life course and how it is affected by a range of factors. Topic 1.2 describes and explains how different types of factors influence the formation of, and changes to, an individual's self-concept. Topic 4.3 will reinforce your earlier learning by:

● Reminding you about the factors that affect self-concept and about the links between self-concept and personal relationships

● Describing how self-esteem, self-image and self-concept are formed

● Explaining how care practitioners can build self-esteem and influence the self-concept of service users by building empowering relationships with service users and supporting service users to develop positive relationships with their family, partners, work colleagues and friends.

Case studies and short scenarios with questions for you to answer are a key learning feature of this topic. You should work through as many of the case studies and scenarios as possible. Applying knowledge and understanding of the development of self-concept and personal relationships will be a feature of the external examination for this unit.

Self-concept reviewed

The idea of self-concept and the factors that affect the way an individual develops their self-concept were first introduced in Unit 1.4. As a brief reminder, self-concept is:

- an individual's view of 'who' they are
- a combination of **self-image** (how we see ourselves) and self-esteem (how we value ourselves)
- continually developing during each life stage
- closely linked to emotional and social development
- the basis of an individual's sense of identity.

An individual's self-concept influences and is influenced by their personal relationships throughout life and affects their emotional development in each life stage. A positive self-concept can give an individual self-confidence, feeling of happiness and help them to form effective relationships with people who are attracted to them. On the other hand, a negative self-concept can result in a person feeling anxious and lacking in self-confidence, feeling unhappy and having difficulty in establishing and keeping good relationships going.

Forming self-esteem, self-image and self-concept

An individual first becomes aware of 'who' they are during infancy. This usually happens between about 18 months and 2 years when the child notices and recognises their reflection in a mirror. At this point the child realises that they are separate, and in some ways different, from other people in the world. Once they realise that they are one of many people in the world, children begin to develop ideas about themselves. This process speeds up as a child's language skills improve. When they can talk and ask questions, children are able to describe and explain things about themselves and also compare themselves to other children and adults. Children also get ideas about who they are and whether they are 'important' and 'valued' through their relationships and experiences. Positive, loving and supportive relationships and good experiences of life during infancy and early childhood lead to a positive self-image, higher self-esteem and a healthy self-concept. The opposite is true for children who do not enjoy good attachment relationships, who are mistreated or who experience emotional neglect, particularly by parents or other close family members.

Friendships, peer groups and relationships with other adults outside of the family, such as teachers and care professionals, are important for the development of self-image and self-esteem during childhood and adolescence. Feeling loved and supported and being valued and accepted as a person, particularly by friends and peers, enables an individual to develop a positive self-image and to feel that they belong and are part of a larger group or community of people.

Intimate, personal relationships as well as friendships, work relationships and relationships within the family are all important for the development of self-image and self-esteem during adulthood. This wider range of relationships means that there are more influences on self-concept during adulthood. As a

self-image

+

self-esteem

=

self-concept

Figure 4.24 Self-image combines with self-esteem to make up the self-concept.

Self-concept starts to form in infancy.

result, adults develop an increasingly subtle and detailed self-concept and greater self-knowledge and self-awareness. Throughout adulthood, an individual's self-concept changes in response to the life experiences they have. Expected and unexpected life events play an important part in these changes. A range of other factors affect the development of an individual's self-concept in each life stage.

Factors affecting self concept

A number of factors affect the way a person's self-concept develops and changes throughout their life. These include:

Age

An individual's self-concept develops and changes as they grow older. An adult or older person is much more emotionally mature and has a much wider experience of life than a child. As a result, their self-concept has been subject to far more influences over time and will be more detailed and based on greater self-knowledge. A person's self-concept will also change as they age because:

- Their body and physical abilities change over time
- Society values people differently as they age, for example older people may be less valued than babies and children.

Appearance

How an individual looks, particularly in comparison to other members of their peer group, becomes increasingly important to the development of their self-image from late childhood. Adolescents can become very sensitive to how their body shape, weight, facial characteristics and hair style compare to those of their peers. Some people choose clothes and hairstyles to identify with a particular group, for example, Goth, Emo or Preppy. The media (TV, magazines, films for example) are also an important source of ideas about 'ideal' ways to look that can have a significant effect on both an individual's self-image and their self-esteem. People who wish, and are able, to mimic these idealised looks tend to believe that they look good and have a positive self-image as a result. People who would like to look like the models or celebrities the media presents as being 'attractive'

Wealth and attractiveness are important features of self-image for some people.

but who are unable to achieve such an appearance may end up seeing themselves as unattractive and develop a negative self-image and lower self-esteem. However, as people get older, physical appearance and the way that they present themselves tend to have a smaller impact on their self-image and overall self-concept.

Gender

Gender refers to the different social expectations of men and women. In Western societies, boys and men are supposed to be 'masculine' (physically tough, active/sporty, strong) whilst girls and women are supposed to be 'feminine' (gentle, more passive and caring). These broad ideas about gender are picked up early in childhood as we learn whether we are boys or girls and what this means. Boys are widely expected to dress and behave differently to girls during childhood and may develop deep rooted ideas about the kinds of jobs and life-roles that they should aspire to. The gender stereotypes that people learn and which are reinforced by parents and others during childhood and adolescence have a powerful effect on self-image and self-esteem. Where people are able to conform to or successfully challenge gender expectations they are likely to develop a positive self-image and good self-esteem. The opposite is likely to be the case for people who feel frustrated by the restrictions that gender stereotypes place on the opportunities that they have in life or which leave them feeling inadequate or unfulfilled.

Some toys and games are more associated with boys.

Social class

A person's social class is usually defined by their occupation, income and wealth. The Office for National Statistics uses the following classification system to define social class:

1. Higher managerial and professional occupations
2. Lower managerial and professional occupations
3. Intermediate occupations
4. Small employers and own account (self-employed) workers
5. Lower supervisory and technical occupations
6. Semi-routine occupations
7. Routine occupations
8. Long-term unemployed.

Most people are able to say which social class they belong to. However, the importance of social class for identity and self-concept seems to have declined over the last century. At the beginning of the twentieth century, a person's social class had a significant effect on their lifestyle, identity and opportunities. Social class differences were much more obvious and important because people were less able to improve their social class position. However, with the growth of free education and changes in employment it is now possible to move from one social class to another. Because social class is less of a barrier to progression and doesn't appear, on the surface, to affect an individual's opportunities and life chances too dramatically, people now tend to see class as a less important factor in their personal development. However, it is still the case that the kind of education and employment a person obtains is likely to be

Over to you!

- How would you describe your own social class position?
- What impact, if any, does your social class have on your self-image and self-esteem?
- How important is a person's social class in modern society?

very similar to that of other people in their social class. People in the same social class are also likely to share attitudes and values and a similar way of life and will recognise each other from this.

Ethnicity/Culture

The ethnic group a person belongs to depends on their racial background, customs, language and religious beliefs. Most people could identify the ethnic group they belong to (black, African-Caribbean or white, European Christian, for example) and are aware that this affects their sense of personal identity or self-concept. As we've seen ethnicity affects self-concept by:

- influencing people's feelings of belonging and community
- giving people a sense of shared values and beliefs
- enabling them to follow and take part in particular traditions and customs.

A person's way of life or culture influences both how they feel about themselves and how others relate to them. An individual's beliefs about what a healthy diet involves, the importance of education and intimate relationships are all influenced by their cultural background. Self-image and self-esteem are influenced by the extent to which people are able to conform to the lifestyle and moral expectations of their ethnic group and culture. A person may also be treated in an unfair, discriminatory way because they are from a minority ethnic group or because their own cultural beliefs and way of life are different to those of other people. This can have a negative effect on self-image and self-concept if the person feels excluded or that they are treated as 'second-class' in some way.

Emotional development

In general, people become more emotionally mature as they get older. One way of thinking about this is to consider that the older a person gets, the wiser they become. Emotional development allows a person to develop self-knowledge and personal understanding and to compare themselves to others. Individuals who are emotionally mature are able to:

- accurately identify their strengths, abilities and personal qualities
- acknowledge their personal limitations or areas where they lack particular skills or aptitudes.

The self-knowledge and personal acceptance that results from emotional maturity is likely to lead to an individual developing a clear self-image and having positive self-esteem.

Education

Educational experiences can have a major influence on a person's sense of who they are. At school, an individual's teachers and fellow students affect their self-image and self-esteem through the way that they speak to and interact with them. This is particularly important during childhood and adolescence when people are sensitive to the views and behaviour of others. Going to college or university may confirm or change an individual's self-image and self-concept depending on whether the individual's experiences reinforce or contradict their beliefs

Expressing ethnicity and culture is important for identity.

Over to you!

How would you describe your own ethnicity? What cultural factors or influences contribute to the way you define your ethnicity?

about what they are good or not so good at. Educational success and the praise and rewards that follow tend to promote a positive self-image and high self-esteem. A lack of educational success, limited praise or a negative experience of school, college or university could, on the other hand, leave a person feeling bad about themselves and negative about their abilities.

Relationships with others

Individuals have a number of important relationships with others that have an influence on the development of their self-image, self-esteem and self-concept. These include:

- Family relationships (with parents, siblings and other relatives)
- Friendships and peer group relationships
- Work relationships (with employers and colleagues)
- Personal, intimate relationships (with a partner).

Early relationships with parents and siblings need to be based on effective attachments. This allows an individual to develop a sense of emotional security and is the foundation of a positive self-concept. Weak or negative family relationships, however, can damage a person's self-concept if they grow up feeling unloved and insecure.

Friendships and intimate personal relationships become more important during adolescence and early adulthood. Feeling attractive, close and connected to others is important for both emotional development and self-concept during this phase of life. People who succeed in finding a partner and maintaining an effective and fulfilling relationship are likely to adapt their self-concept to take account of this close relationship and also see it as a source of self-esteem. Similarly, where people have bad experiences of personal relationships or are unable to find or maintain a close, personal relationship this may have a negative effect on self-image and self-concept if they see themselves as having 'failed' to achieve an important life goal.

Work relationships are often a source of social support and friendship but also provide many people with a status that becomes central to their self-concept. Asking a person what they do for a living is one way in which we find out about other people's status. Somebody who has a high status job or who is very successful in their work life is likely to gain a lot of self-esteem from this. Similarly people who lose their jobs, retire or suffer a loss of work status through illness or disability may experience a reduction in their sense of self-worth and may have to adjust their self-concept to cope with this.

Sexual orientation

Sexual orientation or sexuality refer to an individual's attraction to either a same-sex or an opposite sex partner. Heterosexual people are attracted to an opposite sex partner. Lesbian and gay people who have a homosexual orientation are attracted to same sex partners. Bisexual people may be attracted to people of either sex. Most adolescents and adults declare themselves to be heterosexual whilst a minority of people are happy to declare themselves as lesbian, gay or bisexual.

Close relationships boost self-esteem.

Over to you!

Does homophobic bullying occur in your school or college? Why do you think that lesbian and gay teenagers are often bullied by their peers? What do you think could be done by teachers and fellow students to prevent or minimise homophobic bullying?

People tend to become aware of their sexual orientation in adolescence as they struggle to find and express a personal identity. People who have a homosexual orientation often struggle to accept this and to 'come out' or declare their sexuality to family and friends. This is because there has been, and in some situations there continues to be, prejudice and unfair discrimination against people who are homosexual. As a result a person may find it difficult to come to terms with a homosexual orientation because they are afraid of the way others might respond to them. However, lesbian, gay and bisexual orientations have become increasingly acceptable in society and more people are open about and receive support from their friends and family when they declare their homosexual orientation.

Sexual orientation has an impact on an individual's self-concept and on their social and emotional development. People who are comfortable with and able to express their sexual orientation freely are likely to feel more emotionally secure, have greater self-confidence and higher self-esteem than people who struggle with or are anxious about their sexual feelings and what these might say about them to others. Individuals who are unable to reveal or express their sexual orientation may fail to develop or maintain close intimate relationships and may become anxious and have low self-esteem as a result.

People are now more open about same-sex relationships.

Life experiences

Every individual continually develops their self-concept throughout their life. Each person's self-concept is unique to them and reflects the variety of experiences they have had in each life stage. Expected life events, such as starting school, going through puberty or starting work, and unexpected life events, such as serious illness, relationship breakdown or bereavement all shape an individual's self-concept in specific and unique ways. When older people reflect on their lives they are often able to identify the key moments or achievements that influenced how they developed as a person. Passing exams, getting married, achieving a particular employment status or experiencing a traumatic event might be a part of this. For some people, specific life experiences become the critical factors that shape their self-concepts and influence the direction of their lives.

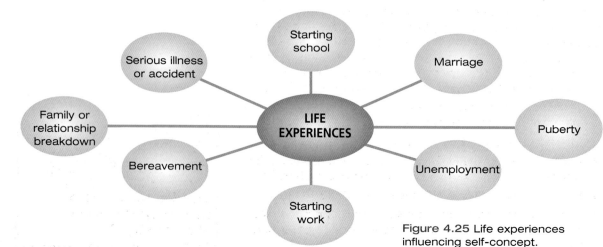

Figure 4.25 Life experiences influencing self-concept.

Building self-esteem and self-concept through care practice

An individual's self-image and self-esteem are strongly affected by the relationships they have with others. Care professionals need to focus carefully on the way they develop and maintain relationships with service users as they are often providing personal physical care and emotional support for people who are feeling vulnerable and who are relying on them to meet their needs. Having an illness, disease or condition can feel threatening and can be disabling for anyone. However, effective care relationships can play an important part in building a service user's self-esteem and self-concept. Relationships with service users which are ineffective and disempowering are likely to undermine an individual's self-confidence and may be damaging to their self-esteem.

Relationship building with service users

Effective care relationships depend heavily on the care professional and service user developing and maintaining trust and mutual respect. Care relationships begin to be formed as soon as a care professional meets a service user. This is usually because the service user has made an appointment or gained access to a service in which the care practitioner works.

Good care relationships begin when the care professional establishes a rapport or personal contact with the service user. Accepting the service user as an individual, respecting their identity and beliefs and being genuinely interested in them as a person enables a rapport to develop. This provides the basis on which a care relationship can develop, as a partnership in which the service user is fully involved. An effective care relationship can be established and maintained when a care professional:

- Achieves the right balance between talking, asking questions and listening during their interactions with service users
- Maintains confidentiality to establish and preserve trust
- Promotes the rights and choices of a service user so that they can maintain an active, independent approach to their life
- Respects the dignity, identity and beliefs of the service user
- Establishes and maintains professional boundaries so that the relationship with a service user is based on partnership and working together.

Over to you!

Think about the relationships that you have with your GP or another care professional. How do they try to establish a rapport and build a relationship with you?

Case study

Emmanuel Johnson is a community mental health nurse. He provides care for adults who have mental health problems. Emmanuel receives referrals from three different GP practices and has a caseload of 15 people whom he works with regularly. Apart from giving monthly injections to some of the people he works with, Emmanuel provides no physical care for the people he works with. Instead Emmanuel is skilled at establishing a good rapport, talking and listening and using relationships to provide emotional support and psychological help.

- What does the term 'rapport' refer to?
- Why do you think that relationship-building skills are important in mental health work?
- What other factors or issues should Emmanuel be aware of when he is trying to build an effective care relationship with a service user?

Care professionals have opportunities to establish and build relationships with service users when they:

- Carry out individual needs assessments
- Discuss and establish care plans with individuals
- Provide treatment, support or other practical forms of intervention to help the service user
- When they talk and interact informally, perhaps at mealtimes or during evenings if the individual is using in-patient or residential care services
- Meet to review and evaluate care plans and care provision
- See service users for after-care or follow-up once they have begun to recover from their health or social care problems.

Effective care relationships result in service users feeling actively involved in and empowered by the care they receive.

Empowerment of service users

Empowering care relationships rely on care professionals using their communication skills effectively when they interact with service users. A service user who is empowered is encouraged to express their wishes and preferences and to make decisions for themselves. This means that care professionals should always consult and involve service users in conversations and discussions

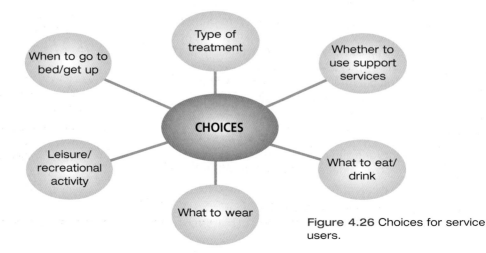

Figure 4.26 Choices for service users.

Empowering service users through choice

Care practitioners can empower service users by:

- Developing a unique relationship with each individual service user
- Adapting their communication style to ensure each individual can communicate as effectively as possible
- Finding out what each individual's likes and dislikes are
- Encouraging service users to express their needs, wishes and preferences
- Encouraging and supporting each individual to do what they can for themselves
- Offering individuals a choice of activities and options about whether and how they participate in them
- Giving service users different options on both large and small-scale decisions that affect them
- Enabling service users to make decisions based on informed choices.

Eating, personal hygiene, leisure activity and sleeping routines all provide opportunities for identifying and promoting individuals' particular wishes and preferences.

about their care rather than making decisions for them. Regardless of the health, social care or developmental needs that an individual has, care professionals should always accept that the individual has the right to make their own choices and decisions. A service user who is empowered through an effective care relationship will feel valued and respected because they are able to make decisions that affect their life. This has a positive effect on self-esteem and is likely to contribute positively to a person's self-concept if they see themselves as capable and independent.

Case study

Beth was born 22 years ago. She has Down's syndrome and a developmental age of 10. Beth has recently moved to live in a shared bungalow with two other women who have Down's syndrome. Beth and her housemates are supported by two care workers who come to the house every day at 8am and stay until 5pm. The care workers are supposed to provide support and assistance where this is needed but also have the task of promoting the independence of the women who live in the bungalow. Beth is currently settling in to the bungalow and she receives more direct help than the other two women. This will gradually change as she will be expected and encouraged to do more for herself.

- What does the term 'empowerment' mean?
- How might living in the bungalow be more empowering for Beth than living at home with her parents?
- What kinds of daily living skills or activities do you think Beth should be encouraged and supported to do for herself?

Health, Social Care and Early Years in Practice

Developing and promoting positive relationships

Service users are the most important people in care settings. Their needs for care, protection and support should be the main concern of care professionals and others who work in a care organisation. The provision of care for any service user should be guided by the aim of meeting the individual's particular care needs. This positive approach to care practice is achieved by:

● Understanding and using care values as a guide to care practice

● Using effective communication to establish a good rapport with a service user and using this to build a relationship

● Finding out about the individual's needs, wishes and preferences regarding care provision

● Respecting the individual's identity, beliefs and rights

● Promoting and supporting choice, dignity and independence.

Positive care practice is based on, and always occurs through, the relationship that a care professional develops with the individuals for whom they provide care.

Over to you!

Using your own ideas or personal experience, describe the qualities and approach an 'excellent care practitioner' should have.

Figure 4.27 Positive care practice.

Knowledge Check

1 What kind of relationship helps a care practitioner to develop the self-esteem and self-concept of a service user?

2 What can a care practitioner do to build an effective care relationship with a service user?

3 What does the term 'empowerment' refer to?

4 Suggest three ways in which a care practitioner can empower a service user.

5 What factors help a care practitioner to build positive care relationships with service users?

Topic review

The box below provides a summary of the areas covered in Topic 4.3. Tick the areas that you feel you understand and would be confident answering exam questions about. If there are any areas that you don't understand or are not confident about, you will need to return to them before you begin your exam revision.

Formation of self-esteeem, self-image and self-concept ❑

Factors affecting self-concept
- Age ❑
- Appearance ❑
- Gender ❑
- Social class ❑
- Ethnicity/culture ❑
- Emotional development ❑
- Education ❑
- Relationships ❑
- Sexual orientation ❑
- Life experiences ❑

Care practitioner's influence on self-concept and self-esteem
- Relationship building with service users ❑
- Empowerment of service users ❑
- Promoting positive relationships ❑

Assessment Guide

Your learning in this unit will be assessed through a one hour and fifteen minute examination.

The examination will consist of a series of structured questions based on case studies and short scenarios.

You will need to show that you understand:

- The development of self-concept and personal relationships.

Topic 4.4

Promoting and supporting health improvement

Topic focus

Promoting and supporting health improvement is covered in detail in Topic 3.4 of Unit 3. This focuses on applying knowledge and understanding of factors that affect health and wellbeing, ways of measuring health and developing health improvement plans. Topic 4.4 will reinforce your earlier learning by:

- Reminding you about the range of factors that affect health and wellbeing in positive and negative ways through the life course.
- Describing the ways health professionals support individuals to change their lifestyles and health-related behaviour.
- Outlining the aims and approaches used in health promotion activities.
- Identifying the links between effective health promotion, support for health improvement and care values.

Case studies and short scenarios with questions for you to answer are a key learning feature of this topic. You should work through as many of the case studies and scenarios as possible. Applying knowledge and understanding of ways of promoting and supporting health improvement will be a feature of the external examination for this unit.

The influence of lifestyle factors on health experiences

All health care professionals see health promotion and illness prevention as a key part of their role. An individual's lifestyle, including their attitudes, the choices they make and their behaviour, are seen as having an important influence on their health experiences. The lifestyles of healthy people are usually seen as being different to and better than the lifestyles of people whose health choices and behaviour lead to ill-health and premature death. Lifestyle is something that an individual has some control over and which they can try to change. As a result, health professionals often encourage service users who have health problems related to their lifestyle to make different choices or to change their health behaviour. The benefits of doing so can include:

- Health improvement and reduction in how often a person becomes ill
- Protection against health risks associated with unhealthy choices (obesity from poor diet) and high risk behaviours (smoking, drug-taking, unprotected sex)
- Improved fitness levels and a greater sense of emotional wellbeing
- Improved life expectancy.

Figure 4.28 Life expectancy, 2005–2007.

	At birth		At age 65	
	Males	Females	Males	Females
United Kingdom	77.2	81.5	17.2	19.9
England	77.5	81.7	17.3	20.0
Wales	76.7	81.1	16.9	19.6
Scotland	74.8	79.7	16.0	18.7
Northern Ireland	76.2	81.2	16.8	19.7

A range of lifestyle factors can affect health and wellbeing across the life course (see figure 4.29). We have already explored a number of these factors and the way they influence health and wellbeing, both positively and negatively, across the human life course in Unit 1 and in Unit 3. You should review these sections as part of your preparation for the Unit 4 external test. The section that follows provides a brief summary of these factors and explains the different ways health professionals can support service users to make changes to these aspects of their lifestyles.

Over to you!

In which country of the UK do men and women live longest?

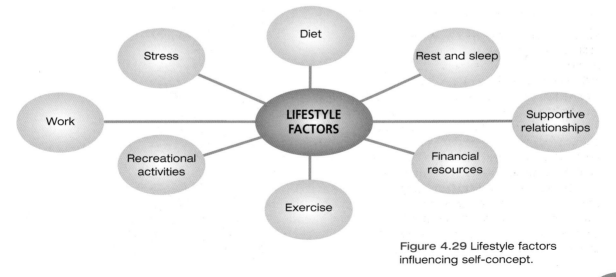

Figure 4.29 Lifestyle factors influencing self-concept.

Health, Social Care and Early Years in Practice

Diet

The food that an individual eats has a major influence on their health, development and wellbeing. A balanced diet is important for health because it:

- Provides energy for the body to function
- Regulates essential body processes and functions
- Builds, repairs and maintains body tissues and fluids.

An individual needs to consume the correct amount of food to meet their energy needs. These change throughout life and depend on a person's lifestyle and circumstances. People who do not consume a balanced diet or who eat too much or too little food are at risk of developing health problems. For example:

- Under-eating can lead to malnutrition which in the long term stunts physical and mental development.
- A diet lacking in essential nutrients can lead to deficiency diseases, such as rickets and osteoporosis (lack of calcium and vitamin D), bowel cancer (lack of fibre) and anaemia (lack of iron or vitamin B12) and increases the risk of people experiencing minor illnesses such as coughs and colds because their immune system is run down.
- Over-eating can lead to weight gain, damage to arteries and organs such as the heart, high blood pressure and tooth decay as the body stores the excess fat and calories that are surplus to the individual's energy needs.

Many people visit their GP and other health professionals with problems that are the result of dietary problems. Approximately one third of cancers are caused by poor diet. People who have long-term health needs because of diet-related heart disease, high blood pressure or strokes are seen more frequently by health professionals such as community nurses, dieticians, occupational therapists and physiotherapists than people who eat and benefit from a balanced diet. GPs and primary care nursing staff monitor diet-related health issues such as weight and blood pressure and provide illness prevention advice, health improvement guidance and in some cases treatment for health problems related to diet.

Regular exercise

Regular physical exercise has a positive effect on health and wellbeing because it maintains and improves:

- Circulation of blood to body tissues
- Heart functioning
- Muscle strength
- Physical stamina, flexibility and mobility (fitness)
- Immunity to infections
- Personal confidence and self-esteem.

Lack of regular physical exercise increases the risk of health problems such as obesity, heart disease and osteoporosis, for example. Exercise is important in every life stage as it helps individuals of all ages to develop and maintain a healthy body that increases their protection against illness and disease.

Health professionals, such as GPs, practice nurses, community nurses, physiotherapists and occupational therapists, will often

Percentages

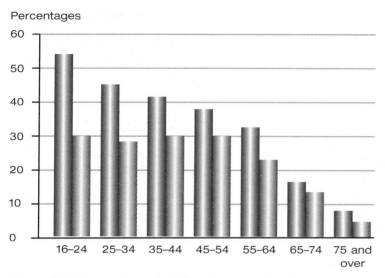

Figure 4.30 Percentage of adults who meet the physical activity recommendations: by sex and age, 2003, England.

Over to you!

What percentage of men under 45 years of age meet the physical activity recommendations? Why do you think so few women aged 16–24 meet the physical activity recommendations?

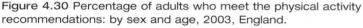

Men

Women

recommend that an individual who consults them about a health problem should increase or change the type of exercise that they do in order to improve their health and wellbeing. Aerobic exercise that increases heart and breathing rates, such as jogging, swimming or aerobics, may be recommended to help a person to lose weight and increase their overall level of physical fitness. Anaerobic exercises that strengthen the body, such as weight training, Pilates or yoga, may be suggested as a way of improving the functioning of the body, particularly where the person is recovering from an operation, an illness or an injury.

Supportive relationships

Do you have good friends and relatives who you care about? Hopefully you will be able to think of a variety of people whom you are emotionally close to. These people are good for your health and wellbeing because they:

- provide emotional security through a trusting relationship
- have a positive effect on self-confidence and self-esteem
- influence the way we develop our self-concept
- help us to develop our social skills.

Relationships with friends and relatives are supportive when the people involved feel emotionally close, cared for and able to trust each other. Individuals need supportive relationships in each life stage to experience wellbeing, and to support their social and emotional development. You may have disagreements and fall out with family members and close friends from time to time, but you shouldn't underestimate the important effect they have on your emotional wellbeing. People who don't have supportive relationships can experience loneliness, low self-esteem and a range of mental health problems that result from feeling 'left out'. Researchers have shown that people who lack close, supportive relationships are much more likely to experience depression.

GPs, community mental health nurses, clinical psychologists, practice nurses and primary care counsellors often see service

Over to you!

How do you think adults can develop supportive relationships with their ageing parents? Suggest ways in which people can build and maintain emotionally close relationships when their parents reach later adulthood.

users whose health problems are really due to psychological or emotional problems. Many of these service users lack supportive relationships with partners, friends and family or find themselves in a position where they are unable to talk openly about their feelings with those close to them. Health care practitioners will often provide supportive counselling, listening to the person and helping them to identify possible solutions. They may also encourage people to seek support from partners, relatives and friends in a more direct way. In cases where a person does appear to lack supportive social contacts, they may encourage them to join social groups or befriending organizations where they can meet others.

Work

How can work help people to experience good health and wellbeing? It is useful to use an holistic approach to health when thinking about this. This means looking at the positive effects that work can have on physical health as well as its possible effects on emotional, social and intellectual wellbeing.

Work can have both a positive and negative impact on an individual's health and wellbeing. For example:

- Work that involves lifting, carrying or other strenuous physical activity, could make a person very fit. Some workers, such as firefighters, builders and fitness instructors, do lots of physical exercise in the course of their daily work. Other jobs, such as nursing and shop work, may not be as physically strenuous but still involve a lot of physical activity. This will contribute to a person's level of fitness and help to keep their body in good condition.

- Some people experience work-related accidents and injuries because of the dangerous or repetitive nature of their work.

- Work that is mentally demanding can also stimulate intellectual development (thinking) and be a big motivating factor in a person's life.

- Work is important for social wellbeing because it provides opportunities to socialise, develop self-confidence as well as a routine and pattern to a person's day. Work gives people social status, confidence and self-respect.

- A person's work life, job status and employment role can all play a part in their self-concept and can be a source of pride and emotional satisfaction. For example, health workers who choose to be doctors or nurses often do so because they want to be useful and make a difference to peoples' lives. So, having a job that you enjoy, and which you feel is useful and important, can be good for your sense of emotional wellbeing.

- Working too much or experiencing too much pressure at work can result in high stress levels, reduce an individual's emotional wellbeing and result in mental health problems.

Over to you!

- Make a list of ways in which work could be good for a person's physical health and wellbeing. Divide your list into physical, intellectual, emotional and social reasons.

- Make a list of ways in which work could have a negative impact on a person's physical health and their intellectual, emotional or social wellbeing.

- What types of jobs do you think would be mentally demanding and good for a person's sense of wellbeing? List five jobs that would stimulate a person intellectually.

Case study

Fiona studied really hard at school and then at university. She obtained very high grades and has gone on to become an accountant. Over the last fifteen years, Fiona has risen to the top of the company she began working for after leaving university. She admits that 'work is my life'. Despite being proud of her academic and work achievements, Fiona is regretful that she hasn't made time for her personal life. She is now 36 and says she would really like to find a partner and have a baby. However, working twelve hours a day for five days a week leaves her feeling quite tired and she has a lot of work responsibilities that preoccupy her. Fiona has recently started to feel stressed and would like to reduce her work hours. When she approached the managing director of her company about this, he did his best to talk her out of it and told her how important she was to the company. Being needed and seen as important made Fiona feel good at the time but she is now starting to feel that her job has also taken over her life.

- Identify one way in which Fiona's job has a positive impact and one way in which it has a negative impact on her health or wellbeing.
- How has work influenced the development of Fiona's self-concept?
- What impact might a change in work-life balance have on Fiona's social and emotional development?

Health and social care professionals, such as GPs, community mental health nurses, counsellors, social workers, occupational therapists and psychologists are sometimes consulted by people who have work-related health problems. Where the problem is a work-related injury, a GP or occupational therapist will diagnose the problem, provide treatment and offer advice and guidance on how to avoid a similar situation occurring again. However, it is more common for people to consult a health professional about their work-related stress or the mental health problems they are experiencing as a result of unemployment or redundancy. In these situations, the health professional will listen and try to work with the person to develop a plan that addresses their worries, sleeplessness or other problems. This might involve making improvements to the person's diet and exercise pattern, making use of supportive relationships and using relaxation activities to reduce stress levels.

Rest and sleep

How much sleep and rest does a person need to be healthy? There is no definitive amount but an individual's need for sleep and rest will vary across their lifespan:

- Babies, young children and adolescents all seem to need quite a lot of sleep to cope with the growth spurts and rapid physical changes that they experience in each of these life stages.
- A four-year-old child sleeps an average of ten to fourteen hours a day.
- A ten-year-old needs about nine to twelve hours.
- Most adults have between seven and eight and a half hours of sleep every night. Others require as few as four or five hours or as many as ten hours each night.

- Adults and older people can often cope with less sleep, and even no sleep for short periods of time.
- During pregnancy, women need more sleep and rest than usual.

Everybody needs regular sleep and rest in order to 'recharge their batteries' and allow their body to recuperate. Sleep and rest are beneficial for health because they enable:

- Tissue repair to happen
- Growth to occur
- Muscles and tendons to relax and recover from exertion
- Stress reduction
- The brain to 'switch off' for a period of time
- Energy levels to be renewed.

However, not everyone takes their need for sleep and rest seriously. Some people work too much or have very active social lives (or both) and spend their life feeling tired. This isn't healthy and can be dangerous. People who are deprived of sleep lack energy and may become irritable. After two days without sleep, concentration becomes difficult. Other negative, and potentially dangerous, effects of sleep loss include:

- mistakes in routine tasks
- slips of attention
- dozing off for periods of a few seconds or more
- falling asleep completely
- difficulty seeing and hearing clearly
- confusion.

Lack of sleep can be very dangerous. For example, many car accidents are caused by people falling asleep while driving and losing control of their vehicle.

Health care practitioners such as GPs, practice nurses and primary care counsellors tend to see people who are suffering from fatigue (lack of energy) or who are having difficulties with their

Over to you!

How many hours sleep per night do you have on average? Would more sleep improve your health and wellbeing?

Working when you are tired can be counterproductive.

sleep pattern because of stress, anxiety or mood disorders like depression. Often the solution to the person's sleep problems is to change their lifestyle or to address the real source of the sleep or fatigue problem. A health improvement plan that promotes a better work-life balance, includes exercise and relaxation activities and which helps them to find sources of support will often enable the person to resume a normal sleep pattern and regain their usual energy levels. In some cases, counselling or other mental health treatment may be needed to help the person address a more deep-rooted problem that is disrupting their sleep and sapping them of energy.

Stress

An individual experiences stress when they have demands placed on them that they find too challenging or difficult to meet. Stress can be caused by a wide range of factors, particularly those that involve major life events – such as moving house, taking exams or becoming a parent – or which involve some form of threat or loss, such as relationship breakdown, an excessive workload or bereavement. Stress can have both positive and negative effects on health and development:

- Stress can be damaging to physical health if it is continual or long-term. High blood pressure, heart disease and mental ill-health can all result from chronic stress.

- Stress can damage self-confidence and self-esteem if the person starts to see themselves as less capable or is self-critical about their ability to cope with the situation that is causing them stress.

- Stress can lead to emotional distress where the person feels out of control, anxious and worried or frightened by some of the symptoms of stress (faster heart rate, dry mouth, feeling of sickness).

- Stress can be damaging to a person's relationships and social skills if it causes them to become irritable, unhappy and withdrawn.

- Stress can also have a positive effect on health and wellbeing because it stimulates 'fight and flight' responses that motivate people to do their best to overcome the challenges and problems that face them. Small, manageable amounts of stress prompt people to protect themselves from potentially harmful or difficult situations and to act in their own interests.

GPs, community nurses, counsellors, occupational therapists and social workers see people who have stress-related illnesses quite frequently. Assessing and treating the physical effects of stress, such as sleeplessness and weight loss, is usually only part of the care offered. Listening to the person explain the reasons for their stress starting and helping them to understand why it is continuing is also part of any health improvement work. A health improvement plan that focuses on changing the person's life or work circumstances, eating well, using relaxation activities and opportunities to socialise as well as increasing exercise levels may be suggested as a way of reducing stress levels in both the short and long-term.

Over to you!

Think about an occasion when you felt very stressed. How did you respond? What helped you to overcome or cope with the stress?

UNIT 4

Recreational activities

Relaxation is important for wellbeing.

Recreational or leisure activities are the things that people do in order to relax when they are not working. Recreational activities include different sports and more sedentary (non-active) pastimes like watching television, going to the cinema or simply going out to meet friends. A good work-life balance should include time for recreational activities because having hobbies, enjoying a social life and simply relaxing are all part of a healthy life. Recreational activities can provide:

- A break from work
- Physical and mental stimulation
- Emotional satisfaction and an opportunity to de-stress
- Opportunities to meet and socialise with others.

Financial resources

Money is an **economic factor** linked to health, wellbeing and development. Having an adequate amount of money enables a person to:

- Afford a good diet, good housing conditions and good quality clothing, which all directly affect physical health
- Go out and use local leisure and recreational facilities, have holidays and join in activities with other people, which all affect intellectual and social wellbeing
- Feel emotionally secure and happy about their standard of living and their ability to meet their daily living needs.

Of course, people don't consult health care professionals because they have enough money! On the other hand, a lack of financial resources may lead to health problems associated with poor diet, poor housing conditions, stress and social isolation. In these circumstances, a health professional would probably make a referral to obtain social and financial support for the individual, perhaps in the form of welfare benefits, debt counselling or social work assistance. Social work and mental health care

Over to you!

What types of leisure and recreational activities are part of your school/life balance? How do these activities contribute to your health and wellbeing?

workers also work with people who lack financial resources to help them with problems related to low self-esteem, lack of self-confidence and lack of skills that can prevent the person from getting work or addressing other issues that would improve their financial situation.

Over to you!

What do you think is 'enough money' for a person of your own age? How might not having enough money affect the health and development of someone your own age?

Knowledge Check

1 Identify four lifestyle factors that can affect an individual's health and wellbeing.

2 Explain why diet is important for health and development.

3 What does the term 'aerobic exercise' refer to?

4 Describe the positive effects on health and wellbeing of taking regular exercise.

5 Which aspects of personal development and wellbeing are affected by supportive relationships?

6 Describe how the work an individual does can have an impact on their health, development or wellbeing.

7 Explain why sufficient rest and sleep are necessary for good health and wellbeing.

8 What impact can high levels of stress have on an individual's health and development?

9 How can financial resources affect an individual's health and development?

Health promotion

Health promotion is the area of care practice that focuses on illness prevention and health improvement. There are many different kinds of health promotion activity. These include:

- National health promotion campaigns targeted at the whole population, such as anti-smoking campaigns

- Health promotion campaigns targeted at specific groups of people in the population, such as breast cancer awareness campaigns targeted at women and testicular cancer campaigns targeted at men

- Health promotion and illness prevention groups run by health care practitioners, such as smoking cessation or weight loss groups

- Health education and health improvement advice and support given by health care professionals to individual service users during appointments.

Smoking may reduce the blood flow **and** causes impotence

Anti-smoking health promotion material.

UNIT 4

The purpose of health promotion work is to give information, advice and support to prevent people from becoming ill or to enable them to make lifestyle changes that will lead to improvements in their health. Health promotion activity often focuses on lifestyle issues and health behaviour that presents a risk to health. For example, smoking, poor diet, lack of exercise, alcohol and drug misuse and unprotected sex are all important health promotion issues for health professionals. However, health promotion activity isn't just about health dangers and giving warnings. Increasingly it is about promoting positive health. For example, you may see health promotion activities that focus on:

- how to lose weight safely and quickly
- how to get the most from local health services
- how to lead an active life after disability
- ways of keeping warm in winter
- healthy eating
- preparation for retirement
- the benefits of exercise
- maintaining personal hygiene
- preventing dental problems
- getting the best out of sport and leisure facilities
- how to maintain desired weight in pregnancy.

Aims and approaches

Health promotion activity needs to be carefully planned in order to be effective. The aims of any health promotion work should be clearly identified from the outset. These might include:

- Raising awareness of health and wellbeing issues
- Preventing ill-health
- Improving fitness levels
- Improving life expectancy.

National health promotion campaigns

Governments often use national health promotion campaigns to raise the awareness of the whole UK population about health and lifestyle issues such as healthy eating, drug misuse and HIV-awareness. This kind of national health promotion provides information to make people aware of health risks and also encourages people to make healthier lifestyle choices. Many large-scale health promotion campaigns, such as the Christmas anti drink-driving campaigns and the summer skin cancer campaigns, are carried out every year. You've probably seen examples of various campaigns in newspapers and magazines, on television or in booklets and posters. You may have come across them at your local leisure centre, sports ground, health centre, library, shopping centre, health food shop, school, college, hospital, nursery or youth club.

Over to you!

Which areas of your own health behaviour, if any, have been influenced by health promotion or health education activity? Try to recall what you have learnt from health promotion activity and how this influenced your personal behaviour.

Over to you!

Identify a health promotion campaign that you can remember seeing.

Explain where you saw the information and describe how it affected you.

Individual health promotion work

> ### Investigate …
>
> Choose any one of the following topics to develop a health message targeted at children:
>
> - dental health
> - balanced diet
> - smoking
> - exercise
> - personal safety.
>
> 1 Identify a message suitable for promoting good health and wellbeing to a group of children aged seven to nine years.
> 2 Identify the health promotion methods that could be used to get this message across to these children.
> 3 Explain why you think your methods would be effective.

Health professionals who work directly with service users often encourage individuals to make lifestyle changes as a way of improving their health and wellbeing. A care practitioner may have given you, or somebody you know, advice or guidance on ways of improving your health or sense of wellbeing. 'Do more exercise' and 'stop smoking' often form part of a health promotion 'message'. As well as raising awareness of health risks by giving information and advice, these health workers also:

- Diagnose individuals' health and wellbeing problems
- Identify lifestyle issues that may lead to health problems and encourage people to adopt healthier lifestyles
- Develop health improvement plans that focus on improving personal health, physical fitness and general wellbeing
- Monitor health and wellbeing through screening and other health assessments and provide services such as immunisations to prevent ill-health from occurring.

Health professionals such as GPs, community nurses, occupational therapists and physiotherapists may work with individual service users to set targets for health improvement after undertaking a thorough assessment of the person's current health status. Part of the health professional's role is to provide support and encouragement when the person struggles to make the necessary lifestyle changes or finds that their motivation to achieve their targets is slipping. Many people feel very motivated to adopt a healthier lifestyle if they believe that it will prevent them from developing heart disease, obesity or other conditions in the future.

Ways of supporting health behaviour changes

People often need support and assistance to achieve their health improvement targets. Health professionals support individuals to change their health-related behaviour in a number of ways. These include:

- Diagnosing health problems and identifying lifestyle areas that could be changed or improved

Group activities motivate people to improve their health.

- Devising health improvement plans in collaboration with the individual, including realistic short and long-term targets for health improvement

- Monitoring of progress to check that the person is moving towards achieving their target in a safe, healthy way

- Providing advice and counselling to encourage the person to maintain their efforts and to motivate them to overcome any problems or difficulties that may affect their progress

- Evaluating the individual's progress against the health improvement targets that were set.

In addition to using individual consultations in which they talk with the service user about their health improvement plan, a health practitioner may encourage the person to:

- Use diaries or a record book to monitor their own progress and their feelings about the plan or the targets they have to achieve.

- Attend a support group, use an online forum or work with a 'buddy' so that they can talk to and support others in a similar position

Case study

Joe, aged 43, has a very busy work life. Despite this he also has a lot of friends and really enjoys going out socialising. Meeting friends for drinks and going out for meals to restaurants are Joe's favourite ways of socialising. However, Joe's hectic work and social life have taken a toll on his health and wellbeing. Joe is 4 stone overweight, does no exercise, drinks about 30 units of alcohol each week and smokes 10 cigarettes a day. Joe has recently become a dad for the first time. This has focused his mind on being healthy so that he can enjoy spending time with his daughter and avoid becoming the victim of an early death. Joe has vowed to make changes to his lifestyle and believes that with the right support he could get fit and healthy again.

- What kinds of health promotion advice do you think a GP would give to Joe?

- Which areas of his lifestyle should Joe consider changing in the short-term?

- Suggest ways in which Joe could be supported by health care practitioners to improve his health and wellbeing.

- Use substitutes such as nicotine patches, or alternative, lower calorie foods or low alcohol drinks to replace less healthy substances.
- Reward themselves when they make progress towards their targets.
- Participate in regular reviews to discuss any difficulties and receive praise and encouragement for their efforts and the progress they have made.

Topic review

The box below provides a summary of the areas covered in Topic 4.4. Tick the areas that you feel you understand and would be confident answering exam questions about. If there are any areas that you don't understand or are not confident about, you will need to return to them before you begin your exam revision.

The importance of lifestyle factors for health improvement
- Diet ❑
- Regular exercise ❑
- Supportive relationships ❑
- Work ❑
- Rest and sleep ❑
- Stress ❑
- Recreational activities ❑
- Financial resources ❑

The impact of lifestyle factors
- Positive impact on health improvement ❑
- Negative impacts on illness experience ❑

Health promotion
- Aims of health promotion ❑
- Approaches used in health promotion ❑
- Ways of supporting individuals ❑

Care values and health promotion
- Promotion of choice ❑
- Respecting identity and culture ❑
- Empowerment ❑
- Promoting independence ❑
- Respecting right to choice ❑

Factors affecting growth and development
- Lifestyle choices
  - diet ❑
  - exercise ❑
  - socialising ❑
  - recreational activities ❑

Assessment Guide

Your learning in this unit will be assessed through a one hour and fifteen minute examination.

The examination will consist of a series of structured questions based on case studies and short scenarios.

You will need to show that you understand:

- Promoting and supporting health improvement.

GLOSSARY

A

Absolute poverty – This occurs when people have insufficient income to meet their basic, daily living needs.

Abstract thinking – High level thinking ability that enables a person to think about issues, problems or situations that are hypothetical.

Acute problems – Health problems which have a sudden onset and are usually short-term.

Ageing – The process of, and the changes that result from, growing older.

Ancillary roles – Indirect care work roles that usually involve organisational work such as administration or cleaning.

Anorexia Nervosa – An eating disorder in which a person maintains a very low body weight and has a distorted image of their body.

Anti-discriminatory approach – An approach to care practice that challenges instances of prejudice and unfair discrimination and aims to counter their negative effects.

Associative play – Play based on imitation and pretending.

Attachment relationship – An emotionally close relationship with a parent or carer through which an infant develops and expresses their emotions and a sense of security.

B

Balanced diet – A diet containing carbohydrates, fats, protein, vitamins and nutrients in quantities appropriate for the person consuming it.

Bereavement – Suffering loss as a result of someone dying.

Biomedical approach – The scientific approach to health used by the medical profession.

Blended family – A family containing stepbrothers and stepsisters that is created when two previously separate families merge into one unit.

Body Mass Index (BMI) – A system for assessing whether a person is a healthy weight for their height that is calculated by dividing a person's weight in kilograms by their height in metres squared.

Bonding – The formation of a very close emotional link between two people.

Bulimia Nervosa – A binge-eating disorder in which a person controls their weight and body shape typically by purging themselves of food soon after eating it.

C

Care needs – The reasons why an individual requires the help or support of health, social care or early years services.

Care package – The range of services and forms of support that are planned and organised to meet an individual's particular care needs.

Care values – The values and ethical principles that care practitioners apply to their work. These are based on beliefs about the proper way to treat service users. Confidentiality, respecting a person's beliefs and behaving in a non-discriminatory way are all examples of care values.

Carotid artery – A large artery found in the neck.

Charges – The amount of money required for a particular care service, such as a private dental consultation or a prescription.

Chinese herbal medicine – An ancient system of medicine of Chinese origin based on the use of herbs and plant products to treat a range of physical and psychological health problems.

Cholesterol – A fatty substance needed by the body and carried in the blood.

Chromosome – Long strands or packets of DNA.

Chronic conditions – Long-term or enduring health conditions that cannot usually be cured.

Client groups – Defined groups of people with similar care needs, such as 'children under five', 'adolescents' and 'disabled people'.

Code of practice – A document that provides guidance on ethically appropriate and recommended ways of behaving or dealing with situations.

Cognitive development – The development of thinking skills.

Cohabiting – Another term for 'living together' without being married.

Commissioning – This term refers to the acquisition or purchasing of care services on behalf of a local population of people.

Communication skills – The abilities and behaviours that allow people to understand and interact with each other.

Concepts – Abstract or general ideas.

Concrete operational thinking – The ability to use logical thinking to solve problems that apply to actual (concrete) objects or situations.

Confidentiality – The protection of personal or sensitive information to ensure that only those who are authorised to have access to it do so.

Conscience – An individual's sense of right and wrong.

Cooperative play – Forms of play in which children collaborate or work together for the same purpose.

Coronary heart disease – A health problem in which the circulation of blood to the heart is inadequate because of damage to arteries or heart muscle.

Culture – Common values, beliefs and customs or way of life.

D

Daily living skills – The range of practical skills needed to live independently.

Dementia-related illness – This term refers to a group of diseases where there is a progressive loss of brain function.

Department of Health – The government department responsible for planning and coordinating statutory health care provision.

Development – The process of acquiring new skills and capabilities.

Developmental norms – These are the points or 'milestones' when particular developmental changes are expected to occur or when skills and abilities usually develop.

DHSSPS – This is an acronym for the Department of Health, Social Services and Public Safety which has overall responsibility for health and care policy in Northern Ireland.

Dialysis – The process of cleaning the blood by passing it through a special machine.

Diastolic blood pressure – The second or bottom figure in a blood pressure result that shows the minimum pressure in the arteries between beats of the heart.

Direct care role – A care role that involves the individual working directly with service users in a care-giving capacity.

Disability – A lack of ability compared to the norm.

DNA – The abbreviation of deoxyribonucleic acid. It is a chemical ribbon that tells cells how to function.

Domiciliary care – Another term for home care.

E

Early years – This usually refers to children under 8 years of age, the care practitioners who work with them or the services provided for them.

Egocentric – This means being preoccupied with aspects of the 'self' whilst being insensitive to the needs and thoughts of others.

Eligibility criteria – These are the requirements or standards that must be met before a person is provided with a care service.

Emotional development – The emergence of feelings about self and others.

Emotional needs – These relate to the feelings people have and which are generally expressed through relationships with others.

Empathy – The ability to see and feel things from another person's point of view.

Emphysema – A disease of the lung that destroys the lung tissue and causes shortness of breath.

Empowering – A process of supporting and giving choice and decision-making powers to individuals or groups.

Ethnicity – A social profile that is used to classify people according to their social and cultural heritage and identification.

Expected life event – An anticipated event that occurs during an individual's lifetime that affects personal development.

Extended Services – A feature of children's services in which schools offer a range of additional leisure, child care and learning services that go beyond the provision normally expected of a school.

F

Fine motor skills – The manipulative movements an individual makes with their fingers.

Formal operational stage – The development of logical thinking skills during childhood.

Formal relationship – A relationship based on a set of rules, such as employer/employee.

Friendships – Co-operative and supportive, non-sexual relationships between people.

G

Gender – A term used by sociologists to describe the social and cultural attributes that are expected of men and women in a society.

Gender stereotypes – Expectations and images of women as 'feminine' and men as 'masculine'.

Genes – Short stretches of DNA ribbon that are located in chromosomes.

Genetic inheritance – The genes received from biological parents.

Gross motor skills – Whole body movements such as sitting up, walking or jumping.

Growth – An increase in size (mass or height).

Growth spurt – A short period of rapid physical change.

H

HDL cholesterol – High-density lipoproteins cholesterol is sometimes called 'good cholesterol' because it can remove cholesterol from the blood stream so that it is excreted from the body through the liver.

Health care – Forms of physical care or treatment, usually focused on the body.

Health Improvement Plan – A series of targets and activities that are designed to improve the physical health and wellbeing of an individual.

Health monitoring – The process of measuring or checking the state of an individual's physical health.

Hierarchy of needs – The organisation of needs in terms of their level of importance.

Holistic – Looking at the whole person.

Hormones – Chemical substances secreted into the blood by certain glands that stimulate activity in other organs.

Hormone Replacement Therapy – Drug treatment that boosts hormone levels which is designed to ease the physical discomfort experienced by women who are undergoing the menopause.

I

Immunisation – The act of creating immunity by introducing a small, controlled dose of an infection into a person's body.

Indirect care role – A job in a care organisation that involves providing organisational support rather than face-to-face contact with service users. An example would be the role of an accountant.

Informal sector – The term given to the large number of largely untrained and unpaid partners, friends and relatives who provide a range of care and support services for people who need care.

In-patient services – Services provided to people who are admitted to and live within an organisation such as a hospital, hospice or care home whilst receiving care.

Integrated Children's Services – Care services for children provided by health, social care and early years practitioners working in partnership.

Intellectual development – The emergence and improvement of thinking and language skills.

Intellectual needs – An individual's requirement for stimulation and learning opportunities.

Intervertebral discs – Discs that support and allow movement of the spine.

L

LDL cholesterol – Low density lipoprotein, also know as 'bad cholesterol' because it can become trapped in the blood vessels.

Learning disability – A condition that limits an individual's intellectual or thinking ability.

Life event – An event in an individual's life that has significance for or influence on their future development.

Life stages – The phases of growth and development that people pass through.

Local Authority – This is an administrative body, such as a County Council, City Council or Metropolitan Borough Council for example, that is responsible for early years, social care and education services at a local level.

M

Material possessions – These are the goods, products and other physical items (car, house etc) that people own or possess.

Maturation – The gradual process of becoming physical mature or fully developed.

Means-testing – This involves assessing a person's income and wealth against a set of criteria to determine whether they are eligible for a specific service or benefit.

Menopause – The period of time during which the menstrual cycle wanes and gradually stops. Usually occurs between the 45th and 50th years of a woman's life.

Menstruation – Approximately monthly discharge of blood from the womb of a non-pregnant woman.

Migraine – A severe headache.

Monogamous – Being married to one person at a time.

Multi-agency working – Co-operation between care practitioners who work for different care organisations.

N

NHS – National Health Service.

NHS Direct – A 24-hour health advice and information service provided by the NHS.

NHS Trust – An organisation that provides health care services on behalf of the NHS in England and Wales.

Norms – Expected standards.

Nutrients – Naturally occurring chemical substances found in the food we eat. They include carbohydrates, fats, proteins, vitamins and minerals.

O

Obesity – A very overweight state, usually defined by a body mass index of 30 or more.

Object permanence – The awareness that objects continue to exist even when they are no longer visible.

Osteoporosis – A bone disease that leads to an increased risk of fracture.

Outpatient services – Care that involves attendance at a hospital clinic for brief investigations or treatment during the day.

Outsourcing – Purchasing services from an external organisation.

P

Parallel play – This happens when children play alongside but not directly with each other.

Partnership working – This term is used to refer to the arrangements that care organisations sometimes make to collaborate or work together in order to deliver care services to service users.

Peer group – Typically a group of friends of approximately the same age who see themselves and are seen by others as belonging together in some way.

Peer group pressure – The emotional and moral influence that a peer group can have on an individual's behaviour.

Percentile charts – Usually referred to as centile charts, these are used to record and compare the growth pattern of an infant.

Permanent care needs – Ongoing or enduring requirements for assistance or support.

Philanthropist – A wealthy person who voluntarily donates their money or other resources to welfare services for the benefit of others.

Physical needs – Health, development or care needs relating to the body.

PIES – This stands for Physical, Intellectual, Emotional and Social needs.

Placenta – An organ rooted in the lining of the womb thatlinks the baby's blood supply to the mother's blood supply, carrying oxygen and food to the unborn baby.

Policy – This is a written document that sets out an organisations approach to wards a particular issue.

Postcode lottery – This refers to the differing chances that people have of receiving care services depending on where they live. For example, some people don't get access to particular drugs or treatment when their neighbours do because they live in an area where the health authority does not fund the drugs or treatment concerned.

Poverty – A lack of resources, usually financial.

Prejudice – A strongly held attitude towards a particular group which will often persist even when shown to be unjustified or unfounded.

Pre-operational stage – A pre-logical stage of thinking that occurs between the ages of 2 and 6 in which children use a lot of imitation and imagination but can't solve problems logically.

Primary health care team – This term refers to the range of practitioners such as GP's practice nurses, community nurses and other health care staff who provide health care in community settings.

Primary socialisation – This is a social process carried out within the family. It involves the teaching and learning of social attitudes, values and the forms of behaviour that are acceptable in wider society.

Principled morality – This is a type of moral thinking that is based on self-chosen principles – such as justice or human rights – which some people develop and use to make judgements about right and wrong from late adolescence onwards.

Private practitioner – Care practitioners who are either self-employed or who are employed by a private sector care organisation.

Private sector – This is the collective term used to describe care businesses and self-employed practitioners who provide services on a commercial, profit-making basis.

Procedure – A document that sets out in detail the particular way in which a task must be carried out or an issue dealt with.

Professional referral – A request by one care professional for care services to be provided by another care professional.

Prosthesis – An artificial replacement for a body part, such as an artificial leg.

Puberty – The developmental period when secondary sexual characteristics develop and reproductive organs become functional.

R

Radial artery – The main blood vessel carrying oxygenated blood, found in the forearm.

Redundancy – The loss of a job because the job is no longer required or necessary.

Referral – This is the process used to obtain access to care services.

Reflexes – Involuntary and almost instant reactions to a particular stimulus.

Registered charity – A voluntary organisation registered with the charity commission.

Regulatory body – An organisation that maintains a register of qualified practitioners, gives guidance on professional ethics and removes those who are unfit to practice. Examples include the Nursing and Midwifery Council and the General Medical Council.

Relative poverty – This occurs when people live below the standard of living normally accepted in a particular society.

Retirement – The point where a person stops employment completely.

Rural lifestyle – A way of life based in the countryside.

S

Screening – A strategy used in a population to detect a disease in individuals who currently don't have any signs or symptoms of the disease.

Secondary care – Healthcare services that are provided by hospital-based specialists for people with more complex or emergency health care needs.

Secondary socialisation – Socialisation that occurs outside of the family. Typically socialisation influenced by friends, peer group, work colleagues and other significant adults.

Secretary of State for Health – The Politician who leads the Department of Health and is responsible for health policy.

Self – The essential qualities that make one person distinct or unique from another.

Self-concept – The combination of self-image and self-esteem that together produce a sense of personal identity.

Self-esteem – The sense of worth or value that a person attributes to themselves, their skills and their abilities.

Self-image – The way a person views themselves.

Self-referral – A direct request by an individual for health care services. Going to see a GP is an example of a self-referral.

Sensorimotor stage – The early stage of intellectual development in which basic learning occurs through the use of the senses and physical, or motor, activity.

Sensory impairment – Damage to or loss of one of the main senses – usually hearing impairment or visual impairment.

Service user – An individual who uses a health, social care or early years service.

Sexual orientation – This refers to the preference a person has for a heterosexual (opposite sex), homosexual (same sex) or bisexual (either same or opposite sex) relationship.

Sibling – This is another term for brother or sister.

Socialisation – This is the process of learning how our society works, its expectations and rules.

Social care – Forms of non-medical support and assistance provided for vulnerable people.

Social class – There are many competing definitions of social class. Central to all definitions is the idea that a person's position in society is determined by their economic circumstances that will then influence their life choices, opportunities and future prospects.

Socially constructed – Something that is 'invented' or 'constructed' by people in a particular society.

Social development – The emergence and improvement of communication skills and relationships with other people.

Social exclusion – A term used to describe a situation where people are unable to participate fully in society for a number of related reasons often including poverty, unemployment, poor housing or homelessness, poor health and poor educational achievement.

Social needs – These refer to an individual's need for interaction and relationships with others.

Social policy – The approach taken to changing or maintaining welfare issues in society.

Social Services Department – The part of a local authority, usually divided into Adult social services and Children's services, that commissions and provides social work, child protection and social care services.

Social Services Inspectorate – The part of central government that inspects social service provision in local authorities.

Social transition – The move from one phase of social development to another.

Solo play – Playing alone.

Specific needs – Care needs that result from particular health or developmental problems.

Statutory sector – The care sector that provides services that have to be provided by law. They are usually provided by public or government-controlled care organisations such as NHS Trusts or local authorities.

Stroke – A disturbance in the blood supply to the brain that can result in physical disability and mental impairment. The medical term for a stroke is cerebrovascular accident or CVA.

Sure Start Children's Centres – Government run and funded centres that provide early years support and services for young children and families.

Systolic blood pressure – This is the first figure in a blood pressure reading. It indicates the maximum pressure in the arteries when the heart beats.

T

Targeted services – Services that are designed and provided for people with specific health, social or developmental problems.

Temporary care needs – Care needs that result from short-term health, social or developmental problems.

Third-party referral – Referral to care services by a some one who isn't a care professional, such as a friend, relative or employer.

Trepanning – Surgery in which a hole is made in the skull in order to treat health problems and to let 'evil spirits' escape.

U

Unexpected life event – An event that occurs without warning – such as serious illness – that affects an individual's personal development.

Unfair discrimination – The unjustified and less favourable treatment of a person or a group, perhaps as a result of prejudice.

Universal services – Services that are provided to meet general health and care needs, such as most GP services.

Urban lifestyles – Ways of life that are based on living in a large town or city.

V

Vaccination – Giving a person the mild form of a disease, usually by injection, to make the immune to the disease itself.

Virtual Wards – A group of care workers who provide care in the community for service users who remain living at home. Virtual wards provide the same staffing and services as hospital wards but without the physical building. The aim is to provide preventative care to people in their own homes.

Voluntary organisation – An organisation that is independent of government and which provides free or low cost care services on a not-for-profit basis. These organisations often rely on volunteer workers.

Voluntary sector – The care sector made up of voluntary and not-for-profit organisations that provide services free of charge or for a small, subsidised fee.

W

Wellbeing – A positive state of physical, intellectual, emotional and social health in which the person feels physically well and psychologically content.

Western societies – This term is generally used to refer to developed countries in Europe, North America and Asia.

INDEX